Liz Harfull is an award-w̶... ...C̶hurchill Fellow. She grew up on a small farm near Mount Gambier which has been in the family since the early 1860s.

She worked for several newspapers before spending twelve years with a leading national public relations business specialising in agriculture and environmental management. In 2006 she walked away from being a co-owner/director of the business to focus on her writing. She is passionate about telling the stories of regional Australia and in 2008 Liz published her first book, the bestselling *Blue Ribbon Cookbook*.

Today Liz lives in the Adelaide Hills, juggling a busy writing career with her voluntary work as president of a national council representing rural journalists and communicators.

WOMEN
of the LAND

LIZ HARFULL

Eight rural women and their remarkable everyday lives

ALLEN&UNWIN
SYDNEY • MELBOURNE • AUCKLAND • LONDON

Unless otherwise marked, all photographs are by the author.
Photograph on p. 235 provided by Catherine Bird

This edition published in 2013
First published in 2012

Allen & Unwin

83 Alexander Street
Crows Nest NSW 2065
Australia
Phone: (61 2) 8425 0100
Fax: (61 2) 9906 2218
Email: info@allenandunwin.com
Web: www.allenandunwin.com

Cataloguing-in-Publication details are available
from the National Library of Australia
www.trove.nla.gov.au

ISBN 978 1 74331 404 3

Internal design by Darian Causby
Map by Mapgraphics, Brisbane
Set in 12/16 pt Sabon Pro by Bookhouse, Sydney
Printed in Australia by McPherson's Printing Group

10 9 8 7 6 5 4 3 2 1

MIX
Paper from
responsible sources
FSC® C001695

The paper in this book is FSC® certified.
FSC® promotes environmentally responsible,
socially beneficial and economically viable
management of the world's forests.

CONTENTS

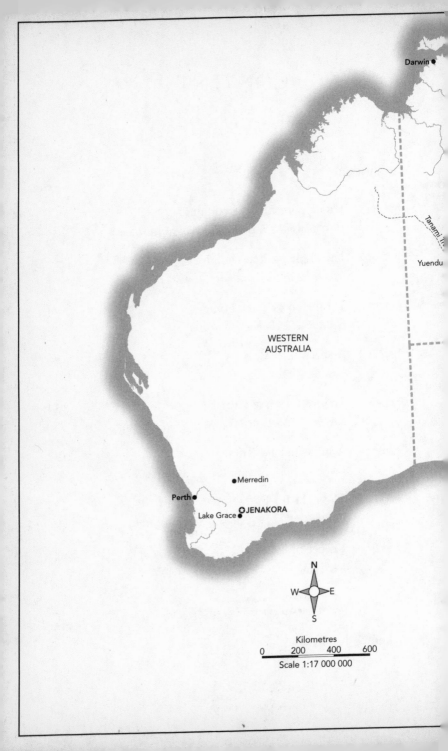

INTRODUCTION

In setting out to write this book, I was told very early on by quite a few people that I would struggle to find women who had willingly taken on the challenge of managing an Australian farm. No woman would be foolish enough to attempt it on their own unless they were forced by circumstance, and I would certainly have a hard time finding women running farms on a commercial, full-time scale if there were able-bodied men in their lives who could take over for them or, at least, share the endeavour equally. What surprised me most is that the people saying this were other rural women.

Having spent most of my working life to date telling the stories of regional Australia in one form or another, I knew it simply wasn't true. In fact, after just a few weeks of very basic research, I had a list of more than 40 potential candidates and I had barely scratched the surface. The greatest challenge was not finding women to write about, but choosing which stories to tell.

In deciding who to write about, I was influenced by my own background as the daughter of dairy farmers from a small farm in a closely settled area of South Australia. Writers, artists and filmmakers have long been fascinated with the outback and the more remote parts of our wide brown land, but there is much more to the Australia that sprawls beyond our urban boundaries. I wanted to share the experiences of women living in some of these places too, as well as their families and communities, and to capture something of their daily lives, personal struggles and extraordinary achievements.

While tragedy and unhappy circumstances may have played a role in some of them becoming farmers in their own right, it is by no means the only reason they are doing what they do. All these women share two things in common—they have made active choices to be farmers, and they love the land. Some are single, some are not, some have children and some do not. Some come from generations of farmers and grew up on the land. Some were actively discouraged by their parents from considering becoming farmers despite the fact it has been their hearts' desires since they were children, not because they were girls but because it can be a tough and unforgiving way for anyone to make a living.

Spending time with these women emphasised the physical challenges that all farmers face. Farms can be dangerous work environments given they usually involve operating machinery and handling livestock, and some of them have experienced life-threatening injuries. While the nature of the work is physical there is more than one way to get the job done, as these women also demonstrate. Because they cannot rely on brute strength, they have found alternative approaches and clever little tricks that enable them to tackle many tasks on their own, whether it be handling a recalcitrant bull, hoisting a sheep onto the back of a ute, or working out the best way to move a stack of fence posts or a 30-kilogram bag of stock lick.

As someone who has observed more than a few farmers at work, I was also struck by their approach to working with others. Before they leapt into the task, they talked about it first to anyone helping out so that everyone was clear on what needed to be done and what was expected of each individual. Believe me this is far from common, as the number of seminar sessions run for farmers on communication skills and managing employees tends to testify. And it struck me that all of them are great networkers, quick to identify people who can provide advice and support when needed, and never ashamed to ask for it or accept it.

One of the more startling aspects of researching these stories was the unexpected points of connection between what at first glance seemed to be a group of women from totally different parts of the country and totally different backgrounds. It is hard to explain the series of coincidences and strange serendipity that kept emerging.

It began with discovering that Cecily Cornish's ancestors made their start as pastoralists in Australia when they bought a block of land from the pioneering John Hawdon, brother of famous overlander Joseph Hawdon, who drove the first mobs of cattle from New South Wales to Victoria and South Australia. John turned out to be Susie Chisholm's great-great-grandfather.

It ended on my final research trip with Keelen Mailman pointing out a distant hill on the station she manages in western Queensland. The hill was given its English name by the colonial explorer Major Mitchell, who climbed it during one of his famous expeditions from Sydney into the unknown hinterland. Only weeks before another farmer thousands of kilometres away in Victoria had taken me to a favourite spot on her farm, pointing out that it was the place where Major Mitchell stood to survey the valley before him on a completely different expedition.

Before starting, the one thing in common I knew all these women shared was that none of them actively seek the limelight.

They are a modest bunch, and it usually took time, observation and conversations with others to uncover the true extent of their achievements. Most had to be convinced their story would be of interest to anyone other than their own family. Often they agreed out of a desire to help bridge the divide in understanding and experience between city and country, and open people's eyes to what is actually involved in producing the food and fibre on which we all rely. Or they were keen to throw a light on the daily challenges of living and raising a family in rural communities where the services and facilities most of us take for granted do not exist or are under threat.

All of them have a deep, spiritual connection to the place in which they live. They believe very strongly that they are only custodians of the land and have a responsibility to leave it in better shape for future generations. None consider themselves heroes, and would dislike strongly being thought of in those terms. But the way they have confronted life's challenges with grace and a sense of humour, their high level of skill as farmers, their compassion and generosity and sheer tenacity despite everything thrown at them is truly inspiring.

It has been a great honour to meet them all, share parts of their lives and tell their stories—a truly life-changing experience for me as both a woman and a writer. I hope their stories will inspire others too.

Liz Harfull

1

TENACITY IN SALT LAKE COUNTRY

Mary Naisbitt, Tarin Rock, Western Australia

For a thinly populated farming district on the edge of nowhere, the Tarin Rock Tennis Club is a remarkable facility. Five tennis courts, flood lit and covered with intense green artificial turf, an undercover playground packed with brightly coloured equipment, an expansive clubhouse and the locals' love of tennis make it the social hub for families from kilometres around. It is a place where they gather at weekends, not just for sport, but to share a meal and a drink or two and, for a few short hours, try to forget the drought which has kept the surrounding paddocks relatively barren for almost three years.

Drought wasn't an issue when friends and neighbours gathered at the club on 3 February 1980 for a relaxed Sunday evening of

1

social tennis. The harvest was in and it would be weeks before the tractors had to start up again to sow the next season's cereal crops. On the other side of the continent, Australia looked like it was cruising to yet another easy victory over England at the Melbourne Cricket Ground, batsmen falling regularly to the fiery bowling attack of Western Australia's favourite son, Dennis Lillee. In a country community reliant on farming for a living and sport for play, all must have seemed right with the world. But life was about to change irrevocably for Mary Naisbitt.

Mary's husband, Joe, was only 46 years old when he collapsed and died that day on the tennis court. Aside from a distraught wife, he left behind four children under the age of seven and a 1828-hectare farm freshly calved from the bush in the salt lake country of Western Australia's extensive eastern wheatbelt. Mary was 350 kilometres away from the support of her own family near Perth and had played no active part in running the farm. Most people expected her to put it on the market, pack her bags and head back to the city with her children. But Mary Naisbitt has never been one to take the easiest option.

Mary was born in the central wheatbelt town of Merredin, about 240 kilometres to the north of Tarin Rock, on 15 February 1943. Her parents, Bozo 'Bob' and Teresa Starcevich, were Croatian emigrants who had come to Australia independent of each other before the Second World War. The son of a woodcutter from a small village in what was then Yugoslavia, Bob had finished the national military service required of all young men in his country and couldn't wait to leave. He wanted a better life and thought Australia would offer far more opportunities. Arriving by ship in Perth, Bob made for the isolated mining community of Kalgoorlie, 600 kilometres further east, in search of work. When he couldn't find any, he headed back along the Great

Eastern Highway, ending up at Merredin where he secured employment on a farm.

Although she also came to Australia from Yugoslavia, Teresa was born in the United States of America. She was the only daughter and middle child of emigrant parents, who also had two sons. Their mother died when Teresa was four and her baby brother was only two months old. Not able to cope with the children on his own her father returned to Yugoslavia, where he married again. However, tragedy continued to mar his life. His youngest son died, as did his second wife and the children he had with her. He married a third time, to his second wife's sister, and had another son, before immigrating again, this time to Australia. He took only his oldest son with him and they worked hard to save money so they could send for the rest of the family.

Father and son ended up at Merredin, where they met Bob. Drawn together by a common heritage, they became good friends, which brought Teresa into Bob's orbit soon after she arrived in Australia with her stepmother and half-brother. Bob and Teresa eventually married. They had two sons, John and Stan, before Mary came along. By then Bob was working part-time for the Public Works Department, carrying maintenance crews to the pipeline which supplied water to towns along the highway from Perth to the Kalgoorlie goldfields. They lived on a 2-hectare block on the outskirts of Merredin, where they had an extensive vegetable garden and fruit trees that supplied produce to the town. Mary can remember spending most of her time outside and playing at being a farmer, using she-oak nuts to create miniature herds of cows and sheep.

When she was about seven, the family moved closer to Perth in search of more reliable work. They settled at Midland, where Bob and Teresa remained for the rest of their lives. Even though he suffered from a bad back, Bob took on a range of physically demanding jobs to look after his family, wrapping his back tightly with a wide band of grey flannelette to keep it warm and support the muscles so he could keep going. At one stage the doctors told him he would never be able to do heavy physical work again, and he spent three months in hospital, leaving Teresa to cope with the children. Mary can remember the strong smell of eucalyptus oil—her father's cure-all for every ache and pain. He shovelled coal on trains, worked on maintenance crews for Perth's water and sewerage systems, and spent his final working years in the railway yards at Midland unloading freight, until regulations forced him to retire on his 65th birthday.

Now a suburb on the eastern edge of Perth's metropolitan sprawl, Midland was then a separate township with a large rail terminus at its heart. Mary remembers a vibrant community of many cultures, with significant numbers of refugees from Italy and eastern Europe. At home, she spoke Slav with her mother, who found it difficult to learn English. Her Australian friends joked that it sounded like 'Double Dutch'.

Mary completed her primary schooling at St Brigid's Catholic School, run by the Sisters of Mercy. Encouraged by her mother, who was an excellent needlewoman, she went on to learn dressmaking at the Midland Junction Technical School, across the road from where she lived. 'Mum was always adamant that no matter what, I was going to learn dressmaking, because she felt that she had missed out on a lot,' Mary says. 'In Croatia, the women used to sit outside on the verandahs and knit socks and jumpers or whatever. Mum always used to watch, and apparently the ladies used to say if you gave her wool she would know how to knit because she was so keen to look . . . She was very much a housewife. She made all our clothes. I can remember my dresses were always made with a big hem that could be let down when I grew.'

While she was studying at technical school, Mary worked part-time in a local grocery store, weighing and packaging up grocery items that arrived in bulk. 'The biscuits used to come in tins and we used to have to pack them in cellophane bags ready for the customers; sugar too and things like icing sugar, dates, prunes and dried fruits. I used to quite enjoy it . . . but I felt I needed to get something permanent rather than just working in a shop. I kept thinking I had missed out on something. I hadn't had a lot of schooling. At that stage getting married wasn't one of the things I thought I had to do and I kept thinking that if I'm going to be working all my life I've got to do something.'

At the age of about eighteen, Mary took herself back to the technical school and studied English and typing, with the idea of finding an office job. She studied part-time at nights, while earning money making shirts at a clothing manufacturing factory set up in Midland by G&R Wills & Co Limited. After graduating three years later, she and a girlfriend decided to head to New Zealand on a working holiday. Aside from adventure Mary thought it might offer a great opportunity to gain some experience in office work so that she could return home and find decent employment. 'It was fantastic,' she says. 'I stayed some of the time with friends my mother had grown up with in Croatia, and I think that helped, but I travelled the whole of New Zealand and worked at lots of different things. I was away for about eighteen months, much to Mum's horror.'

After brief stints in Melbourne and Brisbane, Mary finally returned home and applied for work in the Perth office of an insurance company she had worked for in Melbourne. Although the South British United Insurance Company initially had no vacancies, Mary was soon called back and offered a position handling reinsurances for larger clients whose policies represented too big a risk for the company to handle on its own. Much more responsibility than she had anticipated, Mary is not quite sure why she was offered it.

'It was a very interesting job and it was a job that was generally carried out by a man,' Mary says. 'I was the first woman in that company to do that job. Women were known as typists only, really. I have a feeling there must have been something in the reference they gave me in Melbourne, or maybe they couldn't get a bloke interested in doing it. Some people might think it would be boring, but I didn't.'

In her leisure hours Mary started going to a social club in Perth run by the Catholic church. Young people over the age of 21 would get together on a regular basis at each other's houses or organise social events such as cabarets. 'We used to have lots of fun,' she says. 'It was a fantastic time.' Mary doesn't recall exactly where or when, but she first met Joe at one of these events while he was visiting Perth to see one of his sisters, who was a member of the club. Ten years Mary's elder, it was Joe who followed up the initial encounter and asked her out. In between occasional dates when he was in the city, they wrote letters to each other and she gradually fell in love with the tall, fair-haired farmer.

Missing her company, Joe urged Mary to write longer letters. One day she decided to give him what he asked for, literally, and created an entire letter on a long paper streamer. She kept all their correspondence until just after he died, when the letters were burnt. 'I do regret it now, but at the time I just felt that they were really personal, and there were so many people around and I didn't want anyone going through them, as well-meaning as they were,' she says.

Mary tries to describe the man she remembers: 'Often people used to call him Old Joe, because his hair was thinning out. I do remember when I met him, I suppose because his hair was receding and it was light coloured, he may have looked older than he was ... A lot of people said he used to joke a lot, but I don't know. He was very happy and he had a good sense of humour. He was certainly a very genuine person, and always did the right thing by everybody. He was very well liked among his peers. Anyone who knew him always spoke well of him.

He was always a very fair person, a good listener, and he was good with kids, actually. The kids really missed out because he was the one with all the patience.'

Joe Naisbitt was born in Perth's King Edward Memorial Hospital on 4 November 1933 and grew up on a farm at Tarin Rock, about 20 kilometres west of the town of Lake Grace. His father, Ted Naisbitt, had taken up a 400-hectare parcel of land in 1923, after emigrating from Durham in England with his mother and sister. It was a time when farming in Western Australia was developing rapidly and confidence in agriculture was booming, drawing many immigrants and returned servicemen to the Lake Grace area. Ted worked hard clearing the land for cropping and in 1929 married Win Stacey. Battling through the Depression years, the couple survived with Win milking cows to supplement the family income. They had nine children, with the oldest John and third-born Joe both returning home from boarding school to work on the property in the late 1940s after their father became ill. John and Joe also set up a contracting business to earn extra money, taking on welding and carting grain as well as purchasing half-shares in a bulldozer and ripping equipment to clear land.

Mary was not at all daunted by the idea of marrying a farmer, leaving her life in Perth and moving to the relative isolation of Lake Grace. 'I think I always had it in my bloodstream,' she says. 'I couldn't wait to get out of the city. I worked there because I had to, but I was always more of an outdoor farming person.' Her work colleagues weren't surprised either. They had been expecting for some time that Joe would 'pop the question' and they had a fair idea she intended to say yes. 'They had all expected me to get engaged on my birthday . . . but when I got back there was nothing on my finger. I said nothing to anybody, but we had decided to wait until the long weekend. I remember walking into the office and sitting down, and then I happened to put my hand up to my ear with the phone. A couple of the girls noticed the engagement ring and there was one mighty scream and yelling. The bosses were not overly happy—I was 27 and I have a feeling they had thought I wouldn't be getting married.'

Mary and Joe wed at St Brigid's Catholic Church in Midland on 7 August 1971. Mary entered the church on the arm of her proud father. Joe's brother Michael, who had been ordained earlier that year, officiated at the ceremony with assistance from the local Franciscan priest. All of Joe's large family were there along with Mary's relatives and a few friends who later gathered in the local show society hall for the reception. The couple cut a three-tiered wedding cake made by Teresa and decorated by Mary, who had taken lessons from a lady down the road. Mary recalls that 'the day went without a hitch—a happy, great day. Everyone enjoyed themselves as far as I can remember.'

The newlyweds spent their honeymoon travelling with a caravan up the Western Australian coast as far as Carnarvon, about 900 kilometres north of Perth, before returning to Tarin Rock less than a fortnight after the wedding so Joe could get back to work. The caravan was parked alongside the Naisbitt farmhouse and became their home. With Joe's large family around them and limited personal space it was hard to find time alone, but seven months later they finally moved into their own house on a nearby farm which Joe purchased from Mike and Dot Treasure.

Set on a low-lying ridge about 15 kilometres from town, the property overlooks the expansive, crystalline salt pan of Lake Grace North, part of the massive Lake Grace wetland system. Almost 26 kilometres long and more than 7 kilometres across as its widest point, the lake rarely contains much water. The glistening white salt plain is a spectacular sight which fascinates travellers and provides a distinctive backdrop for the town of the same name, although locals rarely go there because it is so hard to access. Even the Naisbitts had rarely stepped on the crunchy salt-laden lake bed until recent years when their son Kevin started leasing land along its western shoreline.

The lake was not visible at all from Joe and Mary's first home, a prefabricated cottage set low down in a secluded spot at the northern-most edge of the farm. The small house is still there, relatively unchanged, with verandahs at the back and front and only three main rooms. The front door leads straight into the main living space, an open-plan room combining both the lounge area and kitchen. At the back are two small bedrooms which had raw asbestos walls when Mary first saw them; she insisted they were painted before moving in.

Drought has killed off the small square of lawn at the front of the house and most of the garden plants, but she loved the prospect from here, particularly in the evenings when she would watch kangaroos hop up to a nearby dam for water.

Kevin enjoyed it too when he moved in with his wife Sarah just before they were married. 'I loved sitting here with a beer after work; it was really relaxing, I don't know why,' he says.

Mary and Joe soon settled into life in the cottage. Mary was lonely at times but she tried to focus on her new role as a homemaker while Joe worked long days with his older brother on both his own property and the family farm. During particularly busy periods like seeding and harvest, she would pack lunch and take it to him out in the paddock. If he was working nearby on the tractor, Joe loved nothing better than looking back at the house in the evenings and seeing the warm, comforting glow of the lights, knowing Mary was waiting for him. 'He always liked to think when he came home I would be there,' she says. 'I remember one evening I got the dog and went for a walk up around the bush. He came home and he was quite worried that I wasn't there.'

From the beginning Mary loved living in the country although it took her a while to get to know her way around. She can remember failing to locate Joe one day when she was meant to be delivering his lunch, and then there was the time she got lost in a paddock in thick fog, trying to move sheep. The idea seems strange to her now, with every square metre of the farm firmly engraved on her memory, including the 100 hectares of remnant scrub she has protected.

Mary's quiet life ended in 1973 with the birth of Patricia. Known to everyone as Trish, 'never Pat', she was born on Joe's 40th birthday, when Mary was 30—at the time considered old for a first-time mother. 'We didn't wait overly long to have children because I wasn't that young, and he wasn't that young,' she says. 'We always intended to have either two or four children, and Joe always said, "It's up to you. You're the one having them, and you'll be dealing with them." Little did he know how much!'

Trish was born in the hospital at Wagin, about 120 kilometres west of Lake Grace, because there was no resident doctor at the time. Prospective fathers were not permitted to be present during births in those days, but Joe was allowed to see Mary and the baby soon afterwards. He then rushed back to the farm, where shearing was in full swing and all hands were needed. Nine days later he returned for the first time to collect mother and daughter and take them home.

With a second child on the way, Joe and Mary decided they would need a bigger house. They ordered a brand new transportable home in September 1975, on the day Susan was born at the Lake Grace Hospital. The house was placed on a rise with distant views of the eponymous lake and was ready to move into the following January. Only a toddler, Trish took exception to the change at first. One afternoon when Mary thought it was a bit quiet, she found the determined two-year-old heading off across the paddocks towards the cottage with the family sheepdog. 'I am going home,' she told Mary.

The Naisbitt family expanded with the arrival of a third child, Diane, in January 1977. This time Joe was allowed to attend the birth. He was there too when Kevin was born in September 1979. Mary remembers the local, elderly doctor gave her a lecture about having a child at the ripe old age of 35. He accused her of taking risks only because they wanted a son to inherit the farm. 'He really upset me, I can tell you. I went home and told Joe but that is one time I really don't think he supported me. He just said not to worry about him, 'What does he know?''

A loving father, after a hard day's work Joe enjoyed nothing more than relaxing in the evening by playing with his children. 'After tea he would go into the lounge and they would follow because they knew it was playtime, and they would jump all over him,' Mary recalls.

As the oldest child, Trish is not so sure she actually remembers these play sessions, or whether she has adopted the memory and made it her own after hearing about it so many times from her mother, who was careful to talk about their father after he died and answer their questions. 'Sometimes you get confused about whether they're things you actually remember or because you have heard the stories over and over, so you can just visualise it and after a bit you take it as your own memory,' Trish says. 'But I do remember sitting on his shoulders and having to duck going through doorways—the doorframe coming towards me and thinking, "Oh my goodness, I'm going to hit that." And I can remember birthdays. Dad and I shared the same birthday, and I remember my sixth birthday quite clearly. This was in November and Dad passed away the following February. He was 46 and must have made a comment that he was getting too old for birthdays. Kevin was being christened on the same day and he was only about two months old. It was enough for me to think, "Dad is too old for a birthday, Kevin is too young to know about his, this is all mine!"'

With a new baby in the house, three young children underfoot and the crops to harvest, the lead-up to Christmas 1979 was a busy time for Mary and Joe. Most local farming families head to the coast for a summer break in January, once the harvest has finished, but the Naisbitts usually stayed at home, preferring instead to take regular short breaks during the year to visit Mary's parents at Midland and run farm errands in Perth. That year, however, they packed up their brand new Ford station wagon and headed to Albany for ten days, towing a large caravan Joe had bought with his younger brother Herbert. They celebrated Diane's third birthday at the historic port in the state's south-west on 30 January, and drove back to Tarin Rock the next day so they were back in time for Trish to start school.

The following Sunday was a relaxed day. Friends who had been managing the property across the road were leaving the district so they came to lunch. After they left Mary cleared up the dishes while Joe bathed the girls, ready for an evening with other families at the Tarin Rock Tennis Club. The club had far more basic facilities then, but a few people were out on the courts 'fooling around' and playing social tennis, while others gathered in the shed that served as a clubhouse.

A consistent district-competition player in his youth, Joe was keen to revive his skills and start playing more often. He headed to the court with three others for a relaxed game of doubles while Mary sat in the shed. Given the amount of laughter drifting from the court, they seemed to be having fun.

At about six o'clock Mary was talking to a couple of other women, with Kevin asleep nearby in his pram and the girls playing with friends, when she looked up to see people gathered around someone lying on the court. She is not sure how, but she had an immediate sense it was Joe. She jumped up and ran to his side, where several people were trying desperately to revive him. 'I can still hear them calling out, "Come on, Joe". He never responded in any way at all.' Mary stayed beside him while others took charge of the children and kept them away from the traumatic scene.

Trish was playing in a sandpit only a few metres from the courts when she became conscious of 'a lot of commotion' as people ran from the clubhouse and other courts to the spot where she had moments before seen her father, standing by the net, facing towards her. Her next memory is of walking down the road away from the courts, towards the Tarin Rock grain silos, with a group of children and a couple of their mothers. 'I remember walking by Kevin's pram and asking the two ladies, "Was that my dad?" I asked this several times and got no reply from them. I remember being quite confused, not angry but wondering why were they ignoring me.'

Meanwhile, one of the players had rushed to his ute and called his wife on the two-way radio, asking her to phone for an ambulance. It seemed to take an age before it arrived, although Mary suspects the emergency crew covered the 25 kilometres from Lake Grace in record time. A fence surrounding the court was cut down and the ambulance was driven right up to the site. The doctor on board could do nothing for Joe either. He had no known heart condition, but had suffered a massive heart attack. He was most likely dead before hitting the ground.

In a state of shock, Mary travelled in the ambulance to the Lake Grace Hospital, sitting in front with the driver while the doctor rode in the back with her husband's body. A friend later collected her from the hospital and took her to the Catholic presbytery so she could start the heartbreaking process of contacting her family, who all loved Joe. The children were gathered up by near neighbours Philip and Dorrie Gooding, who took care of them that evening.

Trish recalls sitting at their kitchen table, eating dinner with her sisters, when a priest arrived. 'He told us to come into the lounge area and to kneel down and say our prayers because Dad had gone to heaven. I can't recall the next few moments but I remember someone later saying to me to go back to the table and eat my sweets. I am not sure if I said it or just thought it but I remember thinking, "My dad has just died and you want me to eat sweets?" I ran off crying to who knows where and that is all I remember from that night.'

Mary didn't have much to start with when she found herself a farmer in her own right. Joe had left her the property, but there was practically no infrastructure apart from a few fences and dams and a small shed-cum-workshop close to the house. He had run the farm in partnership with his brother John, who provided access to sheep-handling facilities, machinery and machinery sheds on the original Naisbitt property nearby. With Joe's death the partnership was formally dissolved, and most people assumed Mary would sell up and move to Perth to be closer to her parents, but she was determined to stay put and find a way to manage the place on her own. 'I couldn't see myself anywhere else but on a farm,' she says. 'I kept thinking there has got to be a way that I could do it. And then a neighbour actually said to me, "I know a farm adviser that can probably help you."'

Employing a professional adviser to help manage a farm was not common when Mary decided the idea was worth a try. While most farms in the region would today engage consultants to provide advice on at least some part of the operation, back then it was an option mainly taken up by absentee owners or larger enterprises. That was certainly the focus for the farm management business Mary rang in Perth, but the head of the company, Clive Napier, agreed to assess the property and see what could be done. He assigned one of his advisers, Ron Stewart, to provide advice and Ron became a regular visitor over the next few years, heading to the farm every two or three months to see how things were going. He became known as the 'Bunyip Man' to the children because he told them stories about bunyips replacing the Easter bunny. 'He was going to bring us photos, but of course he never did,' says Kevin, with a chuckle.

Clive and Ron very strongly advised Mary that the best way forward was to keep things as simple as possible. The property wasn't big enough to employ a manager, so they suggested she bring in sharefarmers to take care of the cropping side of the business and sell most of her sheep, keeping just the wethers, or castrated males. Cutting the flock back in this way would remove the work involved in managing ewes and lambs, but still give her a regular income from wool production and selling older sheep for export to the Middle East. The sharefarmers would supply the equipment, know-how and labour to grow cereal crops, as well as all the seed, fertiliser and chemicals involved to control pests and diseases, in exchange for keeping 75 per cent of the earnings from the grain. 'So that is pretty much what we did,' Mary says.

Ron placed an advertisement in a farming newspaper and helped screen the applicants, but Mary handled the business negotiations, working with the sharefarmers to draw up something both parties considered fair. A local farmer, Brian Posser, signed up as sharefarmer for the first few years, followed by Philip Gooding, who stayed on for the next twenty years or so, eventually managing the cropping with his son, Daniel. Over time, the terms of the lease changed so Mary was receiving 50 per cent of the earnings from the grain, in return for supplying the land, seed and fertiliser.

Initially, the sharefarmers cropped about a third of the property every year, sowing wheat and some barley. Meanwhile, Mary focused on looking after 1200 merino sheep. 'That was one bone of contention with the adviser. He wanted more sheep but I was always concerned about making sure they were well fed and looked after.'

Within about two years or so of Joe's death, Mary had organised her own silos to store grain for sheep feed, yards to work the sheep in, and a shearing shed. She also named the property so she could register a brand for the sheep and the wool—Jenakora, a combination of Joe's initials and an Indigenous word for dwelling place.

Life on the farm gradually settled into a routine. Mary was usually up by about six o'clock. The first priority was getting the children ready for school and making sure they didn't miss the bus, which picked them up from the farm gate to take them into Lake Grace. Trish was already at school when Joe died, and Susan started a year later. In the early years, Mary packed their lunches but as they got older and the other children started going to school too, they would organise their own food the night before and put it in the fridge ready for the morning.

Never one to sit still for long, Mary would then head straight out onto the farm. Depending on the time of the year, the first tasks revolved around feeding sheep and checking the dams. Checking dams was particularly important in late summer or dry years when water levels dropped, leaving behind thick mud that could easily trap unwary sheep carrying a full fleece. It was a lesson hard-learnt for Mary, who initially bypassed a dam or two. 'We had about 30 young wethers stuck in a dam once. We had to use sheets of iron and boards and God-knows-what to get them out. And what did they do? They turned around and went back in again.'

While Kevin was still a baby and Susan only a toddler, Mary would take them out into the paddock with her while she worked. She was restricted in how much she could do unless Trish was home and able to go with her to help keep an eye on them. Neighbours and friends sometimes looked after Kevin, making the juggling act a little easier, but Mary says the children were very good overall, learning to entertain themselves and not get in the way until they were old enough to help.

Mary can remember many kind acts which enabled her to cope, especially in the early years as she slowly acquired the skills and knowledge needed to run the farm. Far from being intimidated about tackling something new, she proved capable when it came to hands-on skills such as maintaining the machinery, minor building projects and woodwork. She taught herself to weld, learning from her mistakes and the occasional helpful hint from people who dropped by the workshop and saw what she was up to. She taught herself how to put up and repair fences too, joining broken wires using a 'figure eight' method she had seen Joe use. She had a pattern of it made up and carried it in a toolbox, along with instructions on how to use some wire strainers. 'I had to keep the instructions handy when I first started and if anyone drove past I would make sure they weren't visible,' she says, laughing at the idea of being embarrassed by such a small thing.

Neighbours were always on hand if needed but Mary did not want to abuse their generosity so she tried to call on them as little as possible. Even so, in the way of country communities where people tend to keep an eye out for each other, Bobby Walker from down the road would call by with his ute to collect the wool in the days before she had a tractor to lift the bales. He would often pop in for a visit and encourage her to 'sing out' if she needed anything. Then there was the farmer who shared a design for an easier closing mechanism for gates made from wire, star pickets and steel posts. Philip and Dorrie Gooding also proved to be a tower of strength, offering practical advice and providing an impartial sounding board when she was trying to solve problems.

Over the years, Mary also developed the theory that if she couldn't find a ready solution or make something work after giving it a 'good go', it was better to walk away and do something else for a while. 'In the meantime you would think about it and find another way,' she says. 'I don't know if it was sheer luck or not, but it always seemed to work out.'

On Kevin's third birthday, the farm took delivery of a tractor. The little red International with a bucket attached at the front is Mary's favourite acquisition in all the years she managed the property and one of the most useful. She bought it second-hand from a machinery business in Lake Grace. They delivered it to the farm with an offer to show her how to drive it, but Mary refused with a confidence she was far from feeling. 'I just wasn't game to get on it while the tractor bloke was there,' she confesses. 'As soon as he was gone, we worked it out.' Once she was reasonably confident of the basics, Mary invited all four children aboard for a test run. Kevin sat on her lap, while the other three found perches around the three-sided cabin.

The tractor quickly became Mary's 'right hand', allowing her to manage many tasks on her own, especially when all the children were at school. The bucket made it useful for picking up and moving anything from mallee roots to sick sheep, while various attachments were acquired over the years, such as a post-hole digger and even a piece of railway line. 'Mum used to tow it behind, and it would line up all the rocks so we could pick them up more easily. We used to just sit on the tractor and go round and round doing that,' says Kevin.

The Inter remained the main farm tractor for the next 30 years or so until Kevin took over the property. 'We just about killed the poor little thing, to be perfectly honest,' he admits. 'There were a lot of things it just wasn't supposed to do.'

Even though the paint work is a bit faded and it has the odd spot of rust, it's still Mary's tractor of choice, much to her son's amusement. He would rather use the gigantic four-wheel-drive John Deere purchased two years ago with its fully enclosed, air-conditioned cabin, specially designed driver's seat with suspension features to 'enhance operator comfort', and a sound system to help while away the long hours seeding and harvesting. Kevin appreciates every luxury, especially during late-night shifts in the colder sowing season. 'It spins me out sometimes when I hop onto the Inter after the big one,' he says.

Now dubbed 'Nanna's Tractor' by Mary's grandson Griffin and the rest of the family, the little red International still has its uses. A reminder of how much the scale of farming has changed in Australia over the past 30 years, it sits in the machinery shed, dwarfed by the towering green and gold goliath of the John Deere which seems to have been built for giants. Kevin would love to see Mary drive the new tractor. He has a high opinion of her skills as a tractor operator, though the same can't be said of his sisters, who he enjoys teasing about crooked rows and an unfortunate instance when Diane wedged the seeder under a tree, a photo of which mysteriously ended up in the state-wide farm newspaper.

But Mary finds she is no longer game enough to give the big tractor a try, even though she wouldn't have hesitated a few years ago when the challenges were coming thick and fast, and she just rolled from one to the next. 'Sometimes I stop myself and think, "Gee, it's amazing what a few years will do." Now

I'm not looking forward to learning that tractor, and before I would have just got in and done it.'

Like most farm kids, Trish, Susan, Diane and Kevin all learnt to drive at a young age, practising in the farm laneways and paddocks. Trish was the first to experience Mary's skills as a driving instructor. 'That would have to be one of my worst memories,' Trish says, laughing. She was only about eight when her mother came to meet her and Susan one day at the gate, where they were dropped off by the bus after school. Mary put Trish behind the wheel of the old blue Holden farm ute and asked her to drive it up the kilometre-long lane to the house. Susan climbed into the back, joining Diane and Kevin on an old bus seat that leant up against the rear window.

Torn between feelings of excitement and trepidation, Trish slid behind the steering wheel and Mary placed a thick orange cushion behind her back to keep her well forward on the seat and within reach of the pedals. Mary sat beside her and showed the young learner how to move the column-mounted gear shift into first gear and they set off. It was not an auspicious beginning. Trish can remember bunny-hopping up the driveway as she struggled with the gear changes, to the accompaniment of cheerful hoots and derisory yells from the back.

'Just put it in gear, you'll be right,' Mary kept telling her daughter.

'I can't, I don't know where it goes,' replied an increasingly flustered Trish.

Learning to drive the tractor wasn't much better. 'We were up the paddock clearing mallee roots and whatnot. I didn't really want to do it but I can remember Mum saying you have no choice,' Trish recalls. The first thing she noticed after climbing into the cabin was a large notice on the back of the windscreen visor warning that the vehicle may tip over easily. It was not a comforting thought. Instead of sitting beside her, this time Mary was standing next to the back wheel of the tractor shouting instructions above the considerable noise of the engine. But Trish heard her, and put it in gear as requested. The tractor immediately shot off, Mary leaping backwards in fear of her toes being run over.

As the youngest, Kevin started driving, or at least 'steering', the ute when he was much younger than Trish, following the same learner's track up the farm driveway after dropping the girls off for the bus. 'To start with, on the way back, he would sit on my lap and off we would go,' says Mary. As he got a bit older, Kevin graduated to sitting behind the wheel by himself, with Mary in the passenger seat keeping a very watchful eye. A cushion was introduced to help him see over the dashboard after a startled bus driver saw what appeared to be a driverless ute heading down the lane, and made the suggestion.

While Susan was not that keen on the idea, Diane couldn't wait to learn to drive the ute although she was not so confident about tackling the tractor. 'I was very scared of it because it doesn't have a handbrake,' Diane says. 'It was many years before I was game to drive it up or down a hill. I used to stop and make someone else do it.' One day she had no choice. Her mum bogged the ute on wet ground alongside a dam, with the wheels sinking so low their small sheepdog, Cocoa, could just step off the back.

Mary called Diane on the two-way and asked her to bring the tractor to tow her out. 'So Kevin and I hopped on the tractor and hooned off as fast as we could go, and we got up there and we hooked up the ute,' Diane recalls. 'And Mum decides she will sit in the ute while I drive the tractor. So I slowly take up the slack . . . It started pulling and the ute moved a little so I accelerated a bit more . . . and it started coming out but then it did this massive dip down on the driver's side and I thought the ute was going to roll over into the dam, so I just planted my foot and got out of there. I was very aware that Mum was all we had.'

Trish was very aware of this fact too. At least for the first couple of years, she was always anxious to know exactly where Mary was, what she was doing and when she was due home if she was away somewhere or out on the farm working by herself. As she got older Trish worried about how she might cope if anything happened to her mother, especially while her younger siblings still needed looking after. 'I do remember it going through my mind a fair bit, especially as I got older. When I was sixteen, I still had a brother who was ten.'

As the children grew up they all played an active part in running the farm. A relatively willing workforce, they helped remove rocks and mallee roots from paddocks so the cropping equipment could run over them safely, and there were ongoing battles to keep on top of 'poison'—the local generic term for any weed toxic to livestock. 'I'm sure it was like someone had seeded it,' Mary says. 'It was a constant job all the way through . . . and it still pops up. Sheep only have to eat a little bit—even if it's dead it's not good. You just don't leave it lying around.'

The children were all charged to be constantly vigilant, with Mary offering the incentive of 1 cent for every plant collected. Trish recalls the experience: 'We would go off in pairs. One of us would carry the bag and the other one had a pick or a mattock. I used to try and get Diane or Susan because Kevin was too little and couldn't keep up with me. He couldn't drag the bag fast enough or carry the mattock because it was too big . . . We would cheat sometimes because there would be a big bush and we would chop it in two so we would get 2 cents.'

A particularly challenging job which tested everyone's mettle was moving sheep between the home paddocks and a separate block about 6 kilometres away. 'That was a huge job,' Mary admits. 'I used to dread it, but the kids were always quite happy. In fact I think they used to enjoy just going for a run.' Mary would drive the ute behind the mob, with the children running alongside, helping to check gates and fences along the road to make sure the sheep didn't escape into neighbouring properties. If any did, the children would hop over the fence to bring them back.

The real fun started if one of the big, heavy wethers fell behind or went down and had to be carried home on the back of the ute, which had a tray top a metre or so off the ground. 'It would take all five of us to get it up,' says Kevin.

Mary recalls occasions when blokes would wonder 'What's she going to do if a sheep goes down?' But over the years, she developed solutions that relied more on brains than brawn. One of her favourites was a hoist with a sling she had fitted to the back of the ute. 'I'd roll the sheep into the sling and then pick him up and swing him over. That hoist was a great one, even for fencing. You could hook up a big roll of wire with chains, and sling it up and off the ute.' Then there was the little trailer Kevin made while he was in high school, which could be hooked up to the farm's four-wheel motorbike and taken out into the paddock. The trailer was low so sheep could simply be rolled onto it. Mary also bought a portable shearing unit and set it up on the back of the ute so that if she found a fly-blown sheep in the paddock which needed crutching, she could do it on the spot, rather than taking the sheep back to the shed.

Mary admits she didn't know too much about managing sheep when she started, relying on the farm adviser, the state agricultural department's local office, neighbours or the share-farmers for information. Contractors were brought in to handle the crutching and shearing. In tougher times she and the children took on the crutching themselves to save money. 'That was a big mission,' Kevin says, laughing and shaking his head in disbelief at their early attempts. The sheep were big and heavy and the rookie team so slow they might only crutch 30 at a time before they had had enough; even when they had more experience, finishing 150 in a day was 'massive'. Not known for his patience or skill with sheep, these days Kevin can crutch 100 in about 90 minutes.

Kevin recalls: 'We had a little cradle set up to hold the sheep, but we didn't know how to set the handpiece up or anything. We would sit there trying to crutch them and there would be smoke coming out of it. But then one of the neighbours gave us a couple of hints, and we evolved from there. It used to take us longer than contractors to do it, but time wasn't as big an issue for us. We took on crutching and things like that to save money, and if it took us three or four times as long as a normal farmer it really didn't matter.' Mary reckons they also gained a certain satisfaction from doing it themselves.

Not so satisfying was doing battle with the constant flood of paperwork associated with running a farm business. One of Mary's least favourite chores was maintaining detailed hand-written ledgers to track cash flows and getting them to balance every month. 'I remember often hearing her cursing because she would lose a few cents somewhere, and things wouldn't add up,' Kevin says. 'There were a lot of hours in the office, and we used to get told off if we made too much noise while Mum was in there.'

Diane remembers one such day when Mary sent them off to the woolshed to get them out of the way. Their mission was to drench some big wethers for intestinal worms. They took a young sheepdog pup with them, and tied her up in the shed with a piece of rope to keep her from getting into trouble while they filled two drench bottles from a plastic drum standing nearby. Struggling to move the sheep, which weighed more than they did and 'fought tooth and nail', the four children persevered and finally got them into a raceway. Then they climbed in with them so they could grab hold of their heads and carefully administer the correct dose. Kicked, stomped on and pushed around by the big sheep, the children had managed to finish quite a few when Mary appeared with afternoon tea. She was feeling a bit guilty about sending them off to tackle such a big job on their own, and had decided to take pity on them. Meanwhile, the pup managed to wrap her rope around a drum of drench and tip it over. Mary went over to sort out the mess and discovered the children had been drenching the sheep with water. 'So we had to do the buggers again. We were not laughing,' recalls Diane.

When it came to household chores, Trish soon learnt the best way to motivate her siblings was to appeal to their competitive instincts. 'We turned everything into a competition to get it done, even hanging washing on the line. "Who can hang up the first three tops, and they have to be white, and you have to use white pegs?" As a kid myself, if I just nagged all the time it wouldn't work, and half the time I didn't want to do it either.' Mary often motivated them with small treats. Trish remembers her lining up eight little squares of chocolate on the kitchen bench; they could have them only when they had finished their chores. 'Looking back now, two little squares? But at the time it was like, "Oh wow!"'

Housework was something that had to be done. No-one particularly enjoyed it, but there was no shirking. 'It was done because it's got to be done,' Mary says. 'I don't like an untidy house, within reason . . .' She found it particularly depressing to come back inside at the end of a long day and face a sink full of dishes, so Trish and Susan took this chore on most days. Both were delighted when they came home one afternoon to discover a dishwasher had been installed.

At mealtimes, the focus was always quick and easy dishes. Mary describes herself as just a 'plain, ordinary cook', but her daughters remember it differently. By the time Trish was eight or nine years old, she was taking more responsibility for preparing meals to help lighten the load for her mother. 'I can quite vividly remember making sandwiches for school lunches, or helping to cook tea, bathing the younger two, listening to their reading,' says Trish. 'We had a sunroom out on the verandah and sometimes the three of them would be out there playing and carrying on, and I would be inside cooking tea. Sometimes I would wish I was out there playing as well but I really didn't mind. I don't remember Mum saying I had to help more or I had to do more. It was just a natural thing. Either Mum was busy or she might have been cutting firewood or doing something we were too little to do, and tea had to be made . . . We knew no different.'

Mary thought of Trish as her 'right hand'. 'We would all be together, and then suddenly she would disappear and she would be in the kitchen getting a meal ready. Trish really did a huge amount,' she says.

'I can remember Trish almost as a second parent,' Kevin adds, laughing later about Mary's attempts to convince him she deserved a present on Father's Day as well as Mother's Day, because she was filling both roles. While they all liked to tease him, Kevin clearly didn't mind too much the experience of growing up in an all-female household. 'None of the girls were really girlie girls,' he concedes. 'And I used to make them go out and play footy and cricket with me.'

Very conscious of making sure they enjoyed their childhood even though she needed them to help more than might be expected of other farm children, Mary would try to make the farm work as much fun as possible for everyone and it seemed to bring them all closer together. Kevin agrees: 'It was always a family thing where all four of us would pile into our little ute with Mum and go out to the paddock, and pick rocks or mallee roots or that kind of thing, which was generally fun. It was just part of what you did, and there was always a social aspect to it—or family bonding I guess you could put it down to. I loved growing up on the farm—it's a brilliant place to bring up a family.'

'Yes, it was hard work, but it was never torturous,' says Diane. 'It just had to be done. If we wanted to stay on the farm, Mum said we had to bog in and help, and then we could play. Some weekends we had to go and pick mallee roots but Mum would always say, "Enough's enough, let's go home," and we would do something nice together. A few times I built a little fort out of the mallee roots—you just had to try and make games.'

Some of the family's best memories revolve around Sunday picnics on the farm, when they would light a small fire to cook their lunch. Sometimes they caught yabbies from a dam and boiled them, or made a billy of tea. 'I can remember one time we took a Sunshine milk tin to cook frankfurts in, and we put them in there and I put the lid on, but obviously the lid was on tighter than it should be, and when it got warm it exploded,' Mary recalls. The frankfurts flew into the air and landed among the dogs, who raced around eating the unexpected bounty as fast as they could.

'We just thought it was hilarious,' says Trish. 'We didn't realise, of course, that was our lunch going everywhere.'

In the school holidays, they would often go to visit Nanna and Poppa Starcevich, travelling by a different route each time to make the journey more enjoyable. Until she had a stroke in her late 60s and moved into a nursing home, Teresa usually cooked a big pot of macaroni pasta on their first night together, served with her own special sauce made to a traditional Croatian recipe. 'If we arrived during the day and we knew she was making the pasta that night, Pop would take us down the street to a little deli to buy fresh parmesan cheese,' Diane says.

Part of the process was pouring the sauce over the pasta, mixing it in, and then sitting at the table to wait while the macaroni absorbed the flavour. The wait was excruciating for the children, who looked forward to this treat enormously. 'You had to sit there and wait for ten minutes, and it felt like an hour. That macaroni was to die for and I just remember being able to eat lots of it,' says Trish, almost salivating at the memory.

'It must have been how she cooked it because I use the same ingredients and it doesn't taste the same,' adds Mary. Either that, or Teresa had a secret ingredient.

When Mary was talking with her parents they usually spoke Croatian, interspersed with the odd word of English. Except for Susan, the children never really understood it, although they seemed to be able to identify the swear words, and they did pick up on favourite sayings often repeated in the old dialect spoken by Bob and Teresa, such as *zadnji zalagi*. Roughly meaning something along the lines of 'the last little tasty piece', it was applied when handing out the final biscuit or piece of cake.

Even the family's pet cockatiel learnt a few words. The bird would often travel to Midland with them because Teresa liked it so much. One of its favourite phrases was 'go to bloody hell', with the word 'bloody' in English and the rest in Croatian, which the children found hilarious. One day the bird caused a stir at the Narrogin high school when it wolf-whistled at the headmaster. Mary had dropped in on the way through to attend a meeting, leaving the bird sitting in its cage on the school porch. And it was the bane of poor Kevin's life, having learnt to call his name after listening to the family do it so often. If the other children called out 'Who's a pest?' in exactly the right tone, the bird could be coaxed into replying, 'Ke-vin'.

Although money was usually tight, Mary did her best to make sure the children didn't miss out on too much, particularly on special occasions such as Christmas and birthdays. Occasionally, everyone would pile into the family car and they would drive to Katanning, about 130 kilometres away, to go shopping and play in the park before checking into a motel for the night. This was a rare treat, with the children revelling in the luxury of sitting up in bed watching television, munching on fish and chips for dinner.

Mary also did her best to make sure they didn't miss out on too many of the common experiences of their school friends. In Joe's place, she taught Kevin to kick a footy before he headed off to school, and she encouraged him to play football for the Lake Grace Bombers as he grew older. All the children were signed up for music lessons with a private teacher, with Diane really taking to playing keyboard and Kevin enjoying guitar.

With the local school only catering for students up to year 10, all four Naisbitt children joined their peers at boarding school. Most teenagers from the area go to either a private school in Perth or the state-run senior high school at Narrogin for their final years of secondary education. The Naisbitts preferred the latter option because it was closer to Lake Grace so they could go home for the weekend once every few weeks. Mary was no doubt relieved given the lower cost of boarding fees for four children, although she didn't count on all the letter writing involved to keep in touch at a time before mobile phones or email were in use. 'There were a lot of letters to be written. After a while I used to do carbon copies, and then add something on the bottom for each of them.'

Kevin relished living with 40 other boys. Even though it was a co-ed school, it was a big change from home and he made some good friends. A 'less social person', Trish didn't enjoy it quite as much but she loved going to business college afterwards in Perth, where she excelled at her studies and revelled in the novelty of living in the city. She would wander along the mall in her lunch breaks to watch people and window shop; Mary's lesson about always saving 10 per cent of their earnings keeping her from spending too much. Diane hated boarding school, and took a long time to decide what she wanted to do in life. 'One week I wanted to be a teacher, then a nurse, then a farmer, then a butcher,' she says. She eventually studied childcare and is now a teacher's assistant at a college in Perth, where she still lives, going home every term holiday if she possibly can. The 'bookworm' of the family, Susan went to university and then headed overseas, where she has lived and worked for ten years, keeping in touch with her family via skype and email.

'Sometimes I wonder if, because of the situation, they weren't cheated a little bit of their childhood, but then I stop and think, no. I gave them every opportunity. I took them in and out of town for training for their sports, I sent them off to Narrogin, I sent them off to Perth. I don't think any parent does any different, and they just took it in their stride,' Mary says.

For their part, it wasn't until the children were much older that they realised there was anything different about growing up on a farm with a single parent, who happened to be a woman. 'It never occurred to me until I went off to high school,' says Diane. 'The other kids would talk about their dads doing this and their mums doing that, and I began to realise it was different. By the time I had left high school it had really sunk in that Mum took on a lot and succeeded. For me she has just always been there, and I know I can count on her. We all had our share of illnesses when we were little, and if we called out in the night she was there instantly. In these last couple of years I have ended up with a health situation and even though it was the middle of harvest she came to Perth to be with me.'

While everyone adapted after Joe died, because there was little choice, it wasn't until she married herself that Trish began to understand the depth of Mary's loss and the true extent of the challenges she faced. 'She was not only dealing with four little kids and the farm but grieving as well. She had lost her husband.'

Kevin says parenthood has given him a far greater insight into just how difficult it must have been for his mother to cope with four young children on her own. 'I get very lost with exactly how Mum could have handled it as a single parent, even more than running the farm,' he says. 'That is the thing that still spins me out. If either Sarah or I go away for a couple of days and you are left with two kids, it's really hard work. You don't get anything done, farm-wise or housework. You are flat out just taking care of two kids.'

Looking back, Mary cannot think of much that defeated her over the 25 years or so she ran the farm, although a crisis which brought the Australian wool industry to its knees in the early 1990s came pretty close. The industry entered some of its darkest days when the global demand for wool crashed, taking sheep prices with it. The Australian sheep population had peaked in 1990 at an historic high of 170 million, tenfold the national population at the time, driven in part by a price protection scheme which guaranteed farmers would receive a minimum of 870 cents per kilogram for their wool.

Oversupply combined with increasing competition from cotton and synthetic fibres made wool virtually unsellable and stockpiles began mounting up in warehouses around the country. By February 1991, the official stockpile had reached a staggering 4.7 million bales—in Melbourne alone, the amount stashed away was said to be so large, if laid end to end the bales would stretch from Perth to Brisbane and beyond. Arguments raged in country halls, boardrooms and parliamentary chambers across the nation about who was to blame and what could be done to save an industry that had once carried the Australian economy 'on the sheep's back'. Growers and their leaders were so deeply divided that twenty years later the wounds have still not completely healed.

During the early months of the crisis, the Australian government and industry organisations decided one of the quickest ways to dramatically turn around overproduction was to reduce the number of sheep. They set up a program to cut the national flock by 20 million head within a year. In short, farmers would have to sell more sheep for slaughter and if they couldn't find a buyer, shoot them and dump the bodies in pits, either on their farms or at communal sites organised by local authorities. Farmers already struggling emotionally with extraordinary financial pressures now faced the heartbreaking task of destroying healthy animals.

Mary is typically matter-of-fact when she talks about this period, but it must have been devastating to come up against such a monumental hurdle after meeting so many challenges over the previous ten years. She had made running sheep and producing wool the main focus of her own efforts to keep the farm afloat, and up till then she had been successful. 'I remember thinking, "How am I going to do this? How am I going to dig a hole big enough?" Mary says. 'Because I had wethers the authorities came and looked at them, and said they would give me 20 cents each for them. All the neighbours were told to shoot theirs. I lent them my rifle so they had more guns on hand. That was a very hard time.'

It was probably about then that Kevin remembers his mum sitting all of them down to talk about the future of the farm, and that they may need to sell up. 'I only remember that happening once,' he says. 'I was pretty young, and it was obviously a bad year or we were heading towards some sort of financial difficulty . . . And she gave it to us kids to discuss. It's not that we necessarily had a vote, but she wanted our opinion, and we all really wanted to stay.'

Things didn't get any easier with the ongoing decline in global demand for wool lowering prices to just 380 cents per kilogram by 1993, barely enough to cover the cost of running and shearing the sheep. During this time Mary was put under pressure by a visiting wool buyer who implied he wouldn't take her wool unless she agreed to sell her sheep through the same business. 'He was trying to intimidate me,' Mary says. Like a lot of farmers, she had tried over the years to support as many local service providers as she could, dividing her farm business between them. She took out her insurance through one agent, sold her wool through another, and her sheep through yet another. She had found them all reasonably supportive after Joe's death, and happy to trade with her once they knew she had decided to stay. Mary stood her ground with the visiting wool buyer, who never came back.

'Mum was a very tough negotiator in most things,' Kevin says. 'No-one really ever got too much over her. She was aware of the proper value and pushed hard to make sure she got it.' Adds Mary: 'One thing that always stayed with me. When I worked in the shop back in Midland, we had a couple of customers who were vile. We used to duck out the back when we saw them coming and the shop keeper always used to say that, no matter what, the customer is always right when they are in the shop. And that stayed with me. I am the customer, so I get to negotiate.'

At times she wasn't above enjoying the unexpected advantages of being a woman either. She recalls with a smile her ventures into bidding at clearing sales. 'Early on the wives may have gone to clearing sales but there weren't many women out there bidding,' she says. 'To start with, if there was something I wanted I would get someone to bid for me, but in the end I thought, "Stuff this, I'll do it myself." And the blokes used to back off. It was damn good.'

At one clearing sale, Mary had her sights set on a pressure cleaner which someone else wanted too. He gave up when he saw who the other bidder was, saying with frustration, 'Bloody woman, I couldn't bid against her.' Diane remembers going to another auction where Mary decided to buy a pump. A teenager at the time, and reasonably shy, she was conscious of some men snickering when her mother put in a bid, but Mary had the last laugh. 'I think she ended up paying 5 dollars for this pump, and one of the blokes came up afterwards and tried to offer her twenty, but she just laughed at him and walked away.'

At some stage, Mary decided to attend her first farmers meeting. She admits the idea of being the only woman in a room full of men was a daunting prospect, even if many of them were friends and neighbours. 'No women went to the farmers meetings in those days, only blokes, and as much as they all knew me, from my point of view I was very dubious,' Mary says. But the local branch of a state farm lobby group was meeting at the Lake Grace sportsman's club to discuss a controversial issue, long forgotten now, and she wanted to learn about it first-hand. 'You can hear from others, but there is always a different point of view, and I wanted to know for myself.'

Mary discovered the actual experience was nowhere near as daunting as the prospect, and began attending other meetings and information seminars. She was given greater confidence by the wife of a neighbour, who often joined her husband. Before long, other women were showing up too. 'You would be surprised how quickly it changed, so there were more and more women going,' Mary says.

It's early May, and Mary and Kevin are watching the sky for rain. Weather over the next few weeks will make or break the cropping season for the Naisbitts, along with every other cereal producer in the vast Western Australian wheatbelt. It is an anxious time. The past two seasons have let them down, creating one of the region's worst droughts in 60 years, while the eastern half of the continent seemingly swims with water. 'There is a real sense this year will either make us or break us, so people are really quite on edge,' Kevin says.

From the highest point on the property, a sweeping hill overlooking the stark salt pan of Lake Grace North, it is a striking but depressing picture. The farm's 25 dams are empty and many paddocks are completely bare, revealing the flesh-coloured skin of pale dry sandy loam with an underlying skeleton of small stones and rocky outcrops. Puffy grey clouds scud overhead, but this time, like so many others, they do not bring rain. For the past two years the farm has received less than 200 millimetres, compared with the established average of 350. Even in an average year, there is little enough moisture to produce profitable crops, and the wheatbelt's farmers have a long-established reputation for finding innovative ways to cope.

It is one of the reasons the Australian government has chosen the region to pilot a new approach to drought-reform measures for the nation's farmers. For months now local community halls and farms have witnessed a steady procession of politicians and bureaucrats spruiking the program. Like many of his neighbours, Kevin has taken an active interest. He was one of twenty at Lake Grace to sign up for a component that has enabled him to create a comprehensive five-year strategic plan for the farm business and implement measures that will better prepare them for a variable climate. He is not convinced the pilot has all the answers, but he is impressed the approach has encouraged more people to sit down with their families and plan for the future. 'I don't think everyone quite realises what that has done for them yet,' he says.

Kevin is one of the lucky ones. Jenakora has access to water for household and livestock use, thanks to his mum's forward-thinking back in the mid-1990s. When Mary told her farm adviser that she wanted to spend $10 000 hooking the property into the water scheme pipeline running past its northern edge, he thought it was a waste of money. Today that investment has enabled the Naisbitts to hang on to about 1000 sheep at a time when many Western Australian farms have been forced to destock.

It was not the first time that Mary ignored advice to do what she thought best for her family and the farm. In choosing to keep Jenakora and run it herself, she surprised most of the local farming community and seemingly defied commonsense. Once her decision became known, many assumed she was doing it so her son could take over the property when he was old enough. That was not the case. She would have been happy for any of her children to take on the farm, not just Kevin, but she was very anxious to make it clear that none of them should feel under any obligation to become farmers if they wanted to do something else. 'I was really keeping the farm to educate the kids and to bring them up in a good, safe environment, not for any other reason,' she says. 'I had seen too many people who had said to their kids, "Right, you are going to be a farmer." But if you are not a farmer through and through, well, what's the point? You either love it or you don't. If you don't like it, well, no, go and do something else.'

While Kevin was growing up, Mary was not convinced he would in fact one day want to take on Jenakora; however, as time went by, she could see he was becoming more interested. After finishing high school in 1996, he took a year off and worked on the farm and for neighbours while completing a part-time preparatory course for university in agricultural science. Kevin then moved to Northam, about 90 kilometres east of Perth, where he studied for four years at Curtin University's Muresk Campus. Having successfully completed his degree, he took the fairly conventional approach for young Australians and spent a year travelling and working overseas.

During his time away from Lake Grace, Kevin had some serious choices to make. Half of his friends from the agricultural sciences course at university ended up going into support services such as rural banking, agronomy and the rural retail sector. As part of his education, he spent six months working for a wool buyer in Perth who offered him a job before he graduated. 'That was the big decision for me—did I continue with uni, did I take the job and enjoy it, or did I come back to the farm?' Kevin says. The year overseas gave him some perspective and helped clarify his thoughts. In 2003, at the age of 24, he returned permanently to Tarin Rock.

The way the farm operated began to change immediately. Arrangements with the sharefarmers were wound up and Kevin took charge of the cropping program, with helpful advice from Daniel Gooding, who had sharefarmed the property for years with his father. Kevin's first step was buying equipment, including a larger tractor and machinery for sowing the crops, which entailed working out budgets and borrowing money. In what is a common practice for most large-scale grain growers, overdraft accounts also had to be set up with suppliers to purchase seed, fertiliser and herbicides. These enormous upfront costs would be paid off once the crop was harvested and the grain sold.

'Mum was not necessarily the boss, but she still made all the judgement calls. She still ran the sheep flock, and helped me out a massive amount,' Kevin says.

Adds Mary: 'I felt if he was coming home and doing the work, he really needed a say. I think it amazed me where he got all his knowledge from, because he knew what machinery he wanted and all that. The farm adviser was there to bounce ideas off but that is all theory. Kevin was the one doing it. He will still discuss things with me and tell me about it, which I do appreciate because you can't just suddenly stop. On the other hand I was also ready to hand it over. I felt, oh cripes, it's time to do that.'

Succession planning is one of the biggest issues facing Australian family farms; it's often handled poorly, leading to all sorts of personal and financial stress. Mary had come across more than a few examples of problems caused when the older generation did not make way soon enough for the next generation, and plan ahead for the transition. 'A lot of my buddies are just workers on the farm and will be for another twenty years,' Kevin says. 'They don't get to make any decisions and it's silly. They have a degree and they have grown up on a farm, and their knowledge is exceptional.' When Kevin decided to get married and start raising a family of his own, Mary did not want to make the same mistake.

Kevin met Sarah through mutual friends at university. Off a farm near Northampton, about 500 kilometres north of Perth, she worked as a rural journalist and freelance writer after graduating and moving to Lake Grace in 2004 when she and Kevin took up residence in the original cottage. The next year they were married. When a suitable house came on the market in town at about this time, Mary decided she should move too, and leave Kevin to run the farm and make the bulk of the decisions on his own. The kitchen window and back garden of the small townhouse looked out over a neighbouring paddock and she thought she could be happy there, despite the wrench of leaving Jenakora after 35 years.

Moving was a gradual process, interrupted by severe flooding which inundated the town in early 2006, turning roads into rivers, threatening houses and shutting off most access routes. Mary's belongings were shifted into her new home in dribs and drabs over a period of about six months before she made the final move. She found the transition easier than expected. In part, this is because she is encouraged to visit Jenakora whenever she likes, take an active interest in the farm and spend plenty of time with her grandsons, Griffin and Tate. A curious three-year-old, Griffin clearly adores his grandmother and is always keen to go with her when she heads out to the paddock or the sheep yards. Mary remains Kevin's 'chief pusher upperer' during crutching and his best 'right-hand man', helping to check on the watering points and the sheep. During the busy seeding and harvest periods she might be there every day, lending a hand and taking Kevin his lunch out on the tractor, sometimes climbing into the cabin to keep him company for a lap or two of the paddock.

Like Mary, the small country town of Lake Grace and its surrounding farming community have shown remarkable resilience under challenging conditions since the first officially surveyed blocks of land became available for selection in 1911. They were taken up by mainly Scottish and English immigrants, drawn by reports of good soils for growing crops and pamphlets promoting Western Australia as a land of agricultural opportunity. According to *The West Australian* newspaper:

> Many express themselves delighted with the climate and their luck on being able to secure farms so quickly and easily. They appear so far, to be a type of settlers who should do well if they have a few favourable seasons, as they belong principally to the agricultural class of the old country.[1]

But in the early 'bad years' at least, the reality of life at Lake Grace was far different to the visions conjured up by government promotions and the pleasant-sounding moniker. From the beginning, there was a desperate shortage of fresh water for both people and livestock, with everyone reliant on a communal dam built by the government to take advantage of a natural sand soak about 3 kilometres west of the lake. The rainfall proved unreliable and the seasons highly variable. A deputation appeared before the government in November 1911 asking for assistance to secure water supplies because it was so dry and the shortage of water reached a critical stage in the summer of

1913.[2] The following year farmers were lucky if they harvested enough wheat to use as seed, and the year after large areas of crop were affected by fungal disease.

The settlement was also extremely isolated. There was no gazetted township until after the railway arrived in 1916, and the nearest centre offering a doctor or chemist was some 130 kilometres away. Food supplies only reached Lake Grace about twice a year, consisting 'almost entirely of tinned meat, tinned fish, jam, condensed milk, sugar, flour and dried fruit'.[3] Fresh vegetables and meat were virtually unheard of, and people couldn't keep chickens until the first cereal crops were harvested to provide grain at the end of 1913. The diet was so bad people suffered from 'Barcoo rot', the local name for a form of scurvy brought about by vitamin deficiencies. Despite such challenges and setbacks the settlers continued to work long arduous days, clearing land and building humpies to house their families. In a combined effort not so different to that made by the Naisbitts decades later, an early traveller noted men must share the credit for every acre cleared with 'root picking, stump packing mothers, girls and tiny "whackers" of from seven to twelve years of age'.[4]

With the arrival of the railway, a consolidated community started to rapidly emerge. Supplies reached the area on a more regular basis and it became cheaper and easier to ship out farm produce. The first businesses started springing up immediately in the town, which went through a period of rapid development in the 1920s, creating a major service centre for the farming community and significantly improving the quality of life. Since then economic depressions, more droughts and floods, fluctuating wool and grain markets, and an exodus of young people to the city have all had their effect on Lake Grace—but the town is still there.

Despite the latest drought, the Lake Grace community is defiantly making plans to celebrate the fact that it still exists and is in reasonably good shape 100 years on. A member of the committee responsible for coordinating the centenary celebrations, Mary is proud of the way the community works together to get things done and continually reinvent itself. Making her regular walk from home to the post office and the visitor centre, she takes in the well-maintained main street and facilities set up in recent years to encourage travellers and tourists to pause on their way through to Esperance and Perth along State Route 107.

Paved footpaths lead past what used to be a cafe where she took the children for ice-cream after church on Sundays, to the town's only pub where she joined Trish and her husband Grant two nights before for beef parmigiana. Built in the mid-1920s, the Lake Grace Hotel is the only regular option in town for a meal out at night, except for weekends when locals flock to the popular sportsman's club. One of a series of plaques put up around the town to capture historical snapshots of key buildings tells observant pedestrians about high-jinks in the front bar. Apparently a teenage girl once rode her horse among the patrons, and a couple of local lads flexed their muscles by picking up a small car and carrying it through the double front doors.

On the opposite corner is the bank where Trish works, one of three in the town including a specialist rural bank which set up its shopfront a few years before in defiance of a trend that has seen banks close in country towns around Australia as populations decline and on-line services take over. Passing the bank, Mary pops into the local shopping centre where the well-stocked supermarket has been trading since six o'clock in the morning. She wants to check on the community noticeboard and a special whiteboard that has been set up for centenary events. The centre also has a hairdresser, a butcher and a clothing store catering to men, women and children, but the baker and the only chemist in town disappeared some time ago. In an ironic twist of convenience, the delivery van for the bakery based in a larger town further west now delivers prescriptions along with loaves of bread.

Saying good morning to an early shopper who she knows, Mary pauses outside a neat cream building with white-trimmed windows and terracotta-tiled roof. Like many country communities seeking to honour those who served in the Second World War, Lake Grace decided on a much more practical gesture than the memorial statues which sprang up across the country after the First World War. The building was opened in 1954 as a combined war memorial and town library. It is set back a little from the street, behind a small patch of lawn rimmed by hardy standard roses, which also provides a pleasant setting for another memorial of a different kind.

Facing the garden, along the eastern wall of the shopping centre, is a wall mural paying tribute to 48 local women who have been pioneers in some way, from European settlement to the present. There is Scottish emigrant Margaret Lawson, the first European woman in the district, who arrived in 1911 with her husband George and two young children; Effie Padley, who took charge of the first school when it opened in 1914; and Dr Margaret Clark, a graduate from Melbourne University who arrived in Lake Grace in 1932 and served as the town's doctor for 28 years. Mary is there too, for her achievements as a farmer and for her numerous contributions to the local community, where she has served on so many committees it is almost easier to list the ones of which she hasn't been part.

A striking feature of the mural is the backdrop featuring the hospital built on the outskirts of the town by the Australian Inland Mission (AIM) and its legendary founder Reverend John Flynn, who was instrumental in setting up the Royal Flying Doctor Service (RFDS). A much-loved and respected institution in outback Australia, the RFDS continues to provide a vital link to emergency care for Lake Grace. In the mural, one of their early bi-wing aeroplanes hovers over an image of the hospital, which opened in 1926 with two sisters in charge. The two-storeyed weatherboard building provided a home to the nurses and basic medical care for people living in an area of almost 16 000 square kilometres. Patients often spilled over from the ward to the verandahs, where a small operating theatre was set up. The hospital closed in 1952 after a more modern facility was built next door. It served as nurses' quarters and storeroom for another 30 years or so before falling into disrepair. Lake Grace fought to save it because it had played such an important part in the town's history, and was one of the last three AIM hospital buildings left standing in Australia. The heritage-listed building now houses a fascinating museum which allows visitors to experience the atmosphere of rural health care in the early twentieth century and the lives of people who provided it.

Across the road from the mural is the Lake Grace Multi-Artspace building where Trish is helping to organise signage for a centenary exhibition being staged by the local craft group. Mary drops in to have a chat to the volunteers getting ready to open for the first day, and to take a peek at how it has all come together. The carefully arranged display includes an elegant bedroom chair modified and upholstered by Mary, who is part of the group, which meets every Saturday morning. A keen seamstress and embroiderer, she loves going to their weekly sessions to catch up with other women and 'have a good laugh' while working on her cross-stitching. 'We talk while we're working, just about everyday things, and have such a good time,' she says. 'It's just good fun company.'

After making arrangements with Trish to come for lunch, Mary walks on to the cream-coloured building next door. Constructed in the 1920s to house the railway stationmaster, it now serves as the shire's visitor information centre and a gallery showcasing local produce, arts and crafts. Chair of the local tourism committee, Mary has promised to drop in and catch up with the centre manager. She finds Stephanie out the back, taking advantage of a relatively quiet morning to sort out a small storeroom. The two women chat over a cup of tea, admiring the latest items to arrive for the gallery, a popular source of gifts for locals and visitors alike.

Back at home Mary organises sandwiches to share with Trish, who is on holidays from the bank and using the time to catch up on her own volunteer work as chair of the Lake Grace Community Resource Centre and treasurer for the visitor's centre. She is following the example of her mother, who believes you only get out of a community as much as you are prepared to put in. 'After the kids went away to school and whatnot, I gradually got onto a few committees. I just felt, well, okay, the community had given me a lot, it was time to give something back,' Mary says.

In 1993 she took the giant step of nominating for a position on the Shire of Lake Grace council. She had recently attended a community development workshop which challenged participants to think about becoming involved in local government when the next round of elections came up. Finding herself running against two other local women, Mary often wondered 'What the heck am I doing?' and assumed she had little chance of success. Much to her surprise she won. Mary served on the council for the next ten years, a demanding role with the phone ringing often at night and regular meetings to attend, but she loved being part of the decision-making process and working with council to make a difference. She was particularly interested in developing the town's tourism industry and efforts to build new aged-care facilities.

Trish loves volunteering at the local visitor centre too, welcoming strangers to the area and encouraging them to take time to enjoy its sights, particularly the salt lakes and the extraordinary array of rare and endangered wildflowers which carpet the surrounding plains in spring. Keen photographers, she and Grant vie with each other to take the best wildflower images each year and sell them at the visitor centre. 'Grant loves photography and Mum and I really enjoy the wildflowers so we just put the two together,' she says.

Over lunch, Mary and Trish talk about plans for the centenary and the current mood in town. During the previous run of tough seasons, people took a head-on approach to what was shaping up to be a miserable New Year's Eve, and staged a 'Flop Crop' party. It proved extremely popular and no doubt helped more than a few cope with stress and depression, often a farming community's worst enemy in difficult seasons. Thanks in part to awareness-raising campaigns in the bush by organisations such as Beyond Blue, Kevin is well aware of the risks and considers himself lucky in that he is part of a great informal support network of younger farmers who talk openly about the dangers and keep an eye on each other.

With autumn almost over and still no sign of opening rains to sow the winter grain crops, Trish is hearing mixed responses over the counter at the bank. Some farmers have made up their minds to take a punt and start sowing anyway; others are planning to get just a few hectares in the ground so they have a jump-start if it rains but have mitigated the risks; while others are not planning to sow anything at all until they receive a decent amount of precipitation. Meanwhile, with farmers shutting down expenditure on everything but the bare necessities, local businesses are asking staff to take leave without pay and not replacing people who resign. 'It's not optimistic,' Trish says. 'There are a lot of really sad stories out there, and a lot of people on the verge of depression, thinking to themselves, "If it's another bad year, what do we do?" Everybody is praying for rain.'

Reflecting on the joys and frustrations of living in a small rural town, Mary and Trish talk about both the good and the bad of living in a place where everybody notices everything you do and the local grapevine spreads news faster than wildfire. Trish laughs as she recounts how quickly rumours raced around town that she was pregnant. She and Grant had borrowed a friend's ute to go and pick up something in Albany. The ute had a child's car seat in it so they took it out and left it sitting on their front porch. 'By the next week it had gone around Lake Grace that we were expecting. We had no idea what people were talking about, and then it suddenly twigged. We had left the car seat on the porch for just one night,' she says, still bemused. 'There are things that drive you insane about living in a small town, but on the other hand I like being able to walk down the street and say hi to everyone, and that if something is wrong or someone is not well, people will offer to help.'

That was certainly Mary's experience when Joe died. A little later in the afternoon, one of her oldest friends drops in for a cup of tea and apple muffins fresh from the oven. Joan de Vree was one of the people who helped Mary through the first incredibly tough years of being a single parent and trying to run the farm. She and local schoolbus driver Hazel Thiel would occasionally prepare an evening meal and bring it out to the farm to share with the Naisbitts. The children would also go and stay with them at times so Mary could take a break from her responsibilities for a few days or visit her parents at Midland. On the afternoons when the Naisbitt children were the last to be delivered home, Hazel would often drive the bus right up to the house for a cup of tea and a chat. 'It was unreal,' Mary says several times of the support and friendship offered.

Originally from the Netherlands, Joan came to Lake Grace in 1959 with her husband John, who was a builder. They intended to stay for just three months, living in a caravan while John worked on a couple of new houses. Fifty-two years later they are still there, retired to a house which John built. Friends of Joe, they were among the first people in Lake Grace to welcome Mary and attended the wedding.

Joan tells the story of the day she offered to help Mary move the sheep. All four children were away at school and she was anxious about tackling it on her own. Joan showed up in the morning and was put in charge of a young sheepdog. 'It wouldn't stay with me. He would run from the front of the mob to the back, and the sheep got upset. So I took my jacket off and tied one sleeve onto the dog's collar and I hung onto the other sleeve. And I was running to keep up with that dog, and Mary sat in the ute laughing her head off,' says Joan.

Then there was the famous shooting incident, which Mary is still trying to live down. Joan takes delight in recounting the story. Known to be a good shot, Mary had taken great care to instil in her children the importance of handling firearms safely, and never shooting at anything without first checking what lay behind the target. On this particular day, Mary was planning to discourage some birds taking fruit from the trees in her backyard. 'These birds were coming to nick her fruit,' Joan says, 'so she thought, "Right, I'll get you". She shot at a bird and missed. The next thing all this water is running down the hill. She had shot the rainwater tank.'

The Lake Grace Cemetery sits atop a rise west of the town. Tall salmon gums, named for the luscious pink tones of their smooth trunks, stand sentinel in the adjacent reserve. A much softer pink tinges the salt pan of a small lake to the south. Through the main gate, startling splashes of fresh green sprout from large terracotta pots lining the driveway. At the bottom of the rise is a new galvanised-metal shelter with seating for grave-side ceremonies. A new garden area landscaped with drought-tolerant natives is slowly taking root nearby, ready to receive the ashes of those whose families favour cremation over burial.

At the other end of the cemetery, overlooking the main road connecting Lake Grace to Perth, is a discrete area with a bench seat and small statuettes. On behalf of her community, Mary is filled with pride for this part of the cemetery. The memorial garden was created as a place to remember the countless number of stillborn babies buried in unmarked graves somewhere on the southern edge of the grounds, at a time when society and the health system thought it best to hide away such evidence of unrealised lives to spare their parents' grief, unwittingly adding to the pain and sense of loss.

Mary remembers the day this struggling garden was officially opened. There are photos in an album back at her house capturing the occasion. They show her wearing a dark trouser suit, standing with other community representatives and descendants of some of the families whose babies were among those lost. She was part of the committee which drove a project to improve the cemetery, disturbed by the ramshackle sprawl of tipping gravestones, unmarked graves and scruffy pathways.

Ostensibly, Mary has come here to check on the improvements and how well recent plantings are surviving the dry conditions. But strolling only a few metres down the main driveway, she takes a path to the left and quickly arrives at Joe's grave. It is a simple tribute to the husband she lost after less than nine years of marriage. A low platform of rough-cut granite stone is topped with a dark grey slab of polished granite. Full-blown red ceramic roses decorate the small cross which sits below eight rows of gold lettering: 'In loving memory of Joseph Edward, beloved husband of Mary, dear father of Patricia, Susan, Diane & Kevin, died 3–2–1980, aged 46 yrs'. Alongside are buried Joe's parents. In a cruel distortion of the expected order of things, both died after their son. Mary thought very carefully about Joe's grave, where it should be located and how it should be marked. She chose the masonry about twelve months after he was buried, with advice from the local monumental mason. 'I kept it plain, and the wind and the rain wipe it clean,' she says softly.

She recalls that five years or so after Joe died someone raised in concern the fact that she was still bringing his name up regularly in conversation. Worried this was an indication she was not letting go of her grief, Mary consciously tried to stop mentioning him so much, struggling at the same time with a desire to keep his memory alive for the children. She recalls hearing about another woman so affected by the death of her husband that she couldn't bear to even drive by the cemetery where he was buried.

'Different things sometimes catch you out,' she says, in what at first seems an unrelated tangent. 'I can remember being home on the farm and someone came along and shuffled their feet on the verandah. All the hairs stood up on the back of my neck. I don't know that it was something Joe actually did, I wasn't really aware of it, but it certainly sounded like him. And, although I'm getting used to it now because it's caught me out a few times, there is something about Kevin if I catch his side profile that reminds me of Joe.'

Back at home, Mary points out a hand-coloured photo of a handsome, blond boy, on the cusp of adulthood. It is Joe at the age of about thirteen. He wasn't too fond of the picture, which was hidden away when he was alive, but Mary has it hanging in pride of place above the fireplace in her lounge room. 'I reckon it looks good up there,' she says matter-of-factly.

2

THE APPLE PACKERS' LULLABY

Lynette Rideout, Oakdale, New South Wales

Lynette Rideout is inspired daily by memories of her remarkable grandmother. Born Cicely Berenice Robson in 1908, but known as 'Brenda', her life changed forever when her father died, leaving the Sydney family in straitened circumstances. After the funeral they returned home with guests to find bailiffs had removed all the furniture in lieu of unpaid debt. Food carefully prepared for his wake was sitting on the floor. Brenda was only seven, but she vowed there and then to work hard all her life so her family never had to live in poverty again.

True to her word, after completing an elementary education Brenda found work on a production line picking out broken biscuits at the factory operated by iconic Australian biscuit makers Arnott's. It was in Homebush, on what was then the western outskirts of Sydney. Allowed to take broken biscuits home for halfpenny a pound, she developed a particular taste for their famous Milk Arrowroots. First made in 1882 and still in production almost 130 years later, they were marketed for decades as a wonderful source of nutritious starch to help babies grow big and strong. Long past childhood Brenda often carried one tucked down the bib of her overalls to keep her going while she toiled away in the family orchard.

At other times Brenda worked as an usherette at a small picture theatre in Parramatta, close to where she lived. One day she caught the eye of her future husband, Leslie Alfred Gapes, when he went to a movie. No doubt his attention was easily drawn by the willowy brunette, who had recently won a beauty competition run by the theatre. A hand-coloured photograph from the time, which hangs in a large oval frame on Lynette's bedroom wall, reveals a stunning young woman, with wide, intelligent eyes and a kissable, bow-shaped mouth. Brenda was equally taken with Leslie, who she dubbed 'Snow' because of his blond hair.

The couple married and moved into accommodation above a greengrocer's shop at 30 South Street in Granville, which had been in Leslie's family since 1884 and was owned at the time by his father. All but two of their eight children (four sons and four daughters) were born above the store with assistance from a midwife, and Brenda usually returned to work the day after giving birth. 'She gave everything she had,' Lynette says. 'She looked after her family as best she could because she didn't want to see them do it as tough as she had.'

During the Great Depression in the early 1930s Brenda's generosity extended to countless numbers of people who found themselves without work, living on Sydney's streets and going hungry. At night she took vegetables from the shop and offcuts donated by the local butcher and made up a nutritious soup, which she left in a big boiler on the back steps. 'She fed a lot of people,' Lynette explains with obvious pride in her grandmother's efforts. 'She didn't talk about it a lot, but she did charitable acts right throughout her life. She had a heart of gold, she really did.'

In January 1941, Leslie and Brenda sold the shop and moved to Wendyn orchard at Oakdale, south-west of the city in the Blue Mountains, on the edge of the beautiful Burragorang Valley. The strictures of wartime were beginning to bite as the Second World War swept across Europe, and they thought life in the country would be better for their children. Having come to know the district as a source of quality fruit and vegetables for his shop, Leslie had purchased the 33-hectare property on Stevey's Forest Road in 1933, and employed people to plant fruit trees and grow vegetables and flowers. Two of their children, Audrey and Roger, were already living there under the care of the farm manager Cliff Kelly and his wife, but now the rest of the family followed suit.

An astute businessman, Leslie won contracts to supply the army with vegetables and the enterprise quickly grew, with 8 hectares of apples and 4 hectares of stone fruit coming into production, as well as seasonal plantings of cabbages, cauliflowers, potatoes, swedes, turnips, peas, beans and pumpkins. The Gapes also built their own packing shed, and purchased a fruit grader and a press to make the wooden packing cases used to keep fruit safe from damage during transport. After the war, they bought a second property to expand the enterprise. The largest orchardist in Oakdale, Leslie became known as an innovator, keen to explore the latest scientific advice to improve the orchard and to play a part in opening up new export markets. In the evenings, he loved nothing better than to relax by reading the classics aloud to his children.

For her own occasional breaks from the orchard, Brenda would pack up the family and take them on train trips to Sydney. 'She used to love trains and going into the city, because that was her playground as a young person,' Lynette says. 'She used to take the family, lock, stock and barrel. You can imagine it. Eight kids, a nappy bag, a picnic, across the Manly ferry to the zoo for a day. It was a big adventure ... Nanna never drove a motor car. She said they went too fast for her, and she was happy to be driven. In fact I don't think she drove anything all her life, not even a tractor or a horse and cart. They tried to teach her to ride a bike once. And when Pa came home they reckon Nan had enough skin off her to roof an outback dunny. So that was the first and last time she ever got on that "damn contraption".'

Apart from a major hailstorm which severely damaged the fruit crop in 1951, the Gapes led a relatively blessed life when it came to fending off the principal foes of every orchardist in the area—drought, pest and diseases, unseasonal rain and hail. Until 1965. In late November, just days before picking was due to start, a massive hailstorm smashed their entire crop, turning fruit and vegetables to pulp and stripping leaves from the trees. Shortly afterwards, at the age of 62, Leslie died from a cerebral haemorrhage. 'They attributed it to heartbreak,' Lynette explains simply. 'He was so upset because they had a beautiful crop showing, and he just couldn't handle the shame of it.'

Devastated by the loss of her husband, Brenda had the Gapes family orchard label changed so the blue background became black, as a sign of mourning. She took charge of Wendyn and kept it going for the next 25 years, initially with the help of her youngest son, Brian, before he too died tragically young, falling down dead in the orchard with an embolism when he was only 37, leaving behind a wife and three sons.

Over the years Brenda became known for her 'good head for business', a tough but fair woman who worked tirelessly, not only to keep the orchard going but to support her extended family and the local community. She continued to walk around the orchard at least once a day until suffering a stroke at the age of 85, when she moved into a nursing home. Brenda died eighteen months later.

'She was an incredible woman; she gave everything she had. Nanna was the carer—she was the matriarch of her extended family,' says Lynette, the youngest of 25 grandchildren, who spent considerable time with her growing up and loved her grandmother dearly. 'Nan loved progress and always looked forward to the future, planning ahead, being prepared, and encouraging change and innovation. She saw the first mail plane land in Parramatta Park in Sydney, and she saw man land on the moon. It's hard to get your head around,' she adds with wonder.

A third-generation orchardist, at the age of 37 Lynette Rideout is following in her grandmother's footsteps, running her own small farm a few kilometres away from the property where Brenda worked so hard to keep her family from the poverty that scarred her childhood.

Top Forty orchard lies off the winding bitumen road that leads through Oakdale to spectacular views of Lake Burragorang—created by building the Warragamba Dam in the late 1950s and drowning a valley. Lynette has lived all her life on the orchard's eponymous 40 acres (16 hectares), one of two remaining commercial orchards in an area which once boasted more than 150; these days her neighbours are mainly lifestyle farmers and people who commute to Sydney for work.

As the only child of older parents she grew up listening to stories about struggles to overcome the persistent vagaries of nature and fluctuating markets, humorous and gritty yarns of colourful characters who worked in the silver and coal mines which scatter the area, and tales of nostalgia and longing about the lost valley. These stories are woven into the fabric of her family history and her own personal memories, sustaining her passion for the orchard and the legacy left behind by hard-working parents and the tight-knit community that formed an extended family.

Evidence of that heritage lies all about as Lynette gets ready to head out into the orchard and make a relatively late start picking apples. Three months pregnant with her first child, she is pacing herself these days and has spent a bit longer sitting in the tiny kitchen built by her father, Leo. The cupboards he crafted from wooden gelignite cases are still there with the labels clearly visible on the inside of the doors, and so is the Raeburn wood stove which was her mother Audrey's pride and joy. Considered a fourth member of the family, the stove is the heart of the kitchen and the house. Scorning an electric toaster, Lynette lights it first thing most mornings and toasts thick slices of bread in the firebox for her breakfast while the kettle comes to a boil on the hob. Visitors to Top Forty tend to gravitate to the stove, drawn by the magnetic pull wood fires generate even when it isn't cold.

Lynette's husband Chris Keanelly made an indelible impression on his future mother-in-law during one of his first visits, when he parked his backside up against it to warm himself and the bottom edge of his padded nylon jacket caught on fire and melted all over the hotplate. Ironically, the jacket was issued to him by the New South Wales Rural Fire Service (RFS). It was given to Chris as a volunteer crew member helping with rescue and recovery efforts at the 1997 Thredbo landslide so he could better withstand the freezing conditions. Audrey cursed him for about three days. 'Bloody Chris, look what he's done to my stove,' she yelled at her daughter.

Chuckling over the memory, Lynette adds wryly: 'It burnt the entire bottom off, and we had to pat him out. It's the only fire that jacket has ever seen.'

Out on the back porch Lynette is greeted by Bonnie, an Australian stumpy tail cattle dog, and the irrepressible Clyde, a young purebred beagle with Johnny Depp eyes and the breed's notorious fixation on food of almost every kind. He has been sitting at her feet in the kitchen, chewing on potato peelings and a stub of celery. Also waiting is Lynette's 'right-hand man', Elizabeth, a seventeen-year-old student from Wollongong who works on the property during school holidays. She has been feeding the chooks and doing a few other chores before joining Lynette in the orchard alongside the house to pick apples.

Picking apples is without question Lynette's favourite harvest. She enjoys the rhythm of it, the feel of the ripe fruit in her hand, and the satisfaction of gathering up a year's work. 'To be a good apple picker you have to have attention to detail, you have to have gentle hands, and good hand-eye coordination certainly helps so you can use both hands at the same time to pick different pieces of fruit,' she explains, making it clear there is much more to this seemingly simple task than most people realise. 'Anybody can pick apples but picking apples well is a different thing,' she adds.

Unlike many larger orchardists supplying supermarkets and metropolitan-based wholesale markets, Lynette leaves the fruit on the trees to ripen and develop their natural sugars. She washes the apples and then bags them for sale at local produce markets or via the roadside stall outside her front gate. This mild, sunny Friday in mid-autumn, the morning's task is to pick a wooden bin of Granny Smiths. She needs them for a market at Thirlmere on Sunday, and a minibus tour dropping in to the farm on Saturday so people can make a few quick purchases and chat to the person that grew them.

Fading in popularity against trendier new varieties with sexy names like Pink Lady and Royal Gala, Granny Smiths were first grown less than 100 kilometres away in the district of Ryde, in what is now suburban Sydney. Thomas and Maria Ann 'Granny' Smith emigrated from England in 1838 and eventually settled in Ryde in the 1850s, establishing a flourishing orchard. The variety was created by accident from a mutated seedling which grew on their farm from the remains of some French crab apples. By the 1890s it was a popular cooking apple under large-scale cultivation by Australian orchardists.

Lynette loves the idea that she is helping people to rediscover the true taste of this old-fashioned variety. Munching on an apple freshly plucked from a 40-year-old tree, she enjoys the crunch and taste of fruit that is much sweeter because it has been allowed to mature on the tree until April. 'Some people even argue with me that they can't be Granny Smiths,' she says. There are fourteen different varieties of apples and 25 different cultivars at Top Forty, with new trees planted between the old as they become too decrepit and have to be removed.

With an ease that belies years of practice, Lynette plucks apples steadily with both hands, tucking them into a faded canvas bag hanging over one shoulder. When the bag is full, it is tipped into the wooden bin with infinite care so the fruit is not bruised. She was taught at an early age to handle apples gently. No dropping them on the ground, no dumping them into the bin—even bumping the picker's bag against a ladder could damage them.

Lynette has passed these lessons on to Elizabeth, who has become quite adept after three seasons. The teenager started working at the orchard just before her fourteenth birthday. Her grandmother, who lives nearby, noted Lynette needed help during the busy pre-Christmas season and suggested that Elizabeth might like to give it a try. Never known to wear a dress, she jumped at the idea, which offered the perfect excuse to avoid a friend's party with a pink theme.

Elizabeth has been coming back almost every holiday ever since, drawn by working in the fresh air, the physicality of the labour, and the simple fact she likes working for Lynette and spending time in her company. 'There are a few things I don't like, like how tired you can get and how painful your muscles are sometimes,' she says. 'But the really fun bits make up for the others.' With her boss laughing in the background, Elizabeth talks about a particular wet and windy day spent digging potatoes and burning piles of leaves from the garden. They ended up wrapping some of the potatoes in foil and cooking them in the fire for an impromptu feast. Lynette even went to the chook pen and collected a few eggs, showing Elizabeth the old bush trick of using a shovel in place of a pan to fry them over an open fire.

'We sat there eating in the rain, laughing, because it was so funny,' says Elizabeth, trying to explain what she loves most about working there. 'It's the little things,' she adds later, having given the matter more thought. She talks about looking up one day from pruning trees, feeling the wind in her face and looking through the pruned trees to see the setting sun turn the grass yellow and red. 'And one of the best things I will always remember is the smell of incredible fresh coldness and the type of wood Lynette burns in the stove when it mixes with the cold air. If I was on death row tomorrow that would be the last thing I would want to smell,' she says with the insouciance of youth. With plans to spend a gap year in the Royal Australian Air Force after she finishes high school, Elizabeth is not sure yet what she wants to do with her life, but she would be willing to work at the orchard in her holidays 'forever'.

Staying home permanently to work in the orchard was not such an easy choice at first for Lynette. She loved growing up at Top Forty and relished memories of her early childhood, but she had seen the hard toll this life had taken on her parents, and experienced for herself the personal trauma wreaked by the vagaries of extreme weather. 'I fought it and got interested in anything else I could,' she says. 'How things change.'

Audrey Gapes and Leo Rideout met in the 1940s when Leo went to work at the Gapes family orchard. Leo was originally from the isolated Blue Mountains community of Yerranderie, where his father Robert worked in the Silver King mine. A thriving silver and lead mining settlement from the late 1890s until the 1930s, it sits in bushland which is today part of a world heritage–listed wilderness area renowned for its rugged tablelands, sheer cliffs and inaccessible valleys. 'Dad grew up knowing and working in the bush as a kid with his father,' Lynette says. 'They used to harvest wattle bark and tan hides. They had bees, they ran sheep, they had their own poultry, they had their own cows.'

Much later Yerranderie became famous as a ghost town when the last residents were forced to leave because of the new Warragamba Dam. The town itself wasn't flooded, but access to the outside world was cut off by the emerging lake, which was to become the major source of water for Sydney's rapidly growing population. The Rideouts had left years before after Robert developed silicosis, a lung disease caused by inhaling fine mineral particles. They moved thirteen times over five years trying to find a better climate for his lungs and ended up at Oakdale, where he set up a small fruit-transport business.

When the Second World War started Leo was rejected for military service on medical grounds; he had suffered a compound fracture to one leg at the age of seventeen in a motor vehicle accident and it hadn't healed properly. He was working in a factory recycling wooden apple cases, when Leslie Gapes offered him a job at Wendyn.

According to family stories, Audrey's parents were far from pleased when their daughter fell in love with Leo. A good-looking young man of 25 who rode an ex-army motorcycle, loved to dance and was usually seen with a roll-your-own cigarette hanging off his bottom lip, he had a reputation as a 'bit of a rebel'. Even worse, Audrey was only fifteen. 'It's quite a story,' says Lynette. 'They basically said, "Bugger off, you're not having our daughter, she's not of age." But he refused to give up. He came back when she was eighteen and told them he wasn't going anywhere.'

To prove his determination, in 1948 Leo scraped together 100 pounds and bought the block of virgin bush that was to become Top Forty. Working at the time as a timber-getter, felling trees and hauling logs out of the steep local forests, he applied his skills and set about clearing the block by hand in his spare time. Although he was only 162 centimetres tall, he was wiry and extremely handy with an axe. He also owned a former army Blitz truck, which he used to take the logs to a local sawmill where they were cut into timber for frames and floorboards so he could start building a house.

When she wasn't working at a local service station, Audrey walked across from her parents' farm to help. Even shorter than Leo, she was 'a real power pack', who took four sugars in her coffee and had no trouble keeping up with him all day. 'When she was pregnant with me and didn't know, she was jackhammering fence post holes in solid rock,' Lynette says to illustrate the point.

In 1952, six weeks before Audrey's 21st birthday, her parents finally gave in and the couple were married. The rooms of the house weren't lined, there were no coverings on the floor, and the toilet was outside in the backyard, but they had a roof over their heads and were happy.

The initial years of their married life were tough, full of hard physical work, long days and scraping together every cent to establish the orchard and finish the house. They worked together whenever they could to clear the land and sow green-manure crops to improve the soil, but Audrey was often left to work on her own while Leo ran his logging business to earn money, hauling timber out of the Burragorang Valley which was being cleared as part of work to build the new dam.

In 1954, the logging job came to an end and Leo went to work at the Burragorang Coal Mines, taking the night shift so he had some daylight hours in the orchard. 'He worked dogwatch for about fifteen years,' Lynette explains. 'He would start work at eleven o'clock at night and work until seven in the morning. He would come home, have breakfast with Mum, and then he would go to work on the farm until three o'clock in the afternoon. He would go to bed until about ten o'clock, and then Mum would wake him up. She would have tea on the table for him, his crib bag packed and everything ready to go, and he would pick it up and go back to the mine. He took no holiday pay, no long-service leave. He never went on workers comp even though he was injured a few times. He just kept going. He went in as an unskilled person, and came out as a leading hand with a ticket.'

In 1956 the Rideouts were finally ready to plant their first orchard trees—Narrabeen plums, with apples following a year later. While they waited the nine or so years it took for the trees to mature and produce a commercial quantity of fruit, they propagated vegetables and flowers as seasonal cash crops. By 1969 Leo was able to quit the mines and work full-time on the farm, which by then had 1000 Jonathon apple trees, 300 Granny Smiths, 200 Red Delicious and another 200 MacIntosh apple trees as well as the plums.

Not to be outdone by the innovative Gapes family, Leo and Audrey were among the first to start using bulk bins for picking. They invested in a forklift to shift the bins and a rotary grader, which helped keep costs down. With only two small dams to supply water, drought proved a regular challenge as well as hail, which Leo always believed became even more of a problem once the dam was built just over the edge of the ridge, creating a huge body of water. Hailstorms caused frequent damage in the area, wiping out the entire crop in 1969, but the most terrifying experience of their lives came the year before.

Leo and Audrey were out working in the orchard on a hot, dusty afternoon, when they noticed a thunderstorm rolling in.

They decided to go inside for a cup of tea and wait for it to pass. Putting the kettle on the wood stove to boil, they went to stand in the doorway leading out into the backyard and watched the storm's progress. Audrey snuggled in beside Leo, who was leaning nonchalantly against the doorframe. The next thing Leo remembered was waking up on the kitchen floor, the rain falling on his face through the open doorway. Audrey lay unconscious beside him. He tried to get up only to discover he was paralysed down the left side, but he managed to get his right hand underneath Audrey's back and pull her inside the house enough to close the door. When Audrey eventually came round she couldn't hear.

The house had been struck by lightning. According to a neighbour who witnessed it, it wasn't the normal forked lightning but the much more unusual phenomena of ball lightning. It apparently touched down on the house, passing through the telephone line and blowing the Bakelite phone to pieces, stripping the covering off electrical wiring in the ceiling and melting the fuse box. The neighbour realised something was wrong and decided to go over to Top Forty and check. He knocked on the back door of the house. There was no answer. Leo heard him but was struggling to get to the door before the neighbour walked away. He eventually hauled himself up with his right hand and managed to get the door open. The neighbour heard the noise and turned back in time to catch Leo as he collapsed into his arms.

Leo and Audrey were taken immediately to Camden Hospital about 20 kilometres away. Leo recovered enough to be allowed home the next day. Feeling returned to his left side, but he was severely dehydrated and had burn marks on his left wrist, where the lightning passed through his metal watchband, and on the inside of his right wrist, which had been resting on his belt buckle at the time he was struck. 'He went to his grave with the scars,' Lynette says.

Audrey stayed in hospital for three days. Her hearing returned but her body was covered in purple streaks. She was so dehydrated her skin carried the impression of Leo's hand, where he had lifted her out of the doorway, for the next six weeks.

The house survived, but judging by the burn marks along the rafters where the electrical wiring rested, it was a near thing. The damage even extended to the packing shed next to the house, where Leo discovered every electric motor had been fused. The incident made five lines in the local newspaper—their daughter reckons it was worth more.

Audrey and Leo had given up on the idea of having children when Audrey became pregnant with Lynette. They had been married 22 years and doctors thought it unlikely to happen. Instead, the couple regularly filled their house with the offspring of nearby friends and relatives. 'They just accepted that was the way it was going to be,' Lynette explains. 'And then, at 42, Mum didn't feel real good one day so she went to the doctor.'

Leo was sitting in the waiting room when the doctor raced out of his surgery, overlooking normal protocols to herald the good news to the entire clinic. 'Mr Rideout, Mr Rideout, you're going to be a father!'

'He just about had to scrape Dad up off the floor,' Lynette says. 'He couldn't believe it. He really couldn't. He desperately wanted children but for Mum's sake he had acted like it wasn't a big deal.'

Lynette came into the world at Camden Hospital on 30 April 1974. A few days later she was brought home and, as she puts it, 'planted' on Top Forty. Always called 'Bub' by her father, she was an active child who wanted to be part of everything. Leo coped remarkably well with becoming a dad at 53, and often took her with him into the orchard and let her play among the trees to help wear her out. Audrey found the toddler there one day running around in the nude, having the time of her life. She had sat alongside some sprinklers, filling her nappy with mud, and Leo thought stripping her down and letting her go was the obvious solution to keep her happy and allow him to continue working.

At the age of two, Lynette was given her first set of blue overalls, just like the ones her parents wore when they were in the orchard. By the time she was three she was learning how to pack apples, much to the amusement of family and friends who would visit the shed just to see it. A 'gun' packer, Leo had a reputation throughout the district for being able to pack apples quickly and with expert precision so that the right number fitted perfectly in a case, all pointing the same way. He made Lynette a little wooden stool so she could stand on it and help. He would place the apples so the stalks always pointed towards the child, encouraging her to copy and place the 'bums' towards him. Concentrating fiercely, she would attempt to remember this important pattern by picking up each apple, looking at it carefully, and reciting 'bums to oo' every time she put one down.

Lynette often went to sleep in the packing shed while her parents worked. Tucked up safely in the timber apple bin which doubled as her playpen, she was lulled to sleep by the sounds of the grading machine and the roll of apples, in an orchestral-like performance she later came to describe as the 'Apple Packer's Lullaby':

Mum was the maestro standing on her platform where the apples passed by for quality inspection. It was Mum who made the orchestra strike up when she turned the switches on one by one. The first switch was the hum of the big belt that carried the apples down the full length of the sizing mechanism and sounded like the brass section of the orchestra. The middle switch was the string section tuning up as all nine rotary bins squeaked into action, each with a slightly different pitch and rhythm. The last switch was the polishing brushes and main conveyors which were like a grand piano playing strong chords and lending a harmony to the music.

Then after a couple of minutes of Mum's overture, Dad's part in this concerto would begin. The percussion section of the orchestra, of which he played many parts, was strong. The metallic scrape of the steel stand being adjusted along its runner to the next hopper on the grader that was full of apples and needed to be packed out. The scrape and bump of a fresh cardboard box being put onto the stand ready for packing. The squeak and whoosh of a cardboard filler with all its little indentations to hold the apples in place being pushed to the bottom of the box. Then came the part of this concerto that I really liked—the staccato of the apples being picked up by Dad's strong but gentle brown hands and being packed into rows. This was punctuated by another scrape as the next filler was put into place. This sequence repeated itself three or four times depending on the size of the apples Dad was packing, which in turn determined the amount of layers of apples to a box.

The crescendo came when Dad reached for the apple wrap ... Bump of hand onto the paper stack, tap of apple being picked up, gentle slap of apple coming into contact with tissue paper in left hand, scrunch of paper being dexterously folded and twisted around apple, the cushioned thud of papered apple being placed into its spot in the top layer ... The piece of music complete with the whoosh and sigh of the full apple box as the lid was placed on and air rushed out. The case picked up and hefted onto the stack with a gentle thud, and the whole symphony would start again.

Sometimes Lynette was looked after by her father's sister, Aunty Myrtle, who helped teach her to cook in what often turned into a communal activity with half a dozen people crowded into the Rideouts' small kitchen. 'I can remember trying to help cook my cousin's 21st birthday fruit cake. There was my mum's younger sister, Aunty Bev, my cousin Gloria, myself, Mum, and Dad was tucked away in the corner. We were all doing different jobs around the table and Aunty Bev said, "Here, you stir that". And I started to stir the cake mixture and she said, "No, not that way. You're stirring it back to front; the cake will go flat." So I'm stirring this thing, and she's throwing the fruit in, and all of a sudden I got stuck and the sultanas went everywhere. She yelled at me again and, well, that was that. I went to my room and didn't come back for about four hours. She had hurt my very tender feelings,' Lynette jokes.

When she was small, she would often tuck herself under the table in the crowded kitchen and listen to the adults telling stories. It goes a long way to explaining her own talent in this arena. 'I was an only child surrounded by old blokes and ladies all my life and they used to be good storytellers. They would sit around and have a yarn rather than watching telly,' she says.

'Our house always had an open-door policy. There would always be people here, Dad's old logging mates and ex-mining friends, Mum's friends and orchardists in the district, family. They would lob in any time of the day or night. I had an aunt who used to turn up at ten o'clock at night and go home at four o'clock in the morning when her husband needed the car to go to work. She would stay and talk all night. Sometimes we'd come in and find someone had put the kettle on and made morning or afternoon tea. We had been up the paddock working, and they had it laid out and waiting for us on the table . . . And Mum always cooked for at least one extra.'

Not surprisingly, Lynette wasn't too keen on the whole idea of going to school compared with the freedom and fascination of life at home. Despite her potential to be a good scholar, she never really liked school, where she was a bit of a loner and struggled with being self-conscious in her teenage years because she was overweight. By the time she was in high school, there were only a few orchards left in the area, run mostly by older farmers whose children had long since grown up, and she had little in common with other students.

That came home in 1989 when yet another massive hailstorm wiped out the year's crops just days before picking was due to start. With the prospect of a decent harvest so close, her parents had used all their cash reserves to extend the packing shed and buy a second-hand peach grader. Leo was in the shed laying the new concrete floor just before lunch when hailstones the size of golf balls started hitting the roof with the roar of an express train. Audrey and Lynette made a dash from the house a few metres away, where they were preparing lunch so they could be with him. They knew what the storm meant. 'Within twenty minutes we had nothing,' Lynette says. When it stopped the silence was deafening, except for the creak of the roof, shifting under the weight of hailstones stacked almost to the ridge-cap. 'We came outside and it was like we were shell-shocked. Mum and Dad were as white as ghosts.'

Not long afterwards, concerned neighbours started arriving to see what they could do. They were well aware what the storm would mean for the Rideouts, but Lynette says quite a few of her fellow students at high school failed to grasp the seriousness of the situation and gave her a hard time for staying away from school in the days afterwards when she just wanted to be with her parents. She would have quit school altogether if her mother hadn't reminded her how important it was to have an education and career options.

Lynette really didn't need reminding. The storm had broken something in her. She no longer wanted to be an orchardist like her parents and her grandparents before her. 'After the hailstorm

I didn't want a part of it. I decided I would work here, but as far as doing it as my life's work? To see people who had worked hard all their lives go through a trauma like that, I thought, "That's bullshit, there's no way in the world I'm doing that. It's a stupid way to live." So I got interested in anything else I could.' She still helped out on the orchard, but emotionally she tried to keep her distance from the farm because she eventually intended to leave.

In her final years in high school, she found solace in the creative outlet of woodworking, with wood technology offered as a subject for senior students. After scoring well in her exams, she was encouraged to apply for a full-time tertiary course at the highly regarded Sturt School for Wood at Mittagong, about an hour's drive away in the Southern Highlands, which was established in 1985 to teach both the design and making of fine woodwork. She was granted an interview with the founding director, Alan Wale, and accepted into the program, but reality stepped in when she found out tuition alone would cost $10 000, without taking into account the materials and living costs. There was no scholarship and money was very tight because of the hailstorm so she couldn't take up the offer. 'I try to live life with no regrets, but sometimes I think how different life would have been if I had been able to do it. Anyone who came out of Sturt School had a name. It was an opportunity lost,' she says quietly.

So Lynette left school in 1991 and in between helping at the orchard she worked part-time away from Top Forty, tackling a range of jobs from gardening to waitressing. She also took the opportunity to travel to various parts of Australia, and signed up for two training voyages on tall ships sailing the coast of Queensland, relishing the challenge of being completely out of her element.

In her early twenties, she enrolled in a diploma in calligraphy, commuting by train to Chatswood in northern Sydney one or two days a week for lessons. 'The opportunity came up and it was too good to pass up, and it was the right time in my life. I was living at home with Mum and Dad and could still help on the orchard, but I worked at night as a waitress to support myself. I used to get up at 4.30 in the morning and leave home by five to get the train. It was three hours travel to get there, the lessons took three hours, and then I would come home. Sometimes I went straight to waitressing and worked until one or two in the morning. That was only one or two days a week, but the homework was many hours of practice and study and experimentation with paints and papers.'

Lynette found the concentration and fine control required for calligraphy almost like meditation, drawing her into a closed world in which time would pass without her noticing, and she would forget to eat. 'The front room used to be my studio. I would stay in there and put *Phantom of the Opera* on, and keep repeating it. I knew the score and it relaxed me so I didn't have to think, and it drowned out any other noise.' After three and a half years, Lynette earnt her diploma and started receiving commissions to prepare official documents.

Then her father became ill and there was no time or energy for calligraphy. She had to take on more responsibility in the orchard. Lynette says, 'When Dad started to become sick my conscience kicked in. I thought, "Well, the farm isn't going real well, I have to help out where I can. It's time to give something back."'

Leo was diagnosed with lung cancer in April 2000. Less than three months later he was dead. Audrey and Lynette nursed him at home, with help in the final days from a district nurse. There was a steady stream of people to pay their respects and offer support—Lynette can remember only three days in those weeks when they didn't have a visitor. But at nights while she sat beside her father's bed, she had time to think about how she was going to make the orchard work with limited money without relying on her aging mother, who had traditionally handled all the finances and paperwork as well as working on the farm and running the house. She came to the conclusion she would have to scale back the volume of fruit being grown and diversify into other crops that were better suited to changing market trends.

Leo left the orchard to Audrey in his will and mother and daughter became partners in Top Forty, with Lynette taking over from her father as best she could. She soon discovered how much she didn't know. Leo had been a jack of all trades who could turn his hand to building things and making his own repairs, as well as running the machinery and caring for the crops. So much machinery and equipment broke down in the first twelve months Lynette can remember sitting down with her head in her hands. 'Why has this got to be so bloody hard?' she despaired.

It was during this difficult time Lynette began to realise she was fighting her inbuilt love of growing things and what she now thinks of as her birthright. 'Looking back on it, the change was gradual. I had been trying to do other things but it wasn't really working, and I think the heritage within me was pulling me back without me realising it,' she says. 'Mum and Dad always said it didn't matter what I decided to do, they would support me. If I wanted to sell the property and move on, or if I wanted to go and buy another business, that was fine, but when it actually came to it, this was home. There were so many memories tied up here, and it wasn't just about the property, it was the community I lived in.'

In 2001 she finally seized the bull by the horns and decided it was time to put her plans for diversification into action in a big way. Much to her mother's distress, she knocked out hectares of the fruit trees Audrey and Leo had planted together. 'She saw it as part of her life going under the bulldozer. I had grown up under those trees so it was just as hard for me but I had to compartmentalise it. I couldn't afford to be sentimental. I had to put in another crop that was going to make more money, so they just had to go.' Lynette was ready to plant her first *Pinus radiata*.

Mid-afternoon and Lynette and Elizabeth are pruning Christmas trees. The satisfying chop of hedge clippers accompanies their light-hearted banter as they move down the row, tips of sacrificed branches flying past their ears. Elizabeth is wearing a pale green T-shirt and a wide-brimmed leather hat to keep off the afternoon sun. Because the sticky pine sap causes her skin to itch, Lynette is swathed in a red-checked flannelette shirt, long sleeves rolled down over the top of heavy-duty gardening gloves, and the collar pulled up around a yellow kerchief, which is tucked around her neck to stop pine needles falling inside her shirt. Every tree is pruned an average of sixteen times in what is a surprisingly labour-intensive process; it takes four years to produce a symmetrical tree of the preferred size and shape. 'Most people have no idea what is involved,' says Lynette, who admits she didn't either when she put in the first plantation.

The idea of growing *Pinus radiata* for sale as freshly cut Christmas trees came from a comment Leo made one day about how, if he had his time over, he might have looked for a crop that could be grown for a fixed price, which wasn't so open to seasonal vagaries. Lynette chose a particularly awkward moment to announce what she saw as the perfect solution. 'I was fifteen years old and everybody laughed at me,' she says. 'I actually said it in front of the bank manager. He was asking Mum and Dad what future prospects we had on the farm.' Their daughter piped up out of the blue: 'I want to grow Christmas trees.'

'Shush,' hissed Audrey. 'Don't be ridiculous.' And that's where the idea stopped, even though Lynette broached it again later at a more appropriate time. Her parents thought it would never work.

After Leo died Lynette revisited the concept, encouraged by an old orchardist who used to grow Christmas trees himself because they were so reliable in comparison to fruit trees. This time Audrey agreed, recognising the orchard was in Lynette's hands now and that she needed to find her own way to make it work. Chris helped research the idea on the internet and they discovered a nursery at Tumut in the Snowy Mountains which sold stock specifically for Christmas tree production.

'So I put in my first order—for 3000 trees. What a fool I was,' Lynette says sardonically as she chips away at the soft green branches of a 2-metre high pine destined for sale the coming December. The seedlings arrived on 15 August 2001, in boxes and bare-rooted, which raised the novice grower's anxiety levels considerably because she was concerned they would die before she could get them planted. Trying to ignore a freezing cold winter wind blowing in from the west, she spent the next three weeks crawling around on her hands and knees, putting the young plants in the ground. 'I don't think I have ever been so bloody cold in all my life and I thought, "What the hell have I done?"'

Most of the seedlings survived and Lynette was just starting to sell her first lot of Christmas trees in 2003 when fate intervened. Thirteen days into December her heart started palpitating. It was so bad she almost passed out, but Lynette tried to ignore the accompanying dizziness and kept working. Three days later she realised the symptoms were not going away, and couldn't be ignored any longer. Chris's mother, Judy, drove Lynette into the local medical practice at the nearby township of The Oaks, about seven minutes away. They carried out an ECG and were so concerned at what they found they sent her immediately to the nearest hospital at Camden. Camden in turn transferred her to the coronary care unit at the larger Campbelltown Hospital, where a series of doctors and cardiologists carried out more tests to try and find out what was going on. 'You don't expect to be a 30-year-old laid up in hospital with a heart problem. It was a bolt from the blue because I was so fit and so active,' Lynette says.

After spending three weeks in hospital, there were still no definitive answers. She was sent to yet another specialist, this time at St Vincent's Hospital, in Sydney, renowned for its work in treating heart disease and carrying out transplants. The specialist decided to insert a catheter into Lynette's heart and stimulate it from within. The surgical procedure did not go according to plan, and they had to defibrillate her on the operating table. 'When I came to I had burn marks on my chest and my back. I felt like I had been kicked by a mule and toasted.'

But the specialist did work out the cause of the problem—the electrical impulses in her heart were functioning incorrectly, causing her heartbeat to vary dramatically within seconds, from as low as twenty beats a minute to as high as 260. Medication didn't really fix it and she didn't like the idea of a pacemaker, so in June 2004 she returned to hospital for more surgery. Another catheter was inserted into her heart and small pieces of muscle were cauterised to block some of the electrical impulses.

'I had about seven months off work—pretty much invalided and more or less confined to the house. We lost the peach crop and most of the apples. Mum did her absolute best but she was an older lady and there was a limit to her stamina and what she could do. So it was pretty hard. By the time I got back to the Christmas trees they had an extra season of growth and most of them had got away on me. We ended up bulldozing about a thousand because they were just too big.'

At the end of 2004, Lynette finally sold a decent crop of Christmas trees and discovered that, despite the setbacks, her instincts as a fifteen-year-old were right. 'We sold enough to make it financially viable—not as many as I wanted but it gave me a goal to strive for, to hit the 1000-tree mark every season. I haven't quite reached it yet, but that is the goal.'

All the trees are sold fresh off the farm. Customers from as far as Wollongong and central Sydney come at weekends, starting at the end of November, and wander around the plantation to select their own. If they don't want to take them straight away, the trees are tagged and left standing. If they are ready to take them home, Lynette uses a handsaw to cut them down and helps load them in the customer's vehicle. For safety reasons, no chainsaws are allowed and no-one is allowed to cut down their own trees.

After seven years in the trade, Lynette still finds it fascinating to watch families revel in the experience, and how serious people become in their quest. 'You have no idea the amount of time some people spend walking around here trying to find the perfect tree, and the amount of competition for the best trees,' she says. 'We have even had fights. It's really rather funny but not at all in keeping with the Christmas spirit.'

She recounts the story of a spoilt teenager who came late in the season with her grandparents and lost her temper when every tree she liked had already been tagged. And the car load of young blokes who rocked up with a very large chainsaw and expected to be let loose in the plantation. Then there are the countless numbers with 'eyes too big for their ceilings', who choose trees so large they are going to cause problems at home; and others who arrive in a little hatchback car expecting somehow to be able to squeeze in a tree and extract it in decent shape at the other end. Her favourites are the children, excited about the adventure of walking through the small forest and choosing their own live tree. With the exception of one little boy who took a fancy to a dead specimen. 'He wanted the orange one,' Lynette recalls with a chuckle.

Two and a half hours later, 110 trees dutifully pruned, Lynette hops in the ute and drives back to the house for a quick wash and change of clothes before heading off to visit her mother. Audrey is being looked after in a nursing home about twenty minutes drive away, having finally become too ill for her daughter to manage on her own. Lynette nursed her for three years, but during the past year a combination of a broken leg, chemotherapy to treat non-Hodgkin's lymphoma and emerging dementia has seen the 80-year-old deteriorate at a frighteningly rapid rate.

The decision to place her mother in care was not an easy one for Lynette, who is a natural carer and loves her mother deeply, despite the occasional clash of wills. She visited her every day for months, spending as long as five or six hours with her. Now she tries to go every second day, usually at evening mealtimes so she can help feed her. Remembering the powerhouse that was her mother, Lynette is grateful Audrey was still living at home and well enough to attend her wedding.

The apples are picked and Lynette is sitting atop her old tractor, moving a fruit bin into the packing shed. She knows this tractor and all its little foibles as well as any member of the family. It even has an affectionate nickname—Greasel—a combination of the words grease and diesel, because it is covered in one and powered by the other. The Massey Ferguson was bought second-hand by her father when Lynette was about four. She can remember being very put out when she wasn't allowed to sit on his lap and help drive it the 40 or so kilometres home.

When the tractor broke down not long after her father died, Lynette came to know every part of it as she took on the unfamiliar challenge of rebuilding the engine, with help from an old family friend. He wasn't well enough to do the work but he sat for hours on an old apple box, watching over her efforts and patiently explaining the various parts and what needed to be done.

'I love this tractor,' Lynette says before starting it up. 'It is like an extension of me. I spend hours on it. I am at home in the world when I am on this . . . This is where I solve problems—some people do it on the toilet, I do it on the tractor,' she jokes. 'I put the headphones on, turn the music up, I can still hear the engine, but I plan, I solve, I come to terms with things that are worrying me. This is my happy place.'

In more ways than one, this little red tractor brought her and Chris Keanelly together. Lynette was up to her elbows in grease rebuilding the engine when he came to visit with an old schoolfriend. They had come with an offer to help fix another tractor sitting in the shed, so she had something to use in the orchard. 'He said to me, "If I can get the tractor going, will you have a beer with me?"' Lynette says. The other tractor is still sitting in the shed and doesn't go, but she went out for the beer anyway.

Ten years after they started going out Chris asked Lynette to marry him. They decided on a simple wedding in the garden at Top Forty, with family, friends and the community gathered around them. It was going to be a long guest list between the usual relatives and friends, and the extended 'family' of people they had both come to know growing up in the area and through active involvement in community organisations. Both were members of the local RFS brigade and Lynette had belonged to The Oaks Historical Society since she was fifteen. She worked alongside her parents and other volunteers to create the Wollondilly Heritage Centre and make sure it opened to the public every weekend.

'We just wanted to have a happy day,' Lynette says, trying to explain the unusual approach she and Chris took to their big day. 'In this day and age we gather so much for sad occasions, and I knew it would be the last time a lot of people would see Mum because she was declining, so I wanted to make it special. Chris proposed to me on his birthday, 12 April, and from the next day on I started to plan.'

She decided to combine her not-inconsiderable cooking skills and her mother's wood oven, and bake a high tea for 350 people using recipes from an historical society cookbook. It would be followed a little later in the evening with roast pig on a spit for a smaller group of about 150 guests. The ceremony would take place on Leo's Lawn, a formal garden in front of the house which Lynette started landscaping while her father was ill.

With only six months to make it happen and a very small budget, Lynette hit the internet. In the end, she bought only two things by visiting actual shops—her veil and a small pompom handbag. Even her wedding dress was ordered on-line. Made especially for her in China and appropriately featuring a design with tiny flowers, vine-work and leaves, it arrived by parcel express within four weeks of being ordered and fitted perfectly after small adjustments to the sleeves and hemline. Small muslin gift bags for the wedding guests also came from China, for the staggering price of 1 cent for every 50 bags. 'The total charge on the credit card was $3.01, including postage,' Lynette says. Her hair accessories came from Singapore, and the wedding invitations were printed in Belgium to her original design.

Just before the wedding day in October, Chris gave Lynette her wedding present—a bright blue Iseki tractor fitted with a bucket front-loader. Not every bride's idea of a wedding gift, Lynette thought it was perfect. Returning the favour, she bought Chris a tractor too—a tiny model that sat on the wedding cake—and a set of Ferguson tractor cufflinks, which she purchased online from the United Kingdom. 'I ordered them about three weeks before the wedding, and I waited and waited . . . and in the last mail, on the Friday before the wedding, they arrived.'

On their wedding day it was Greasel which carried the bride to her groom. Wanting it to be a surprise for the guests, Lynette had quietly gone about giving her favourite workhorse a new coat of tomato-red paint. Unfortunately, she was forced to use it in the orchard two days before the wedding and had to wash off the mud and polish it up again. 'That is the first and last time you will ever catch me polishing a tractor,' she says, laughing.

As the guests gathered in front of the house for the ceremony, the bride was around the back with her second cousin, Kelly, climbing onto a small platform attached to the rear of the tractor. But Lynette and Chris hadn't counted on the unpredictable spring weather, which turned freezing cold and dumped 100 millimetres of rain on their wedding day. Determined to carry on, the bride and her matron of honour sheltered under a large black and white umbrella, and warned the tractor driver, friend and former Top Forty volunteer helper Ryan, not to go too fast. By the time the ceremony started, the rain was pelting down so hard the guests couldn't hear the tractor coming as they huddled under marquees and a vast array of umbrellas in an effort to keep dry.

'It was coming down in sheets,' Lynette says, flabbergasted at the memory. 'I have never seen so many soggy people in my life, but they were entertained by the fact we went ahead anyway. I can remember stepping off the tractor, and when I looked up all I could see was this sea of umbrellas. People were dressed up to the nines with matching everything, but they were carrying the shittiest umbrellas which they had to grab at the last minute. It didn't matter if they matched or not—they were desperate.'

Lynette was accompanied down a temporary aisle of squelchy carpet by her cousin Ian, who handed her over to a gobsmacked Chris. He was knocked completely sideways by the sight of his future wife in her wedding finery. Until that day most people had never seen Lynette in a dress; in fact more than a few half-expected her to show up in her favourite flannelette shirt and workboots.

Following behind the bride was Kelly, dressed in a long gown of deep iris purple. Lynette's closest friend since childhood, she had flown down from Queensland with her family to act as matron of honour. As the official party gathered in front of the local RFS chaplain, Elizabeth led in Bonnie and Clyde, the designated ring bearers. Resplendent in a bow tie, Clyde was bribed into reasonable behaviour by the dog treats Elizabeth carried in her pocket, but much to everyone's amusement Bonnie took exception to Glen, the best man, growling in the back of her throat as he leaned forward to untie the rings.

After exchanging vows they had written themselves, the newly married couple moved towards a spot on the lawn to plant a cerise pink hawthorn. 'The hawthorn is the Celtic tree of love, betrothal and marriage,' explains Lynette. 'We decided we would incorporate a tree planting ceremony as part of the wedding, and that would become our family tree where we would meet in times of trouble and times of joy.' Everyone laughed as the ever-practical Lynette pulled a pair of gardening gloves from her little handbag. One wag even called out boldly, 'Don't you ever stop gardening?'

As the ceremony ended guests threw apple blossom gathered by a relative as a surprise for the bride. 'That in itself was just really special,' she says. Taking advantage of a break in the rain, the official party then headed off to a very soggy orchard to have their photos taken. Enjoying the quirkiness of the occasion, the photographer had fun setting them up around the tractor, at one stage calling for the farm toolkit so she could capture Chris and Lynette having a mock swordfight with spanners over the top of the shiny red bonnet.

By the time they were finished everyone was frozen. As the afternoon wore on, Lynette and Chris handed out anything they could find in the way of extra coats, jumpers, beanies and hot water bottles to help warm their guests. Fellow RFS crew members from the Oakdale brigade ended up towing bogged cars out of the orchard with the fire truck, and Lynette eventually succumbed—partly in jest and partly from necessity—and donned thick woolly socks and her workboots. 'When it came time to take the garter off and I pulled up my skirt, everybody just about died,' she says. 'It was all about entertaining ourselves and everybody else. We certainly did it our way.'

Six o'clock on a Sunday morning and Lynette and Elizabeth are heading to the market at Thirlmere. It is one of several regular local events she attends in an effort to take back control of the way her produce is marketed and sold. Her parents sent most of their harvest to the wholesale markets at Flemington in Sydney, where there were times they ended up losing rather than making any money despite all their hard work. 'The last season we sold fruit at Flemington we picked 400 trays of peaches. There was 3.5 kilograms of fruit in a tray. The trays cost $1.51, the green liner cost 16 cents, the labour cost 11 cents per tray, and it cost 50 cents to get them there. The agent sold them for $2 a tray, and they were beautiful fruit. It was just so disappointing. So I decided to grow less, handle it myself and deal direct with the public.'

Like an increasing number of primary producers she has found one answer to controlling her farm's destiny is farmers' markets. Top Forty has become a regular stallholder at Camden, Picton and other more general weekend markets within a 30-minute drive of the orchard. Thirlmere is a relatively new event set up in a small park opposite the Trainworks heritage rail centre to take advantage of tourists and visitors arriving by steam train at the town's historic railway station. Elizabeth helps Lynette to unload the ute and set up the stall in a prime spot on the main walkway. Taking pride of place are the Granny Smith apples picked fresh from the orchard two days ago and an old wheelbarrow piled high with a staggering array of heirloom pumpkins.

Growing rare and unusual varieties of pumpkins has proven an absolute winner in Lynette's strategy to diversify her business. She planted 45 different varieties last summer, searching the catalogues of seed companies in the United States and Great Britain for new and unusual kinds. Her customers are fascinated by the extraordinary range of colours and shapes, from the pale green of Queensland Blue, to the bright yellow of the Gill's Golden Pippin heirloom variety originally bred in Oregon, and the exotic stripes of the Mexican Chihuahua, a 'small pumpkin with a bit of an attitude'.

This morning Lynette also has a few quinces, the last tomatoes for the season, and a few Dutch Cream potatoes. It is just a tiny but seasonal reflection of the extraordinary variety of fruit and vegetables grown at Top Forty these days, in deliberately small quantities. Reciting them all is something of a memory test even for Lynette. There are 25 different cultivars of apples alone and multiple varieties of stone fruit such as the heirloom peach variety Fragar, out of favour with supermarkets because they grow too big and are so difficult to transport without damaging. 'The biggest we ever grew was 585 grams. They used to be a world-renowned dessert peach, but you just about need to sit with a bib in a bathtub to eat them,' Lynette says.

Taking advantage of the different altitudes, temperatures and soil types within the property, there are also nine varieties of citrus, with the small, sweet 'mini' mandarins especially popular. Lynette also grows figs, pomegranates and mulberries, and is preparing to plant persimmons and cherries in the coming winter, as well as chestnuts to expand the range of nuts she is already growing in small quantities, including pecans, walnuts, hazelnuts and macadamias.

A separate patch of the farm close to the house is devoted to trellised crops, with black and banana passionfruits and kiwi fruits vying for space alongside red and white raspberries, boysenberries and thornless blackberries (Elizabeth reckons they lied about them being 'thornless'). Ground crops range from potatoes and French shallots to garlic, which is proving so popular Lynette can't grow enough to meet demand. Then there are various melons such as the old-fashioned jam melon popular with home preservers but impossible to source in supermarkets, and whatever other short-term crops take her fancy. For flower lovers, she also propagates 3000 daffodils and 200 varieties of iris to sell as bulbs or corms as well as flowers.

True to the philosophy of the burgeoning farmers' market movement, Lynette only sells what she grows. She seizes every opportunity to give her customers a sense of seasonality and the true taste of produce left to ripen properly and sold within days of being harvested. It worries her enormously that this knowledge has been lost from the collective memory in a country where most people are at least one generation removed from the once-common practice of growing their own fruit and vegetables. 'Supermarkets have dumbed us down,' she says. 'We have been spoilt for choice instead of having to think about seasonality, which is so important. I would spend half my time talking to people about what is in season and what is about to come in.'

Importantly, she sees the farmers' markets and bus tours of the orchard as a way to bridge the gap between city and country, increasing people's understanding of life on the land and how their food is produced. 'I spend a lot of time trying to change perceptions, and that's a challenge in itself,' she says. 'As a farmer I am always planting seeds—it's just whether they are in the ground or in someone's mind . . . As a person on the land I have got a choice. I can either do nothing or I can try to break the barriers down. I give people information to the best of my knowledge without making them feel like idiots. It's just a matter of passing on what I know, and if I can change somebody's perspective and enlighten them in some way then maybe I have done some good and helped the next generation somewhere along the line.'

Her sense of urgency about all this has become stronger as she contemplates the birth of her baby, and the possibility that she or he might one day want to carry on the family business. 'Before Chris came on the scene I had never seen myself with a life partner. I had figured I was going to be one of those old spinsters on the farm all by myself. But my life changed and I realised that maybe I would have a family one day, and have someone to pass the farm on to,' Lynette says.

'I want them to have the experience of what it is like to be a farmer, whether they decide to go on with it or not. I want to give them every chance of growing up the way I grew up, or the best I can given things are changing. They won't have the apple packer's lullaby to go to sleep by, but they will have the sound of the mopoke owl at night, fresh air and dirt, and running free and wild through the paddock not having to worry about traffic. That is all pretty special.'

3

TILL THE COWS COME HOME

Jan Raleigh, Timboon, Victoria

Dawn is almost an hour away and the crickets are still singing when Jan Raleigh heads towards the dairy with her girls—191 doe-eyed cows, udders bulging softly with milk. Despite their size and number they move quietly through the darkness, up the gentle slope of the dirt laneway to concrete-paved yards where they shuffle closely together in the dark. An older cow is breathing heavily, soloist to a chorus of softer sighs around her. The wiser matrons in the herd, and the just plain cunning, are pushing their way towards the light spilling from the milking parlour, first in line for the bovine equivalent of cereal.

Jan has already eaten breakfast. In a routine that rarely changes from one day to the next, she woke up at five o'clock, staying in bed just long enough to listen to the ABC news on her alarm clock radio. She gets dressed, plaits her hair and winds it into a tight bun set low on the back of her head before heading into the kitchen to make a cup of coffee, rich with thick, creamy milk from her own cows. Weeks away from surgery to replace a worn-out hip joint, she takes a painkiller to help ease her into the day and sits quietly in a favourite lounge chair while the pills take effect.

By six o'clock she is walking out the back door into the pitch black of a mild, dry late summer morning. Waiting to greet her is Chocky, a decidedly chocky-in-build, eleven-year-old brown Labrador, who doesn't move too far from the house these days; and the exotically named Juliette, a sleek white kitten brimming with energy and the joy of all nine of her young cat lives. Juliette disappears as Jan climbs onto a four-wheel-drive motorbike parked in the small corrugated-iron shed alongside the house, and Chocky heads back under his favourite shrub for a bit more sleep. Once upon a time he would have run after the bike but these days he often waits until the sun is up before wandering down the dirt track that connects the house to the dairy about 200 metres away.

The dairy is a small plain building of grey, concrete bricks. A large, galvanised-iron door slides open to reveal two large stainless-steel vats where the milk is cooled and stored until it is collected later in the day by tanker. Stainless-steel pipes bring the warm, frothy liquid from the parlour next door where Jan's cows are milked just once a day instead of the usual two practised on most dairy farms. Built to what is known as a Herringbone design, this part of the building has two parallel, raised platforms. Fourteen cows stand side-by-side, close together on each side, munching on rations of special stockfeed while the milking machines are attached to their udders.

Jan works behind the cows in a central concrete pit, dodging frequent splatters of urine and sloppy, green manure. Milking cows is a messy business, which accounts for her long green plastic apron, ubiquitous black rubber boots, protective rubber sleeves and bright red baseball cap. The cap is worn backwards so she can lean in close to place a rubber-lined cup on each teat. The placid, elegant Aussie Reds stand quietly throughout the process, soothed by the sounds of their favourite radio station (most dairy farmers swear their cows milk better to the ABC), and the pulsing shoosh of the machines. This is one of Jan's favourite times of the day. She loves working in the dairy and moves between the cows with a natural rhythm despite her bad hip, in a choreography made smooth through years of practice.

By about ten o'clock the milking is finished, and Jan is faced with one of her least favourite chores—cleaning the milking parlour and the yards with a high-pressure hose to wash the manure into a large effluent pond alongside the shed. Happy to have an excuse, she delays the exercise to check on a sick cow—something you could safely say she is overqualified to do, thanks to her career before becoming a dairy farmer.

There is no doubt Jan loved farm life from an early age and would rather have stayed home with the animals than go to school. But after finishing his formal education at the age of twelve, her father was determined his children would have a good education.

Robert Raleigh was born at Arthurs Creek, about 50 kilometres north-east of Melbourne's city centre, on the 'hill next door' to his future wife; one of nine children, her family had the neighbouring apple orchard. When Bob was still a young boy, the Raleighs moved to a farm near Melton on the western outskirts of the city. Today a sprawling suburb with shopping centres and densely packed housing developments, Melton was then a small rural village kilometres from the edge of the city, with little more than a few shops dotted along the main street.

Like many country children at the time, Bob finished his education at the end of his primary school years, and then worked on the family dairy farm. He ended up taking responsibility for the property, his mother and two sisters after his father died when he was only eighteen. 'He did it pretty tough, poor old Dad,' says Jan. She's not sure how Bob and Sylvia reconnected years later, but they eventually married and continued running the Raleigh farm, milking cows and growing oats. Meanwhile Sylvia had her mind set on moving to the rolling, green hills of Timboon where her sister, Muriel, and her husband, Keith Bassett, had bought a small dairy farm.

'Mum asked them to keep an eye out if any other farms became available, and one day Uncle Keith rang up and said this farm was on the market and the person who was going to buy it couldn't come up with the money,' Jan says. She is not sure how much they paid, but at the end of 1945 the Raleighs became the proud owners of 90 picturesque hectares set either side of Scotts Creek, about 5 kilometres north-east of Timboon. It proved to be a sound choice, with fertile pastures, reliable rainfall and plentiful supplies of good quality water—assets which continue to make the general vicinity some of the best dairying country in Australia.

First settled in the 1870s, the Timboon area began to flourish when a railway line from Cobden opened in 1892, supporting the development of a thriving timber industry, with up to eighteen mills processing about 13 000 tonnes of timber a year at its height, and a local lime quarry, which is still in operation. It also created one of the town's lasting assets—the Heritage-listed Curdies Creek trestle bridge, which today forms part of a popular 30-kilometre walking and cycling track.

When the Bassetts arrived in the 1940s, the township was very small and they had to rely on Cobden, about 30 kilometres away, for most supplies. That situation changed in the 1960s as returned soldiers and their families began to take up farms created as part of the nearby Heytesbury Settlement Scheme. The last timber mill closed in the 1970s, followed by the railway line in the mid-1980s, but Timboon remains a thriving service centre for the dairy industry, which is today the mainstay of the local economy.

The Raleighs took up residence in the area in January 1946, with their three children: five-year-old Royce, three-year-old Jimmy and Jan, who was only six months old. Their first home on the property was a timber house only 100 metres or so from the road; it is derelict now, with Jan comfortably ensconced in a nearby orange-brick house built by her parents in the late 1970s.

On top of a high, steep hill at the back of the farm was the dairy, a simple shed shaded by a big old pine tree, where the Raleighs milked about twenty cows by hand. Jan grew up with stories of being carried to the dairy in her bassinet and left to amuse herself in a playpen. It was set up in the 'milk room', a small room used to store the milk and a hand-operated separator, which separated the cream from the milk by centrifugal force as the handle was turned. Only the cream was sold. It was loaded onto a horsedrawn sledge, pulled along the track which wound down from the dairy, and then sent to the Cobden Butter Factory.

After a few years a new dairy was built in a more convenient location on the flat, closer to the house and the road. The new milking parlour was fitted with the latest milking machines, powered by a petrol motor, started by pulling a cord. Jan can remember that although she wasn't all that big in stature, her mother had the knack of starting the motor, and was often called on by a neighbour with a similar set-up who wasn't so blessed. 'He couldn't pull the cord hard enough—he was a great big bloke and Mum wasn't that big but she was very fit. She played in an A-grade tennis final the day before Royce was born,' Jan recalls with a shake of her head.

Tennis was a favourite pastime for Sylvia. A court was built next to the farmhouse so she and the rest of the family could play whenever they liked. It also hosted games for the local community, with Sylvia playing a leading role in setting up the Scotts Creek Tennis Club before they built their own courts a few kilometres down the road. No doubt benefiting from such ready access, Royce went on to play for Australia and won many tournaments.

His sister played tennis too, but what she really wanted was her own pony. She can remember the day her father brought home a big horse, half Clydesdale, which he used to bring in the cows. Jan was warned not to go near it because it was 'as wild as a March hare'. 'Of course I snuck out and the next thing I'm riding it around the paddock—no bridle, no saddle. Mum and Dad nearly had a fit but it loved kids, and just hated adults,' she points out.

Jan didn't get her own horse until she was in her early twenties. She can remember taking a pony shared with her brothers to the first meeting of the new Heytesbury Pony Club and winning a horse-powered version of a treasure hunt. 'I found the treasure, which was a packet of columbines, but this boy belted me up and pinched them, so Mum wouldn't let me go again,' she says, smiling at the apparent injustice of it. As an adult, Jan helped out at the club, which today has its own highly regarded cross-country course, and has twice hosted the State Horse Trials Championships. In 1998, they presented her with life membership in recognition of meritorious service, for many years of assisting with administration and supporting club activities.

Jan started her education at Yan Yean after being sent to live briefly with one of her aunts while her mother was recovering from illness. She soon returned to Timboon, where she completed primary school. Then she joined her brothers at Camperdown High School, with their mother driving them part of the way to catch a bus. Once the boys had finished school, her mother wasn't keen on making the trip for just one child, so Jan headed back to Timboon for her final three years of secondary education.

If Jan had been given her way she would have joined her parents at home on the farm the minute she finished high school. But like many farm parents anxious about their children's prospects, Bob and Sylvia Raleigh were keen for her to learn another occupation with the prospect of a more regular income. Her mother suggested nursing, and knowing she had little choice, Jan applied to train at the Royal Children's Hospital in Melbourne. If she must give up the idea of being a farmer and looking after cows, she would nurse children instead.

Before she could pursue this option, there was at least one major hurdle. Jan had only finished fifth year in high school after repeating her studies to pass, and applicants were required to have completed their sixth and final year before they would be considered. Showing a determination that has stood her in good stead over the years, she travelled to Melbourne and begged the matron in charge of nurse training to bend the rules and give her a go.

Who knows whether it was Jan's pleading or because the matron saw promise in the eighteen-year-old dairy farmers' daughter, but Jan started training in July 1963, just four months after Queen Elizabeth II officially opened the hospital's new premises on Flemington Road, in the inner northern suburb of Parkville. Founded in 1870, the original hospital had developed an outstanding reputation for pioneering work in paediatrics. With a nurse-training school dating back to 1889, it had transformed from an old-fashioned charity hospital into a highly regarded modern teaching institution by the time Jan donned her trainee's uniform.

One of 24 student nurses who started training at the same time, Jan moved into the nurses' home alongside the hospital, where she quickly made new friends. She missed the farm and her family, but her older brother Royce wrote every week from Malaysia, where he was teaching at a school for the children of Royal Australian Air Force personnel stationed in Penang. Jan says, 'If I was on night shift I would stay up waiting for the mail to come in, and the old girl down on the front desk, she used to say, "For heaven's sake, go to bed. I'll put the letter under your door if it comes."'

Jan found the first year of studies tough, with so many new concepts to learn and understand. Like many of the other students she failed and had to pass a supplementary exam to continue. But at the end of the three-and-a-half year course she was among just thirteen who successfully qualified. She was also more determined than ever to nurse children, who she found complained far less than adult patients and often recovered much faster. Her conviction was reinforced by an experience at the Royal Melbourne Hospital, where she worked for six months as part of her training. 'The first night I went to the Royal Melbourne I was put in charge of the medical ward—all old people—and five died. I was really upset about it at the time.' The sister in charge of the hospital that night took Jan aside and told her not to worry about it because it happened all the time. But it was enough for Jan. 'It just turned me right off looking after old people,' she says.

After qualifying, Jan spent a much more fulfilling six months working as a theatre nurse at the Royal Children's, where she was part of a surgical team performing groundbreaking operations on very young children. 'It was really great. We did some huge operations and it was really nice to be part of it, and then to see these kids afterwards and how quickly they got better.'

In 1967 the young nurse decided to go to Perth for twelve months and study midwifery. Western Australia had a reputation for offering more comprehensive training because nurses in the state often had to deliver babies in isolated outback locations without ready access to additional medical support. 'I remember one of the questions in the exam paper was something like, if a woman had a baby and she had a retained placenta and she started to haemorrhage and the doctor was in the pub 200 miles away drunk, what would you do?' she recalls, laughing at the idea. While Jan welcomed the extra training in coping with a medical crisis, she was not so keen on the personal insights she gained into another type of emergency.

Jan was on the second floor of the King Edward Memorial Hospital when the building was rocked by an earthquake at 10.59 a.m. on 14 October 1968. Measuring 6.9 on the Richter scale and focused just 7 kilometres below the earth's surface near the small town of Meckering, it was one of the largest recorded in the seismic history of Australia. The earthquake's effects were felt across the southern half of the state, opening up a series of surface fault lines that extended over 200 square kilometres, injuring twenty people and damaging buildings as far as Perth, some 130 kilometres to the east of Meckering, which was virtually destroyed.

'I tell you what, I was ready to jump off the balcony and they reckon I went as white as my uniform,' Jan says. 'The girls in the nurses' home, which was only four storeys high, they said it swayed that much the pictures were sitting out from the wall. They had expansion cracks built into the floors of the hospital, and after the earthquake some of them were that wide you had to step over them. We didn't sleep in the nurses' home for two weeks afterwards—we weren't game.'

'We survived, but I tell you what, it shattered my nerves, it really did,' she says. 'We sat our exams the day after the earthquake, and of course 24 hours later we're sitting there and there's another earthquake. Everyone leapt up out of their chairs, about to bolt out the door, and the old sister in charge of us said, "Sit down, it's only an aftershock".'

A month or so later, she travelled to Meckering with a few friends to see the worst of the damage for herself. She found the crumbled buildings, buckled railway lines and large cracks in the earth 'incredibly eerie'. Jan is telling me this story a little more than two weeks after a massive earthquake hits Christchurch in New Zealand on 22 February 2011, killing 181 people. It has stirred memories from more than twenty years ago and she empathises with Christchurch residents.

Returning to Victoria after gaining her qualifications as a midwife, Jan was appointed matron at the Cobden Hospital. The job meant she could visit her parents at weekends and help on the farm. After six years she moved east to the Colac Hospital, not far to travel either, taking time out from her nursing duties to gain even more qualifications, this time in infant welfare. When the hospital in the nearby provincial city of Geelong announced it was going to offer a twelve-month course in coronary intensive care, Jan signed up for that too. She flew through the studies and was put in charge of night shift in the coronary care unit, where she stayed for the next four years or so. In her last year, she acted as night supervisor for the whole hospital whenever the usual supervisor was away.

Reflecting on her nursing career, Jan clearly enjoyed the twenty or so years she devoted to it, and the regular studies to improve her knowledge and skills—a love of learning that she took straight into farming. She made the most of having a steady, independent income, travelling overseas during holiday leave. 'If I had come straight home to the farm I wouldn't have been able to do any of that,' she admits. But most of all she enjoyed the friendships made along the way, particularly with other trainees who started at the same time; half a dozen of them continue to hold occasional reunions.

And Jan still treasures a tiny, toy seal given to her by the sister in charge of the first ward she worked on, by way of thanking her for standing in a queue to buy a ticket for The Beatles when they performed in Melbourne in 1964. Jan didn't go, but she joined other nurses and patients on the hospital balcony to watch the band pass along a packed Flemington Road as they drove into the city from the airport. Jan named the seal after her favourite Beatle, Ringo. 'Funny the memories you have of different things, isn't it?' she muses, picking up the little seal from the lounge room mantelpiece.

Jan returned permanently to the farm in 1983, the year after her father died. Her mother held things together for about twelve months, with help from Jan whenever she could take a three-day break from night shifts at the Geelong Hospital. Sylvia milked 80 cows by herself in a walk-through shed, which meant leg-roping each animal to hold them still and bending down to put on the milking machines, a back-breaking and labour-intensive process compared with today's ergonomic set-ups where everything is within easy reach at waist height.

Despite the fact it was obviously a heavy responsibility for the 70-year-old widow, she did not ask her daughter to give up nursing and come home full-time. Jan is not sure why. 'It was very difficult for her,' she says. 'Every time I came home she would be in tears because something was wrong, something had happened or something was broken. And I just got to the point where I couldn't stand her looking like that every time I came home. She didn't "welcome me with open arms" type of thing, but I think underneath she was really pleased that I did come home.'

Recognising that considerable work was needed to bring the farm up to modern standards, Jan applied herself straight away to more studies, this time in farm management. She signed up for a twelve-month, part-time course offered by the well-respected agricultural college at Glenormiston, about an hour's drive north. She also joined a local discussion group, where dairy farmers came together once a month to talk about what they were doing, and learn from each other and expert guest speakers.

Jan knew there was enormous potential to make the farm more profitable, and her studies helped give her the confidence to have a go. 'I knew what needed to be done, not that people necessarily thought I did,' she says. 'When I first started going to discussion groups they would all think, "What does she know? She hasn't been farming long." I was the only woman at a lot of them, but I stuck it out and the tide turned.'

The changes Jan needed to make were going to cost money, and Sylvia didn't want her daughter investing anything without first sorting out what would happen to the farm after she died. In the end, Sylvia went to a solicitor and made a will which spelt out that Jan was to inherit the farm, and pay each of her brothers a set amount within six months of her mother's death to compensate them for their share. 'Once she had that sorted she was quite happy for me to put my money in,' Jan says. 'She had a real head for figures and had done all the farm book work . . . She put me on a 50:50 share basis, and I started ploughing a few paddocks and sowing new grass, because nothing had been sown for years . . . At the start, I just did things without even telling Mum. She knew things were improving and what I was doing was right. She may not have thought that I was capable of doing it at first, but I proved to her I was.'

Within about eighteen months of Jan coming home, her mother was not well enough to leave the house, and some years later, after she broke her hip in a fall, Jan was applying her nursing skills once again to care for Sylvia in between running the farm. She honestly didn't find this a burden, given that her parents had worked hard all their lives to provide the best they possibly could for their children.

Sylvia Raleigh died in 1996 at the age of 83. Jan was making most decisions on her own by then, but she still misses being able to sit down and talk to her mum about the farm and what she plans to do next to improve it.

When Jan first came home, the property needed a massive amount of work to turn it into a modern dairy farm. The grazing area was divided into just one day paddock and one night paddock, which made it extremely difficult to manage. The pasture was of poor quality, there were no proper laneways to move the herd around, and the dairy was well past its use-by date. The Raleigh women borrowed some money to put up new fences, install all-weather tracks, and build a new dairy.

Jan also wanted to expand the herd, and to make that more feasible she decided to buy more land. She can't remember exactly when she started, although her mother was still alive at the time, but she began with a small block of about 8 hectares tucked in an oddly shaped corner on the north-eastern edge of the farm. She added a few more adjacent titles as neighbours decided to sell up, gradually expanding the property to cover more than 130 hectares, which is a reasonable size for a dairy farm in this part of the world.

Then about three years ago she really got carried away and bought another 33 hectares on the opposite side of the road. She was so worried her brother Royce might have thought it a step too far that she was scared to tell him. In a rare treat for herself rather than the farm, she was also installing a new kitchen complete with the latest appliances. She decided to invite him down and surprise him with both investments at the same time. Jan was gobsmacked, and more than a little relieved, when he heartily congratulated her on both counts, obviously proud of his sister and what she was achieving.

Neither of her brothers were interested in farming at all. After attending teachers' college at Geelong, Royce spent most of his career teaching in the Wimmera region of Victoria, having settled in the Wartook Valley on the north-western edge of the Grampians. He and his wife Jeanne raised three children, Jeannette, Ruth and Peter, who are regular visitors to the farm. Over the years they devoted most of their spare time to creating an award-winning native garden with more than 1000 species of plants, and they often brought seedlings to plant at Timboon. Jimmy joined the Royal Australian Navy, reaching the rank of captain before retiring to Canberra. He married Jane, the sister of a naval mate, and raised three daughters, Caroline, Philippa and Elizabeth, who Jan doesn't see as often because they live further afield.

As Jan tells it, she was never as bright as her brothers, but her achievements in formal education, both in nursing and agriculture, prove she is no academic slouch. Aside from her extensive nursing credentials, she holds an Advanced Diploma of Applied Science in farm management with the University of Melbourne and an Advanced Diploma of Agriculture in dairying, granted by the university in 2000. In 1997 she was named a finalist in an award run by the Swinburne University of Technology's National Centre for Women, recognising the achievements of women in non-traditional areas of work and study. She failed to impress the judge during the final interview process; it was union heavyweight and future Labor parliamentarian Greg Combet, and Jan says she wasn't at all surprised as it was pretty clear he knew nothing about farming. In 1998 she was selected among 40 Australian women to attend an international Women in Agriculture conference in Washington DC.

'Let's face it. In this life you don't stop learning. If you stop learning, you stop still,' she says later, contemplating a neatly typed resume running to several pages, with a long list of all the courses she has completed over the years and the community groups in which she has participated. Apart from highlighting her belief in the benefits of ongoing education, it also neatly summarises all the skills a modern farmer must own to take on dairying—soil nutrition and fertiliser management, cow nutrition, artificial insemination, record keeping and financial management, running high-tech milking equipment, and operating heavy machinery.

Jan's skills in the latter are demonstrated every afternoon in the autumn, when she heads to a small open-sided shed next to the dairy and picks up a bale of hay or silage for the milking herd. Usually made by cutting and fermenting green pasture, silage is one of the main sources of supplementary feed for southern Australia's dairy cows. Farmers often rely on it in the summer and autumn months when there is less grass growing in the paddock or the paddock feed isn't of good enough quality to provide most of the nutrition a cow needs to produce plenty of milk.

Jan climbs up onto her red Massey Ferguson tractor, donning a set of bright yellow earmuffs over the top of her black-peaked baseball cap, and starts it up. The front of the tractor is fitted with hydraulically powered tines, which she slips into a bale of silage. Standing more than a metre tall and often weighing more than half a tonne, the bales are impossible to shift by hand but the tractor makes light work of it. Jan deposits the bale with precision into a curved steel cradle emblazoned self-importantly with its brand name, 'The Boss', in big, capital letters, and then turns the tractor round so she can attach the cradle to the back. She climbs down off the tractor and uses a pocket knife to rip away the pale green plastic wrapping that keeps air and water out of the silage and helps to control the fermenting process.

The whole task has taken only a few minutes, and Jan is ready to head to the paddock. She is planning to move the milking herd from one field to another before feeding them. At this time of the year, the cows usually spend the morning on a pasture of specially grown summer crops, such as turnips. It is a treat they enjoy and so rich in readily metabolised energy they only need to spend a few hours on it each day. It takes a load of silage to tempt them away from the turnips to the 'night' paddock, a mix of ryegrasses and clovers which also contain plenty of protein.

Knowing just how much energy each pasture type provides, and how much of it a cow needs to eat every day, is part of the complex business of managing a dairy farm that Jan has to think about continuously, like a sports nutritionist nurturing the performance of super athletes. She must plan well ahead to make sure she is growing enough grass or fodder crops, and she must take into account that at different times of the year when it is dry or cold it takes plants longer to recover.

If she gets it wrong, the cows go hungry and the amount of milk they produce declines, cutting into her profits. Jan knows the average cow will eat as much as 3 per cent of her entire bodyweight every single day—that's almost 4 tonnes of feed a day for the whole herd—and sheer volume is not enough. It has to contain the right blend of protein and carbohydrates to fuel the energy-hungry process of converting feed into milk.

The cows know it's time for afternoon tea, and they are lined up at the gate waiting for Jan as she drives the tractor down the laneway, past a small dam landscaped to provide a refuge for waterbirds and frogs. When she reaches the night paddock, Jan turns on the cradle and small tines start rotating under the bale to tease out the silage and drop it behind the tractor as it moves slowly across the paddock. A long, narrow trail emerges, giving every animal a chance to eat their fair share without trampling their neighbours.

As the herd moves sedately from one paddock to the other, the cows stretch out into a parade of gently swaying, angular hip bones and swishing tails. It is a pastoral scene with a timeless quality, set against a background of dark green blackwoods. The day has been overcast like so many others this wet summer, but the sun breaks through the clouds as the cows settle in to eat, burnishing the rusty red coats of the Aussie Reds which make up most of the herd.

Jan loves these cows and the hours she spends with them. It is easy to see why. They are beautiful creatures, calm and curious, easily coaxed into a routine that sets the rhythm of every day. One of the fastest growing dairy breeds in Australia, Aussie Reds are a relatively new breed in their own right, combining exotic infusions of Norwegian, Danish, Swedish and Finnish red cattle with traditional English red breeds such as Ayrshire and shorthorns, and Australia's own Illawarras, created by dairy farmers in the Illawarra region of New South Wales in the 1800s.

Jan first heard about Aussie Reds in 1990, only a few years after the breed was officially recognised, when she read a story in a farming magazine. She had completed a part-time course at a nearby agricultural college in how to artificially inseminate cows with semen that could be bought in from a range of bulls, rather than having to rely on one or two bulls held on the farm. Jan thought it offered a faster and more cost-efficient way to improve the family herd, and that buying some semen from Aussie Red bulls was worth a try.

Her parents had traditionally favoured shorthorns, rather than the more popular, cream-coloured Jerseys of the day, or the larger black and white Holsteins soon to take over dairy farms across the nation because they could produce large volumes of milk. Jan didn't want to go down either line, and the Australian government had recently banned the importation of cattle semen from Britain—the breeding stronghold for shorthorns. There was escalating concern about the risk of infecting local cattle with bovine spongiform encephalopathy, or mad cow disease, which saw millions of cattle slaughtered in Britain in an attempt to eradicate it and put fear into the hearts of farmers around the world.

Jan liked the sound of Aussie Reds because they could apparently produce high levels of protein and butterfat. These are the solid components found within milk and dictate, more than liquid volume, how much a farmer is paid because they are essential to make butter, cheese, cream and ice-cream. The cattle also seemed to have calm temperaments so they would be easier to handle in the dairy, and they were known to experience far fewer problems than the smaller Jerseys during calving, especially young cows, or heifers, giving birth for the first time.

Jan got in touch with the breeders featured in the story and bought some bull semen. That first year an extraordinary number of cows gave birth to twins, which is not necessarily a good thing because it can affect the reproductive health of a cow and create problems at calving. She pauses to recount the story of the day she went in to tell her mother that yet another set of twins had been born from cows impregnated using artificial insemination. 'Jan, you must be giving them too much stuff,' Sylvia said. Jan later told the story to a social gathering of farm women and says the entire audience cracked up. 'She did have a sense of humour, although it was hard to find at times,' she muses.

Twenty years after the initial experiment, Jan has her own registered Aussie Reds cattle stud, Blackwood Park, inspired by her farm's beautiful blackwood trees. The herd is now recognised as one of the best in Australia, based on the performance criteria used to objectively measure dairy cows. Known as ABVs, or Australian Breeding Values, they help farmers work out the genetic merits of dairy cows and bulls, and their potential to produce cattle with particular characteristics. The main focus is on the 'business end' of the cow and what can be measured, rather than how good she looks.

Jan studies the figures every year when she is working out which bull semen to buy, and she records her own cows' individual performances so this information can go into a national database for the breed. Even though she is still trying to build up the herd and doesn't sell cows to other farmers, as a stud breeder she believes contributing to knowledge about the national herd and how it is performing is essential to making gradual improvements. She gathers information about her own cows once a month in the bovine equivalent of a physical fitness test. Known as herd testing, it is no small undertaking—only about half the dairy farmers in Australia bother because of the time and paperwork involved.

To make it feasible, every cow in Jan's herd has its own number and is fitted with an electronic ear tag. As they walk into the dairy to be milked on herd-testing day, they pass through a gateway fitted with a scanner, which reads the number recorded on an electronic chip placed in the tag. A separate sample of milk is collected from each cow, labelled and sent away to a laboratory, where it is weighed and tested for protein and fat content and somatic cell count. Somatic cells are white blood cells within the milk, and they tell farmers a great deal about the health of the cow and her udder. Normal milk contains as many as 200 000 of these microscopic cells per millilitre, but when a cow is suffering from mastitis the count increases dramatically.

All the results are recorded in a handwritten ledger. Figures from the last test show some of Jan's better cows have produced more than 250 kilograms of butterfat in just 200 days. She is very pleased with the overall results, which indicate production has fallen only 15 per cent since she cut back to one milking a day about two years ago. 'When they were being milked twice a day I was trying to get most of the cows over 250 kilograms of butterfat per year and that was at a time when I couldn't cull the worst cows because I was trying to build up herd numbers. They say an average lactation is 300 days, so they're doing really well.' A separate book the size of a large poster keeps track of the annual history of every cow—the day she was inseminated, who the sire was, the sex of the calf and its identification details, and the date the cow 'dried off', or stopped producing milk. Green lines are drawn through the cows she has sold, and orange lines through the ones that have died. There are very few of either.

Seeing the meticulous nature of these records, it is not hard to accept that Jan is recognised for her excellent record keeping, using a combination of the ledgers filling one end of her dining room table, electronic spreadsheets updated in a tiny office opposite the kitchen, and the small notebooks she always carries in her pocket to make running notes. For her own satisfaction, she also keeps track of the 'big picture' on a large wall chart. Drawn in fading chinagraph pencil, the graph charts overall production since she first came home in 1983 when there were only 80 cows producing about 1000 kilograms of butterfat, or about 60 kilograms per cow per year. Within twenty years the farm was producing four times that amount.

❖ ❖ ❖

The care Jan takes of her animals is among the reasons Liz Coghlan finds her an inspiration. The tall, slim blonde is one of twenty veterinarians working for The Vet Group, which Jan calls in whenever she has a cow in trouble. 'I was very excited when I met her,' Liz says of Jan. 'At first I thought this woman is as tough as nails, and then I had to tell her one of her cows wouldn't make it and we might have to euthanase her, and she started crying. She does everything she can to try and save them. She has a lot of determination, and it is amazing the things she can do.'

One of the largest practices in Australia focusing on dairy cattle, The Vet Group covers hundreds of farms across south-western Victoria, providing advice on all sorts of aspects of managing a dairy herd as well as treating sick animals. Finding a woman vet in a rural practice was rare until quite recently, with conventional wisdom being they couldn't manage the physical challenges of working with large animals. But a significant percentage of veterinary students qualifying these days are young women, and many are drawn to work in regional areas where there has been a desperate shortage of vets.

Liz comes from southern New South Wales, where her family operates one of Australia's largest red poll beef cattle studs, Eurimbla, at the foot of the Tabletop Mountain Range near Albury. She decided early in life that she loved cattle and wanted to work with them. Nothing gave her a greater buzz than helping a cow having trouble calving to deliver a healthy calf. 'When you pull a live calf, it's the best feeling ever,' she says. But she found school a challenge and thought she would struggle to secure the academic results needed to study veterinary science. Then she was lucky enough to get into the course at Charles Sturt University, which takes into account life experience as well as academic achievements.

Six years later, after extensive study and on-the-job practical experiences in places as far flung as Paraguay in South America, Liz emerged fully qualified and headed to her first job at Timboon. 'Driving to the practice on the first morning I thought how beautiful the area was. I just knew this was it.' That was almost two years ago, and the conviction hasn't worn off, despite long hours and often having to work in cold, wet conditions.

'I always wanted to work with large animals,' Liz says. 'Every female in the class came off a farm or had spent a lot of time there. Just over half the students were female and most were going into rural or mixed animal practices.' She believes her training taught the importance of stopping to think before tackling something, not just to consider potential occupational health and safety issues but to find the smartest way to do it without relying on brute strength. 'Every female veterinarian here can do everything the males can do. There are smarter ways to do things.'

Liz has found so far that most farmers do not have a problem with a female veterinarian showing up to treat their cows, although she mentions a recent visit where the farmer queried she and another female vet being allowed out on their own. 'On the whole there is not much scepticism, although we do get a few that are a bit traditional. I think a lot of it is because I look young,' she says.

Jan has no such problem. She walks across the yard in front of the dairy to welcome Liz as she climbs out of one of the practice's four-wheel drives. Jan explains she has a cow which is slobbering heavily and giving very little milk, and Liz suspects a mouth problem that is preventing her from eating. The cow has been kept aside after milking and is being held in a small yard alongside the dairy. Jan encourages her to move into a cattle crush, a strongly built steel frame which will hold her safely for closer examination and treatment.

After prising the sick cow's jaws open and taking a closer look, Liz is convinced the problem is woody tongue, which can be treated with antibiotics. The condition is caused by a bacterial infection and usually occurs after soft tissue under the tongue is abraded by something coarse in the feed. Jan wonders if it's something to do with the fact silage-making was interrupted so much last spring by wet weather, making it difficult to cut before the seeds developed.

The Timboon area was badly affected by floods in August 2010. Jan didn't lose any livestock, but she watched the water rush down Scotts Creek, sweeping away fences and trapping three cows in a paddock on its bank before she had a chance to move them. Reaching a level last seen by her parents the year they took up the farm, the water covered the wooden bridge connecting the dairy to most of the grazing paddocks and took three days to clear. Jan wasn't too worried it would reach the house, which sits on a slight rise, but she was concerned about the trapped cows. In the end all three swam out, one somehow getting through five fences before reaching dry ground. 'She had scratches all over her, but she was okay,' says Jan.

It was not the scariest moment of Jan's years farming the property alone. That came about six years before when she was thrown off a four-wheel motorbike, breaking her neck, although she didn't know it at the time. She was about 2 kilometres away from the house, in a back paddock leased from a neighbour, when she unwittingly headed at speed through the single wire of an electric fence. The wire hit her in the chest, flinging her backwards off the bike. Faced with the option of climbing back on board or walking about a kilometre out to a road that experienced very little traffic, she decided to ride slowly back to the house. That involved getting off the bike to open six gates, with her body screaming in protest the entire way.

Eventually arriving back at the house, Jan rang the local medical clinic, where the receptionist very strongly recommended she call an ambulance. Then she rang her cousin Clyde Bassett, who had taken over his parents' farm on the other side of the hill. Sensing the urgency, he jumped on his own bike and rode the shortest possible route overland while his sister Marilyn raced around to the house by road. 'They waited with me until the ambulance came. I just flopped in the chair.'

Jan was taken to the Warrnambool Hospital, where they did not find any significant injuries, and after a day in casualty she was sent home. Convinced there was something wrong—'my head felt really heavy, and it was hanging down'—Jan went back to the local clinic, where she saw a locum doctor and had more X-rays. He suggested she see a physiotherapist, who took one look at the X-rays and said, 'I'm not touching you with a 40-foot pole until you've seen a neck specialist.'

So Jan drove herself to Geelong, where an orthopaedic surgeon was appalled at what he saw and the risks she had unwittingly been taking. A week later she was having surgery at the Austin Hospital in Melbourne. 'I had been riding the motorbike around, milking the cows, driving the tractor. I could easily have become a quadriplegic,' Jan says.

The incident highlights the biggest challenges Jan faces as a sole farmer. 'If something goes wrong or you have an accident, there is nobody around, and because you have nobody else around to help you do things, you have to really think ahead,' she says. 'But I suppose one of the biggest things, mainly, is not having anyone to talk over problems with, whether they be minor or major. If someone else is there you can say, "Well, what do you think?" But it's your decision and that's it.'

When it comes to larger decisions her mainstay is Chris Hibbert, one of the principals of The Vet Group and a farm consultant, who has been providing her with advice for almost twenty years. 'I don't think I would be where I am today if I hadn't had him to give me the confidence to do things,' she says. 'I don't always do what he says . . . but it's got to the stage where he knows what I want and what I am capable of doing.'

Jan honestly doesn't believe she faces challenges that are different or more difficult to those a man would face running a farm on his own. 'I have always said all along you can do anything if you really want to. There are things you mightn't do as quick or as fancy as the fellas do, but you get there in the end.'

She is surprised people like Liz find her an inspiration, and she certainly does not actively seek the limelight for her achievements, but she is very pleased to be able to help if other farmers seek her opinion on something. She particularly enjoys the quiet sense of achievement running the farm alone gives her, revelling in the independence of doing things her own way, at her own speed, and of living alone. 'Never found the right fella, never really went looking,' she says with a laugh. 'I am much happier being a free agent.'

But at 65, Jan realises how useful an extra pair of hands about the place can be, and has decided to take on a sharefarmer to help run the expanding property and enable her to increase the milking herd to about 220 cows. She is missing Rachel, who worked on the farm part-time for six years up until a few months ago. Rachel would hose down the yards, feed the cows, carry out routine tasks like spraying for weeds, and feed the calves which start arriving in August. 'She was my right-hand man,' says Jan.

❖ ❖ ❖

Mid-afternoon and Jan is high on the hill at the back of the farm, taking in her favourite view. One of two wedge-tailed eagles that also favour this spot glides by on thermal currents as it searches for prey. Jan often contemplates installing a bench here so she can sit in comfort and enjoy the vista. The wandering line of elegant blackwoods she loves to see in flower, and the towering sugar gums marking Scotts Creek. The patchwork of rolling green paddocks, stitched out in the native trees she has planted to create shelter belts and stabilise the hillsides. The orderliness of the connecting laneways she and Sylvia installed, and the dairy they built in the early years after Bob died. The herd of beautiful, healthy Aussie Reds Jan has bred and nurtured, grazing peacefully in the distance. A solo red gum standing in the middle of a paddock where her niece Ruth planted it when she was about five, disappearing one afternoon with some seedlings brought as a gift by Royce from his garden at Wartook.

'I love it because it's just so picturesque,' she says simply. Trying to explain why this place means so much to her, she talks about how most of the farm is tucked away in a hollow, sheltered from the howling southerlies, but offering mild temperatures in summer. Jan hates the heat. She would much rather cope with the area's notoriously wet and cold weather, protected by the waterproof pants and coat she wears most days in winter because it's nearly always raining. And she knows that when she gets back to the house it will be 'warm as toast' because her parents had the foresight to incorporate underfloor heating in the main part of the house.

What would they say if they could see what she has done with the farm over the past 28 years or so? 'I don't know what Mum would think, but I know she wouldn't say anything,' Jan says. 'That is something that really frustrated me all my life. She would never congratulate me or say I was doing a good job, but she would tell everybody else I was doing a good job. I found that out from other people. And Dad must be watching me from up there and thinking, "God, she has turned into a real property baron, hasn't she?"'

4

A SHEEP LIKE ALICE

Nan Bray, Oatlands, Tasmania

The official start of winter is still two days away when Nan Bray heads out into the paddock, rugged up in multiple layers of warm clothing topped with a padded ski vest. The minimum temperature dropped to −5 degrees Celsius for the second day in a row this morning, coating the bare, rugged hills and highland plains of Tasmania's central Midlands with a crisp, white frost more reminiscent of Europe than Australia. It has taken hours for the sun to gradually dissipate the accompanying fog. Fence wires coated with ice turned into strands of spun gold as the first rays of sunlight broke through the dense, damp blanket at about the time Nan was completing a few yoga stretches in her front room. By ten o'clock the fog had shrunk to thin pillows below a pale blue sky, revealing the strong lines of Lemon Hill, after which her farm is named.

Given the weather and an unexpected rush of morning visitors Nan is making a late start. Her wily sheepdog Mac is racing ahead, keen to get to work and not always that mindful of waiting for his mistress. Calling back the intractable border collie, she walks steadily up the hill towards a mob of ruminant royalty—superfine merino sheep descendent from some of the oldest and most respected bloodlines in the world. From a distance they are camouflaged by the soft-feathered stands of long, dry grass which cover the paddock. But Mac spots them quickly and moves up close in the low, stalking crouch which comes instinctively to a well-bred sheepdog.

'That'll do, Mac,' Nan calls as the mob turns to face her. The sheep stand calm and resolute, a cohesive social unit watching her approach. Every animal is looking straight at her, ignoring the dog approaching silently from the other direction. This is unusual behaviour for Australian sheep, which are normally raised in large mobs where they are all the same age. These sheep have the extra confidence that comes from having your family at your back.

Nan moves across to open a gate into the adjoining paddock, leaving Mac to turn the sheep towards it. A sharp noise from the whistle she is carrying tells him what is required, although he seems to think he already has things in hand. 'Mac is one of those guys that you love, but they drive you crazy. He is like the bad boy that you can't help loving,' Nan says, with wry humour. 'We had a battle of wills through his early training because he has this idea that he really doesn't need me to work sheep. He thinks that I should stay home and let him go do it.'

Nan stands in front of the mob, a few metres out from the gate. An experienced shepherd, she knows just where to place herself and how to position her body so the sheep are encouraged in the right direction, with a little assistance from Mac. In one hand she holds an old-fashioned crook with a distinctive handle made from ram's horn; the carved and painted figure of a border collie in working pose runs along the outer curve. Nan finds the crook extremely useful to guide sheep and steady herself while walking in rough country, as countless generations of shepherds around the world have done before.

In the distance, Nan's stockman David Carnes is piloting a four-wheel motorbike across another paddock, moving a separate mob. He is being ably assisted by his favourite dog Janie, a sweet-natured, tricoloured border collie who loves to work and lives to please. With every fibre of her small being she worships Davey, who patiently restored her confidence and salvaged her career after an unhappy time with an inexperienced handler. A 'wizard' with animals, Davey treats them with respect, building a mutual regard which creates a true sense of partnership.

In fact, running Lemon Hill is all about partnerships—partnerships between human and dog, partnerships between nature and farming, partnerships between the formalities of academic science and life's wisdom. And at the heart of it all the seemingly unlikely partnership between Nan, an American-born oceanographer who has spent most of her life in sunny California, and Davey, an 84-year-old stockman who acquired his deep understanding of sheep from a lifetime on the land and the generations that came before him in a tradition stretching back almost 200 years.

There is little resemblance between Nan's merinos and the first sheep to arrive in the penal colony known as Van Diemen's Land, in September 1803. Records show sixteen ewes, four ewe lambs and three wether lambs were taken ashore at Risdon Cove in the island's south. Historians believe the early mobs were a motley lot, crossbred from small Bengal sheep which had thin hairy wool and Cape sheep, known for their fat tails and course, dark wool. But the fibre didn't matter—their primary role was to provide meat for European palates tired of kangaroo and wallaby.[5]

Things started to change under the influence of Governor Philip Gidley King. As the senior representative of His Majesty King George III in the British colony of New South Wales, which then encompassed Tasmania, King took an active interest in improving colonial sheep flocks. He sent some merino rams of the 'Spanish type' to Tasmania in 1805, with a view to improving the fleeces. With the push well and truly on to build an export trade in wool to supply British mills, Tasmania's Lieutenant Governor William Sorrell also bought 300 rams in 1820 from the famous Camden property established by the Macarthur family near Sydney.

However, one of the most influential figures in changing not only Tasmanian but Australian merinos forever was not a government official but one of Nan's predecessors in the Midlands—a remarkable woman by the name of Eliza Forlong. Born Elizabeth Jack in Scotland in 1784, she married a Glaswegian wine merchant at the age of about twenty. They had at least six children but by the 1820s most of them had died of tuberculosis. When one of their two remaining sons showed signs of contracting the disease, the Forlongs decided they should move to a healthier climate. After some methodical research they settled on the idea of becoming woolgrowers in New South Wales, where they believed it was possible to make good money running Saxon merinos.[6]

A refined strain of the merino breed first made famous in Spain, these precious sheep were bred in the northern German province of Saxony under the enthusiastic patronage of the local head of state. Spanish merinos were limited in number and could only be exported with royal consent, but the elector of

Saxony was cousin to the king of Spain. He not only convinced the king to part with some of his precious stock, but set up a shepherd school to encourage the best management practices. By 1800 there were 3400 purebred merinos in Saxony, nurtured by special diets and sheltered in purpose-built barns. Wool from these cosseted animals soon started fetching high prices in England, attracting considerable interest in Australia, where efforts were being made to establish a large-scale sheep industry.

In June 1827, Eliza travelled to Germany with her two sons, William and Andrew. According to an early biographer, she spent considerable time in Saxony over the next four years, learning German so she could conduct business direct, and meeting with woolgrowers and all the great wool houses to find out as much as she could about breeding and managing sheep and producing the best quality wool. While her oldest son William worked in a sorting house to absorb as much as possible about preparing fleeces, Eliza bought sheep that would become the foundation of their new family venture on the other side of the world.

Unlike other colonists sourcing merinos from Saxony at the time, she did not engage an agent. Instead, she sewed gold sovereigns into the stays of her garments for safe-keeping and walked up to 25 kilometres a day from farm to farm, selecting her own sheep and negotiating the purchases. Once paid for, each animal was fitted with a special collar with a lockable tag or seal and stamped with a stylised letter 'F' so there was no danger of it being swapped or sold again before she could return to collect it. Having purchased all that she needed, Eliza then walked from farm to farm, gathering up the sheep and droving them to Hamburg, where they were loaded onto a ship for England.

Eliza sold the first lot of sheep she purchased to another venture, and then returned to Saxony to buy some more for her own family. The second mob of 97 was given into the care of William, who was only a teenager at the time he set sail for

Sydney aboard the *Clansman*. When the ship reached Hobart Town in November 1829, he decided to stay in Tasmania rather than continue on to his original destination. He filed an application for land and despite his young age was soon allocated a grant of 612 hectares, with another 408 hectares in reserve. William eventually selected a site at Cleveland, about 60 kilometres north of where Nan farms today.

Meanwhile, Eliza returned to Saxony and gathered up yet more sheep for her younger son Andrew and her husband's sister, Janet Templeton; a widow with nine children, she had decided to emigrate too. In late 1830, Eliza finally set sail for Australia aboard the *Czar*, with her husband John, Andrew, Janet and her children. When the ship arrived in Launceston on Tasmania's north coast in January 1831, she disembarked with Andrew and 76 sheep. But Janet took a strong dislike to the place and decided to continue on to New South Wales with her share of the flock. John went along to help get her settled, before returning to his own family a few weeks later.

Together at last and with enough high-quality Saxon merinos to make a start, the Forlongs intended to set up a 'model' farm and build their reputation and fortunes as leading wool producers. But the next few years did not go according to plan. Despite letters of recommendation and extensive negotiation with the authorities, they failed to secure grants for what they considered to be sufficient land suitable for the enterprise. The grant given to William was not large enough and there was no reliable water supply on the land where sheep could be washed before shearing, an essential process to remove sand and dirt from the fleeces.

In 1834, John, Eliza and Andrew returned to Britain so they could negotiate in person with authorities about securing more land. John died about a year later. Andrew returned to Australia and briefly took up land across Bass Strait in the emerging colony of Victoria, where new pastoral country was opening up, but he eventually left the colony altogether and settled in the United States. William married a cousin and also moved to Victoria. He established properties at Woodstock, west of Melbourne, and Seven Creeks Station near Euroa, in the state's north. Historians are not certain when Eliza returned from England but she died at Seven Creeks on 5 August 1859.

The Forlongs' attempts to set up a model farm in Tasmania may have failed, but Eliza's keen eye for fine wool sheep and the energy and determination she devoted to traipsing across Saxony have made an extraordinary mark. Descendants of the Saxon merinos she so carefully selected can still be found in many of Australia's best superfine-wool flocks, including the sheep at Lemon Hill, where Nan is using bloodlines from the renowned Winton Stud at Campbell Town. Winton was founded by David Taylor in 1835 with sheep purchased direct from William Forlong.

The stud remains in the hands of the Taylor family six generations later, the oldest and most famous of the sheep breeding enterprises which have made Tasmania's Central highlands world renowned for its superfine merino wool—fibre so soft and fine that textile manufacturers and international fashion houses have been known to pay as much as $320 per kilogram.[7] A considerable number of today's producers are the descendants of families who have been breeding sheep on tightly held pastoral runs for generations. Once considered the wool kings and queens of Australia, these families were the backbone of an elite grazing aristocracy created in the nineteenth century by pioneers from mainly middle-class backgrounds.

Nan had little idea of the history and long-standing traditions she was buying into when she decided to become a superfine-wool producer near the historic Georgian village of Oatlands, about

80 kilometres north of Hobart. Although she was returning to her roots, they came from a family tree planted in an entirely different place.

The Brays have been cattle ranchers in the United States for four generations. Nan's great-grandfather, Benjamin Bray, was among the pioneers who travelled to Idaho by covered wagon in the 1870s, drawn north-west by the prospect of taking up new agricultural land and building a better future for their families. Many of them made the arduous journey in wagon trains, following the legendary Oregon Trail that stretched some 3200 kilometres from the Missouri River in the Mid West to Oregon on the West Coast.

Like most settlers the Brays experienced some tough years, at one point wintering in a cave dug out of a riverbank. In 1881 the family took up land in south-central Idaho, in a picturesque valley about two hours east of Boise. Surrounded by rock-rimmed canyons, it had its own hot springs and a meandering creek, but it was sage brush country, often dry and harsh, and difficult to farm. Nan's grandfather Solon was born here in 1882, reputedly the first non-Indian child born in the county.

Solon married in 1915 but his first wife died three years later, leaving him with two young sons. In 1920 he married again and moved to Oregon to try and earn a better living. He and his second wife Ada had another two children, a daughter and Nan's father, Donald T. Bray, who was born near Oregon City in 1922. During the Great Depression, when Don was about ten years old, his parents returned to the family ranch, where they ran mainly cattle and a few dairy cows. Sheep were referred to unflatteringly as 'range maggots' and not part of the operation.

Life didn't get any easier when Solon died in 1936 at the age of 53. One of Don's older half-brothers took over the ranch, and Ada worked hard to keep the family together. 'My grandmother did lots of things, but her main independent source of income after her second husband died was to cook for shearing crews.

At the time there were a lot of sheep in the area and she was a fabulous cook,' Nan recalls.

Don proved to be an extremely bright scholar. He set his sights on going to the University of Idaho in the state's north to study science. 'They didn't have a lot of money but they had enough to get Dad started. He would tell stories about that first year. He had to pay for his books, his room and board, and his tuition, and he had 25 cents left. He would carry that in his pocket the entire winter so he had the feeling he had a little something in reserve. It wasn't that he wasn't going to survive but it took absolutely everything to get him to university.'

Don was in love and only a year or two into his studies when the Japanese shocked the world by bombing the American naval base at Pearl Harbor in Hawaii in a surprise military strike on the morning of 7 December 1941. The attack killed more than 2400 people, wreaked havoc on the United States navy and forced the country to enter the Second World War, fighting in both the Pacific and Europe.

Like thousands of other young men, Don responded by signing up for the Reserved Officers' Training Corp, a university-based program which produced officers for the United States Armed Forces. In 1943 he married his college sweetheart Fran and left for Georgia, where he trained as a second lieutenant in the army, in preparation for joining the fight in Europe. After the war ended in 1945 he served as part of the occupation forces in Berlin. Then he returned to civilian life and his studies, graduating with a masters degree in chemical engineering in 1950.

An exceptional scholar, Don was selected from about 500 applicants in the same year to attend the newly established Oak Ridge School of Reactor Technology in Tennessee, which focused on peaceful uses for nuclear technology. He gained the equivalent of a doctorate and in 1954 joined ten other graduates in starting up a nuclear engineering consulting company which they named Internuclear. At some stage during this period, the

Brays moved back to Don's home state so he could work at what became known much later as the Idaho National Laboratory. The federal facility was established in the desert west of Idaho Falls in 1949, and went on to lead the world in developing nuclear energy as a source of usable electricity.

Nan was born on 5 May 1952 while the Brays were living at Idaho Falls. They already had a four-year-old daughter, Kathy, who Nan recalls being very frail and quite spoiled. Kathy was a 'blue baby', born with a congenital heart problem, and required special care. Another daughter, Amy, followed about two years after Nan.

The family moved around a great deal during Nan's childhood, including going to Europe for two years when she was five. Her father was part of a team designing Italy's first civilian nuclear power plant on the Garigliano River between Rome and Naples. Internuclear became part of a working group established in 1957 to develop the project, which was funded by the World Bank. Construction was due to start in late 1959 but tragedy saw the Brays return to the United States before it was really underway. Nan does not remember much detail, but her sister Kathy died in an accident which fractured her skull. She was only eleven.

Back in America, Don found work as a senior engineer with the General Atomics Company in San Diego, California, where he became fascinated with developing technology to desalinate seawater. This area of engineering was not so far removed from the world of nuclear energy as it might appear—a field of thought at the time was that nuclear power plants could be used to provide cheap energy for developments such as desalination plants, or that the two functions could be combined in a single sea-based plant that produced both electricity and fresh water.

Don later said his interest was heightened by memories of the family ranch, where water was not only scarce but often brackish. He went on to become a pioneer in the field of water treatment, developing and patenting numerous inventions, techniques and systems that could be used both in large-scale plants and much smaller residential systems. In the late 1960s he started two companies, Desalination Systems Inc for the commercial-scale plants, and Nimbus Water Systems Inc for the home-based systems, building an empire that he hoped, one day, Nan would join.

Meanwhile, he and Fran had divorced. Nan and Amy continued to live with their mother in San Diego, and Nan played a significant part in looking after her sister, who became increasingly difficult to manage. 'It is only in the last few years that I have really learned more about who she really was because families create stories, and the story around Amy was that she was mentally unstable,' Nan says. 'But I think the truth was that I was this disgustingly well-behaved, highly motivated, not to say kiss-ass child . . . and Amy was pretty much normal. She was stroppy and never learnt how to manage either of my parents, but in the end I really think the combination of the three of us—Dad and my mom and myself—really did make my sister nuts and she ended up having quite a struggle with mental illness through her teenage years.' Amy committed suicide in 1976 when she 21.

'It was not an easy family to grow up in,' Nan admits quietly, with great candour, reflecting on the difficult years of her youth and young adulthood. 'I really loved my dad but he was a very hard man . . . He softened up later in life, but he was really tough to have as a father, and my mother was not very easy either. That is part of the reason why I am on the other side of the planet. I very consciously just shut the door on my family, and I did it in different ways at different times, although I reconnected with both parents in later years.'

One of those instances was when Nan ignored her parents' request to stay in San Diego for her college years, and applied to study science at the prestigious Stanford University. A big part of the attraction was that it was almost 800 kilometres away, near San Francisco. 'I was just so out of there. I got myself a scholarship and I got out.'

In what Nan now admits was probably an attempt both to impress her father and to make sense of her family life, she started out determined to study psychiatric medicine, but she almost failed the required subject of chemistry and decided to switch to psychology. The student with the highest academic ranking at her high school, Nan was not used to failure. 'I was pretty much an overachiever,' she confesses. 'Anything I set my mind to, I expected to get.' When she couldn't settle into psychology either, she tried human biology and even music, which remains a passion.

After two years struggling to find direction, Nan decided to take a year off and rethink her future. Certain that she did not want to return to Stanford, she decided to transfer to the University of California at Berkeley, where they were offering a degree in the emerging discipline of environmental science. It was not such an unusual choice for the twenty-year-old, who loved hiking and camping in the wilderness and spending holidays at the family ranch, even though one of her earliest memories of the place was 'freezing my butt off' on a winter cattle drive on horseback when she was about ten. But after just one semester Nan dropped that program too, concerned it lacked academic rigour so early in the discipline's development.

'I look back and it's probably one of the few decisions I regret,' Nan says. 'Knowing what I know now about myself, it's a pity I didn't stay with it. It's probably the closest I came to who I was. To have become a ranger or a wildlife ecologist or something like that would have been a career path that was more about what I really cared about, as opposed to doing something to be an achiever . . . There are some things I have a native talent for but mostly I didn't go for those things because it was more about impressing my dad and trying to get his attention.'

Contemplating what might have been, Nan reaches for a copy of her favourite book, *A Sand County Almanac*. One of the most influential and widely read nature books ever published, it had a deep and lasting impact on Nan, although she didn't realise it at the time. She was introduced to it as a text during her brief flirtation with environmental science, when she took a course in wildlife biology. Published posthumously in 1949, it was written by renowned American conservationist Aldo Leopold, who shared his observations in a series of essays capturing changes in the ecology from one month to the next on his farm in Wisconsin. The book reinforces Leopold's view that people have a responsibility to look after the land which they inhabit and preserve the delicate balance of nature.

'I found it again about three years ago and reread it,' Nan says, struggling not to cry as she recalls the deeply emotional experience. 'It was like coming home. I had read it, taken it in and absorbed it, and then forgotten about it. When I read it again, I couldn't believe I had forgotten about it, but I hadn't really in the core of me.'

The impact of *A Sand County Almanac* on Nan's approach to running Lemon Hill seems obvious in hindsight. Childhood visits to the sage brush country of Idaho may have prepared her eye to see beauty in the windswept hills, sparse vegetation and distant mountain views of the Tasmanian Midlands, but the book opened her mind to a way of observing and caring for the land and animals which she puts into practice every day as a farmer. 'It's all about balance,' Nan repeats many times as she carefully explains her approach to managing pastures, her sheep, and the biodiversity of native plant and animal species found on her property.

At the heart of Nan's philosophy lies the principle that sheep, just like people, need a diversity of things to eat. No matter how rich and green a pasture might be, if it's made up of just one or two plant species, it's like dining on nothing but oysters and caviar. While the idea might seem appealing at first, actually having nothing but oysters and caviar to eat for days on end would soon have most people longing for the mundane joys of a Vegemite sandwich. Not to mention the long-term health implications.

Nan was encouraged to explore the surprising complexities of what a sheep might want and need to eat by a sick merino ewe called Alice. Nan and Davey found her in the paddock one day, cast among the tussock grass. Casting is when a sheep lies down and cannot get up again under its own steam. It happens quite frequently to those carrying the bulky weight of a full fleece or to ewes after a difficult lambing. If they are not found soon enough and helped back onto their feet, they can become distressed and die quite quickly. Alice had given birth to a lamb which Nan and Davey found dead beside her and she couldn't stand, so they took her back to the hospital pens set up in a shed near the house.

Nan hates losing animals and has been known to try absolutely everything possible to resuscitate them, but even she had her doubts about saving Alice. They propped up the ewe with bales of hay so she was lying on her chest, and kept a close eye on her. Alice started to make progress but her knees became infected, so Nan treated her with antibiotics and bought a sling on an aluminium frame to support her while she stood up to graze. 'Right from the start she wanted to eat and drink so she wanted to live,' Nan says.

With the help of the frame, Nan would move Alice every day out to an area behind the shed where there just happened to be a huge variety of plants for her to eat—lucerne, clover, different grass species, and a range of perennial herbs sometimes grown in Australian pastures, such as chicory and plantain. 'I would go out every couple of hours and move the sling, and I would stand and watch her. I realised she was very selective,' Nan says. 'She would start with the lucerne first, then the chicory, then plantain, then clover, and then the grass . . . she was incredibly specific. There was a definite pattern and a clear preference.'

Alice eventually recovered and rejoined the rest of her mob, but Nan kept thinking about what she had witnessed. A short time later she raised the question with a group of researchers visiting from the United States to talk to local farmers about reducing the impact of grazing on the natural environment. They told her about the work of Professor Fred Provenza, a former ranch manager from Colorado who went on to become an award-winning scientist recognised for his groundbreaking work on the feeding habits of grazing animals, and the implications not only for animal health but managing farmland more sustainably.

As Nan describes it, somewhere during the conversation two neurons suddenly connected in her brain. Two years before an adviser from the local environment department had given her a DVD put together by Provenza's research group but she had never watched it. 'Of course you never pull out a DVD on grazing when you sit down in front of the television and want to watch a movie,' Nan says laughingly in her own defence. 'Every time I would look at it and think, "I really should watch that". Then these guys came over and we had that conversation about Alice, and I realised they were connected. So that very evening I came in and put the DVD on. I was just blown away.'

As a graduate student in the 1970s, Fred Provenza had set out to research the grazing patterns of goats in sage brush country in the United States. According to Nan years of work led him to realise that if you can provide enough diversity of feed to animals which have enough knowledge to recognise the different varieties of plants available, they will adapt their grazing to not only make sure they eat a balanced diet, but to take advantage of the plants' medicinal properties and self-medicate.

Known as 'nutritional wisdom', this phenomenon involves sheep learning about different plants and the effects they have on their metabolism. The effects are driven by various chemical compounds within the plants, which can vary not only between species, but within the same plant at different times of the day or year or in different weather conditions. With enough wisdom, a sheep can improve its overall health, with potential to grow faster, produce more wool and become more resistant to disease, flystrike and intestinal worms. These are all major issues for most sheep producers which not only chew up a lot of energy to manage, but cost a lot of money in the form of extra labour, veterinary chemicals and lost production.

The theory is well and good, but to make it work in a practical setting Provenza tells farmers they have to make sure of two important things—every animal on their farm needs to acquire the knowledge of which plants to eat and when; and they need to have daily access to enough diversity and quantities of plants to be able to choose what they eat. Achieving the first means allowing lambs to stay with their mothers long enough to learn, rather than weaning them at a very young age and putting them into separate paddocks with the rest of their age group. Achieving the second means not only increasing the diversity of plants available, but adjusting the amount of stock being carried on the farm so there is more than enough feed to go round.

'Once I found out what Fred was really on about, it was the missing piece for me,' Nan says. Within days she had decided not to wean that season's lambs. Instead of removing them from their mothers when they were about four months old as per standard practice, and running her sheep in mobs divided up according to age, she would keep them in family groups with multiple generations and see what happened.

'I thought the idea of family groups was so cool,' she says. 'Basically it reflects what every mother knows—babies learn best from their mums. The research in sheep is suggesting a year to eighteen months, but I think it takes closer to two years for the knowledge to be transmitted in such a way that the young animal is really prepared to fend for itself well in that environment. What do we do in our standard production systems? We wean them at three to four months so we have these babies wandering around totally clueless.'

Nan's epiphany came in October 2008. It was the end of lambing season and she had more than 700 ewes with baby lambs at foot, including quite a few twins. The numbers were much lower than previous years when she had run up to 2000 sheep, because three very dry seasons had forced her to sell all the older animals. Her pasture wasn't in good shape either. Lemon Hill had received half its normal rainfall every year since 2006, and the paddocks had been eaten out more than Provenza would like because Nan had held on to too many sheep. She had kept them going by setting up a temporary feedlot and feeding them grain—it had not only cost a fortune, but even though the sheep looked like they were in good condition, she and Davey agreed something wasn't quite right.

After talking to Davey, Nan decided the first thing she needed to do was reduce the number of sheep even further, at least until the seasons improved. She worked out how many the property could carry without buying in extra feed, and cut the numbers down to the equivalent of a bit more than two sheep per hectare—less than half the rate it was carrying before the dry. It was a far from easy decision after all the care and attention she had put into breeding them, raising them and keeping them going during the drought, but it had to be done.

There was one exception—Alice may have been getting on in years and in the target group for culling, but she would be staying. She had earnt the right. But when the day came for yarding up the mob of older ewes so they could be loaded onto a truck for the abattoir, Nan couldn't find her. 'I was quite sad because I knew she was in the mob somewhere . . . I didn't want to look at them because I knew what was going to happen.'

Realising this was far from courageous, she turned to the mob and said out loud: 'All right, girls, I'm sorry you have to go but I want you to know I really appreciate all you have done for me over the last few years.'

Nan couldn't believe what happened next. 'Out of this mob, swear to God, walks Alice. And she was looking at me as if to say, "Get me the hell out of here". I had maybe twenty minutes before the truck was due so I called up Davey and said, "Get over here, I've found Alice and we have to get her out". So we did. She has had three more lambs since then.'

The next challenge was finding the best way to divide up the remaining sheep so there was more than one generation in each mob. They were currently being run in five separate groups—four divided according to the year they were born, and a small flock of ewes which had delivered twins and needed extra care. Nan decided to keep it simple and leave the ewes and their lambs where they were. The four-year-olds and their lambs were given blue ear tags to help keep track of the family unit, the three-year-olds and their lambs became the nucleus of the 'yellow family', and the two-year-old ewes and their lambs became the 'red family'. The single teenagers, the one-year-olds, were divided up randomly between the three new family groups, and the flock of twinning ewes which were various ages were kept together to create a fourth family.

The easy part was done. Now the sheep were sorted Nan had to deal with the implications for running the farm on a daily basis. Her whole approach to management up to then had been designed around the sheep being divided into year classes. For a start, the lambs must be left to wean themselves or, at least, until it came time for their mothers to be mated again to produce the next lot of lambs. At this point the ewes were removed and put in a different paddock with the rams. The lambs were left in the familiar environment of their home paddocks so they would be less stressed from being temporarily separated from their mothers, but safe from the dangers of unwanted teenage pregnancies. After six weeks enjoying the sheep equivalent of a honeymoon with the rams, the ewes returned.

The approach had to change at shearing time too. Nan talked to the contract shearing team that comes to the farm every September, and was pleased to find they didn't object to working with mixed age groups. She decided anyway to separate out the young sheep, or hoggets, about to be shorn for the first time; they could be kept in the shed as backup, so there were some dry sheep available to shear if it rained.

While Nan and Davey were coming to grips with a new way of running the sheep, Nan also had to pay attention to sorting out the pasture side of things. When Nan first bought Lemon Hill, it was a rundown farm which had most recently been used to grow potatoes and graze prime lambs. There was very little remnant native vegetation, with only a few sparse white gums standing on top of the highest hill. Years of overstocking had contributed to soil erosion, and most of the paddocks contained only a few different pasture species. Today the pasture is much more diverse in line with Provenza's principles. Nan introduced new mixtures of perennial plants, including the chicory and plantain that Alice enjoyed so much. In areas described as 'semi-native' there are now 50 or more species for the sheep to choose from, and on the rocky hillsides Nan has found up to 100 different species—a relative sheep smorgasbord.

Mid-afternoon and Nan is heading up to the top of her property and her favourite spot on the farm. It is three o'clock and the sun is already low in the sky, casting a long shadow from the western hills. Beyond their reach the afternoon light is turning clumps of native spear and wallaby grass white-gold as she heads across the lowest paddock. Behind her to the east is Curly Sedge Creek, which has been fenced off to preserve remnants of the threatened water-loving species after which it is named.

The ute chugs up the first rise. In the spring this hillside is covered with tiny vanilla lilies, as well as small, flowering herbaceous plants known as forbs. This is Davey's monitoring spot—the place he uses to judge how well the whole property is going in terms of the amount of feed available.

Nan enters Butterfly Gully, a small gorge which takes its name from the endangered species of Ptunarra brown butterfly found there. An inconspicuous insect of unremarkable brown, the butterfly only appears for a couple of weeks around the autumnal equinox, fluttering between clumps of the silver tussock grass that is its sole habitat. Pathetic flyers, if they dare to go too high and the wind catches them, they are not strong enough to get back. The butterflies were documented by a biodiversity expert during a government project to help landowners identify native flora and fauna on their properties and come up with plans to protect critical 'hotspots'.

Lemon Hill proved to have more treasures than Nan expected, with several pockets of threatened and endangered species, especially in the gullies and on the rocky slopes. There is a grassland greenhood orchid (*Pterostylis ziegeleri*) that has virtually disappeared from the Midlands, flax lilies, knawel weed, and native grasses that are becoming increasingly hard to find after decades of sowing exotic pastures. In what Nan dubs the Wallaby Tenement, there is a colony of red-bellied pademelons, small marsupials related to kangaroos and wallabies that were once a favourite snack for the now-extinct Tasmanian tiger. Much to her delight a pair of wedge-tailed eagles also routinely hovers over the farm, and she is pretty sure there are signs of bandicoots. 'One of the things I find really encouraging about the future of farming is that if you give even a clapped-out place like this a chance to breathe, it is amazing what comes back,' she says. 'We haven't completely stepped over the threshold yet, and that really matters to us as farmers.'

Passing through the gully and onto a higher slope, Nan takes a small detour to admire one of her merino families. Among the mob are lambs born eight months ago, long tails swinging happily behind them as they turn and move away from the ute. They are almost as tall as their mothers and looking healthy. Further up the rise Nan comes to an area that was badly overgrazed when she first saw it in 1999. The intersection of three runs is in the lee of the hill, where sheep used to camp for shelter and to access water. It is also the point where Nan started to have an inkling she might be interested in buying the farm on inspecting it for the first time. On the other side of a gate is the highest point and sweeping views to Table Mountain in the west. The mountain has become a 'bellwether' for Nan and Davey—if they see the weather closing in there, they know that within about twenty minutes it is going to snow, hail or rain on Lemon Hill; if it's clear, they can expect fine weather for at least an hour or so.

Much closer is the hill after which Nan's place is named. Flat-topped, with a smattering of trees and a phone tower, it bears the moniker of a notorious bushranger, Richard Lemon, who terrorised the area in the first decade of the nineteenth century. Involved in several murders as well as robberies, he hid out in a rough bark hut not far from Oatlands with two cohorts. He was eventually shot and, in a grisly end, his head exhibited on a stake in Hobart Town.[8]

A larger-than life silhouette of the criminal holding up a man on horseback now stands near the top of Lemon Hill, overlooking the Midland Highway. It is one in a series of sculptures handcrafted from steel plate which were placed along the road that connects Tasmania's north and south, as part of a local arts project celebrating the region's rich heritage. Ironically, Lemon Hill now stands on the opposite side of the highway to Nan's farm. She is not sure when they became separated but the road was realigned in the 1980s to bypass Oatlands. The new road passes within 100 metres of her house.

Nan has become used to the highway being so close, but originally she was a little dismayed. 'I didn't think much of this property when I first drove onto it. I only realised this in retrospect but I really had a bit of a bush block in mind. I drove onto this place and it was such a mess, you could not believe it. It was very cheap—347 hectares for $320 000—but I thought it was never going to work, and then we drove up top, and it fit something in the image I was carrying inside of me . . . I would prefer it wasn't alongside the highway in many ways but I have gotten used to that. The place itself I have had a real feeling for from the moment I got up to the top.'

From the highest point of the farm the stretch of black bitumen is not as visible and there is a greater sense of isolation. While most of the rest of the property is bare of significant trees, here there is a smattering of beautiful old gums. 'It looks more like the sort of place I had in mind,' Nan says, contemplating the view.

Long before she set foot on Lemon Hill, Nan's first trip to Australia was as a graduate student in 1979, when she was invited to speak at an International Union of Geology and Geophysics conference in Canberra. 'I was just petrified, but it went okay as far as I can remember,' she says.

Not long married, she was accompanied by her husband Dean. After the conference they stayed a few extra days to climb Australia's highest peak, Mount Kosciusko, in the nearby Snowy

Mountains. The adventure was slightly disappointing for people used to hiking in California's majestic Sierra Nevada mountains, where the highest peak is more than 4420 metres. The summit of Mount Kosciusko is only half as high and by comparison a pleasant stroll, except for summer plagues of small black flies. 'I had never experienced anything like it,' she says. 'We kept saying to each other, "That's all right, tomorrow surely we will be above the fly line . . ." If you hike in the Sierras, you get to 10 000 feet and you are above the tree line and the mosquitoes and other insects drop away. But there is no place above the fly line in Australia!'

About three years later Nan and Dean were approached by the CSIRO to work in Australia. The oceanography division was on a recruiting drive; it had recently been relocated to Hobart and a considerable portion of staff did not want to leave Sydney. The young couple seriously considered the offer, but they decided from a career perspective it was better to stay where they were until they had gained a little more experience. They were working at the Scripps Institution of Oceanography. Based at the University of California, in San Diego where Nan grew up, it is one of the oldest, largest and most important centres for ocean and earth science research in the world. Nan ended up there in 1982 after studying engineering physics at the university's Berkeley campus and then completing a doctorate in oceanography in a joint program run by the Woods Hole Oceanographic Institution and the Massachusetts Institute of Technology on the east coast, where she met Dean, who was studying in the same program.

Fast forward thirteen years to 1995 and life had changed dramatically for Nan. Her marriage to Dean was over and she was looking for a change. 'I just needed to get away from San Diego and Scripps, and I didn't really want to live in a big city any more. I was offered a job on the east coast but it is like a whole different country and I just couldn't do it.' So she certainly wasn't thinking of migrating to a different continent when she took advantage of the relative proximity of a research cruise in the Indonesian Archipelago to visit her peers at the CSIRO Division of Marine Research in Tasmania. She hadn't been to the island state before and proximity was the perfect excuse.

It was March and the early autumn weather was perfect. She accepted an offer from a local guy she had met on the work cruise, and travelled all around the state with him for a week by motorcycle. 'I just fell in love with the place, not with him, but with the state. I actually extended my visit by another week, and by the end of that time I had decided that I wanted to emigrate,' Nan says.

She talked to the man in charge of the marine division about working from Hobart for a year on sabbatical, bringing her research team from Scripps if they wanted to come. It was Nan's way of being cautious. She knew in her heart that Tasmania was where she wanted to be but, after all, she had only spent two weeks there when the weather was warm and sunny. It would be smarter to experience the place for longer as a working resident rather than a tourist, and get a better feel for the climate and the culture before making a final decision. 'I just thought I would be a little more conservative and not just leap out of a good career job in the US, at a university where I had tenure.'

All six members of Nan's team back in California jumped at the opportunity to work Down Under for a year, so in March 1996 Nan packed up her small garage apartment and her office, shipped what she needed to Australia and hopped on the plane. Waiting for her in Melbourne was Brooke, one of her border collies, who had been sent out ahead because she had to spend four months in quarantine.

By the end of her temporary year in Tasmania Nan was absolutely convinced moving to Australia on a permanent basis was the right thing to do. The next challenge was obtaining permission from the Australian immigration authorities. She figured the best potential lay in securing full-time work with the CSIRO so they could sponsor her visa application. There were only a couple of suitable jobs going in the marine division. One of them was for division chief, and she decided to put up her hand.

Figuring most of the cards were stacked against her, Nan never really believed she would succeed. The CSIRO had a reputation at that time as a conservative organisation and a bit of an 'old boys' network. She was not old, not a boy, and not even Australian. But her academic achievements and research background were impeccable, and she did have experience in management and administration at Scripps, where her last position was director of the physical oceanography division.

The initial application process involved much more than Nan expected. With only a week to go before the closing date, she discovered every applicant must respond in full to each one of 36 selection criteria listed for the job, rather than submitting an initial brief expression of interest as an interim step. Having rushed the paperwork Nan was amazed when she made the short list of three candidates. Next was a formal interview and seminar presentation before the selection panel, and Nan was reasonably pleased with how she performed. Then came the final hurdle, billed as an 'informal talk' with CSIRO chief executive Sir Malcolm McIntosh.

Dr McIntosh was one of Australia's most outstanding scientific leaders, admired not just for his energy and vision but for his skills as a communicator and the rapport he had with the organisation's 7000 staff. Nan found the mental gymnastics required to keep up with his insightful mind exhausting and not a little exhilarating. 'For 45 minutes he took me everywhere. I really knew I had been interviewed.'

Her biggest concern was having absolutely no idea about Australian politics and managing the division's relationships with government ministers. 'I couldn't be anything but honest with him. But he said if they offered me the job he would teach me that stuff,' Nan says. And then he changed the topic of conversation to chat about sheepdogs. He had kelpies and knew that Nan bred and competed with border collies.

About a month later, Dr McIntosh rang her personally to let her know she had the job. She was one of three women appointed as division chiefs during his tenure, which ended with his untimely death from cancer in 2000.

Nan took up her appointment as the nation's senior marine scientist in September 1997. For the next six years she was responsible for 350 people at three sites across Australia. 'I spent half my time catching planes,' Nan reflects. 'Part of the irony of the situation was that I wanted the job so I could be in Tasmania and work with the people I loved working with during my first year at CSIRO. Half the time I wasn't in Tasmania, and the people in the division I really cared about now backed off because I was chief.'

While the travel wore her down, she loved working with the division's younger scientists to help them become more confident, and she enjoyed learning about the Australian political system and how to work within it to raise support for the division and its scientists. The process of setting scientific directions was 'excruciating', but in the end she found it 'very satisfying'.

A few years into the job, Nan decided to buy a farm. She had no fixed ideas about where it should be in Tasmania, but she definitely wanted to run merinos and produce superfine wool. 'I knew that is what I wanted to do, but not for the right reasons, ironically. It's a bit silly, really,' she admits, laughing and shaking her head. 'When I went to work at CSIRO I didn't have anything approximating a suit, and I was going to be doing this high-level administrative job. I used to work in my bathing suit during summer because I was a coastal scientist, and mostly I just wore jeans. So I went shopping and found these very wonderful, very expensive suits—made of merino wool. They don't wrinkle and they're warm. I thought they were superfine merino so my thinking was if I had bought one and it cost $1800, then there had to be a market for superfine merino.'

The irony was the suits turned out to be made of 22 micron wool, which is not classified as superfine at all. Not only was the connection spurious, but so was the perception that because the suits cost a fortune there was a fortune to be made in growing wool. 'We have since learned differently,' she says wryly.

Nan's initial idea was to lease a farm and 'put her toe in the water'. She would buy a few sheep, hire a manager and visit at weekends to take a break from the crazy pace of work and give the dogs a good run. It was a 'step along the track' in a journey which began with holiday experiences at the family ranch in Idaho. 'For a long time, from childhood, I had this secret longing to be a farmer. Not that I really understood what that meant but I liked the actuality of the farm, and I think some of that must have been passed on genetically. There was this affinity for land and doing something with land,' Nan says.

'But both my parents were adamantly opposed to the idea that you could make a living from farming, and they may have been right—I haven't completely proven them wrong yet. So I never felt it was going to impress my dad much if I went into farming, and then in the early 70s my uncle sold off most of the ranch and ran the rest into debt. My dad had bailed him out a few times but he wasn't going to do it any more. He waited for it to go into foreclosure and then he bought it. So there's my dad, who doesn't believe in farming as a way to make a living, with a farm. It wasn't much of a farm, but my dad's company was doing really well so over the years he started buying back the bits that my uncle had sold off and then he kept going. He ended up with about 8000 acres [3265 hectares] . . . At some stage, something kind of clicked in me. If it's okay for him then I can do it too.' Don hired a manager to run the ranch while he concentrated on his companies. The manager turned out to be dishonest so Don's ex-wife, Fran, took it on for a while. Then it was run by one of his stepchildren and her husband, who continue to manage it after Don's death in February 2011.

When Nan bought Lemon Hill she also hired a manager, but it didn't work out too well for her either, adding to the stress building up from working up to 80 hours a week in a job that was becoming increasingly demanding. After the first twelve months or so she came very close to giving up on the whole idea. 'It wasn't fun. The dream balloon had definitely burst,' she says. 'A pocket of land cut out of the corner of my property came on the market and I just couldn't bring myself to make an offer. I thought the last thing I need to do is add more to this.'

It was during this difficult period that Davey came to the rescue. It would be too trite to describe him as a knight in shining armour, but he was a gentle and thoughtful man, riding a well-trained stockhorse, and he was more than happy to work for a raw beginner even if she was his first female boss. 'I could see from the start that she had some affinity for the land,' he says.

David Carnes was only thirteen when he took on his first full-time job as a stockman. It was wartime and Geoff Green was short of men to work Middle Park, his grazing property at Antill Ponds, just a few kilometres north of Oatlands. Mr Green no doubt recognised the pedigree of the young boy with his 'little old horse and dog from up bush' when they showed up in his yard one day looking for employment.

Born at Evandale in 1927, Davey was the son of a shepherd from Bothwell, who was also the son of a shepherd from Bothwell. From the age of about eight, when he wasn't at school Davey would climb onto his pony and follow his dad to help with the sheep. 'My old father was a restless sort of bloke, and four years was as much as he ever stayed in any one place. He worked on different properties all around the state,' Davey says.

For a time Davey lived with an older sister at Longford, where he went to primary school. His formal education ended abruptly during a major outbreak of polio, which killed more than 80 Tasmanians in the late 1930s and resulted in health authorities introducing severe restrictions on the population in a desperate effort to control the epidemic. Davey packed his bag and headed back to his parents. 'I managed to get home before they quarantined everyone. I was lucky, and from then I finished my bit of schooling by correspondence,' he explains.

The young stockman enjoyed his first full-time job at Middle Park, a 2500-hectare property which ran a flock of prize-winning Corriedales. He was paid the princely sum of fifteen bob a week and returned home most nights to his parents. Later on he worked on some of Tasmania's most notable stations with some of the country's most respected pastoralists, including Colonel Allan Cameron at Mona Vale, who used to shear about 50 000 sheep; the Burbury family's Glen Morey station, then under the guiding hand of J.V. Burbury; and the historic Connorville station of about 11 430 hectares at Cressy, which hosted Queen Elizabeth II overnight when she visited Tasmania in 1954.

Davey had three horses during his time at Connorville, so quiet he could trust them with children. 'To get to where our main work was we had about 5 miles to travel from the homestead. We would go off on the horses at half past seven, and canter the 5 miles or so. Then you would do your work. Going back 50 years it was all horse work . . . I always used to say, doing stockwork in the hills, if you had a good horse and a good dog it was a breeze.'

The horses proved handy for carrying sheep too, something Davey says couldn't be done now because sheep are generally so much larger. 'When I was a young bloke we always had a sack bag cut down about halfway, and then sewn to another sack bag, and you tied that over your horse so you had two bags, one each side . . . You could put young sheep in those saddle bags,' he explains. Larger sheep were sometimes thrown on top of the horse, across the front of the saddle. 'There were many times that we threw them up on the horse and got up behind. You couldn't get them up on a flaming horse now, not even the smaller ewes.'

It's not the only change he has witnessed over the decades. Davey has lived through the widespread introduction of superphosphate fertiliser and exotic pastures, which increased dramatically in Tasmania with the start of aerial application in the late 1940s. Horses have made way for motorbikes, and properties that once employed 50 workers and were communities in their own right now only employ a handful, with support from contractors for major seasonal tasks such as crutching and shearing.

Davey reckons the most dramatic period of change was the 1950s, during the booming post-war economy when the price of wool jumped from about 2 shillings for a pound of wool to a pound a pound. It was generally a boom time for producers, with the exception of 1950–51 when the prime minister, Robert Menzies, unwillingly introduced a tax on wool sales and a 10 per cent increase in income tax to stem rising inflation and shore up the currency. 'He brought in what was called at the time a horror budget. People had received all their money for their wool, and a lot of them had spent it. A lot of people went broke. I remember it so well.'

In particular, 1956 lives in Davey's memory as a 'bonza' year because wool prices had risen again and the seasonal conditions were wonderful. The year 1958 wasn't bad either, at least for Davey, who was a keen sportsman playing both cricket and Australian rules football with local teams. That was the season he won the best and fairest medal for the Oatlands District Football Association and his team, Tunbridge, took out the grand final by a substantial 44 points. 'Just after the war, country football here in Tassie was brilliant. The soldiers had come home from the war and they were ultra fit, and they didn't want to go anywhere else. They just wanted to be here with their families,' he says, remembering the glory days of country football with obvious nostalgia.

As time went on Davey's reputation grew as a stockman with a particularly good eye for superfine merinos. Modest, quietly spoken and from a generation when the boss was always respectfully called 'Mister', he made the most of every opportunity to learn as much as he could. 'For some unknown reason Colonel Allan Cameron asked me to help class his sheep every year. I learnt a lot from him, and from J.V. Burbury,' he says. Davey got to know Mr Burbury in about 1960 when he bought Middle Park. 'He said, "You've worked on it, you know it, come and work for me." He was a very clever man and he taught me a lot about how to run the place. He was an excellent sheep man.' Davey also helped to class the famous Connorville sheep one season, working alongside their regular woolclasser. All these experiences taught him a great deal about wool and what makes a good sheep. He has been applying that knowledge to help Nan for about ten years in what has become an extraordinary partnership.

The seemingly unlikely combination first met at a sheepdog trial at Huonville in southern Tasmania, where they were both competing. Davey was curious about Nan's American-bred border collies and they got talking. 'At the time she knew nothing about sheep herself and she didn't know that I did either,' he says. Nan ended up giving the stockman one of her pups, Russ. Davey trained him and competed in trials in which the dogs have to move three sheep through a series of obstacles, but Russ tended to be overshadowed by another one of his dogs, Ted, a large black and white border collie who often won. 'He was a magnificent dog. He was handy. I got him from a top handler here in Tassie, Malcolm Taylor, and I was talking to his wife one day and I asked why Malcolm gave me Ted, and she said it was because he couldn't do anything with him.' It proved a point on which Nan and Davey both agree—sometimes dogs, no matter how well bred and trained, will only work for certain people.

When things started going badly awry at Lemon Hill, Nan turned to Davey for help. He kept an eye on the property during the week, while Nan drove up every weekend from her home at Woodbridge, south of Hobart. Gradually she began to enjoy the farm once more, and in 2002 she finally packed up her belongings and the dogs and moved permanently to Oatlands. For another year or so she commuted to the city. Although she claims the travelling wasn't so bad, Davey could see she was worn out. 'She used to come home very tired,' he recalls. 'I can remember when she said she was going to throw it in. I said, "I don't blame you, Nan, but it won't be anywhere near as lucrative."'

Nan replied with conviction: 'With your experience and my science we'll make this work.'

To make a fresh start, one of the first things Davey did was introduce her to some trustworthy livestock agents who could help purchase decent sheep. 'Being in the game all my life I knew good auctioneers, good sheep men,' Davey says. 'One bloke had loaded her up with a rotten lot of sheep. She went over to the mainland and paid good money for them but, God, they were cows of sheep. And I said to Nan those sheep are just no good, and they weren't.' The new agent took Nan to see Allan and Carol Phillips from the Glen Stuart Stud at Evandale, who were destined to become a regular source of rams and ewes for Lemon Hill and good friends.

Davey recognised Nan's thirst for knowledge and with the wool clip finally heading in the right direction, he decided the next step in her education should be attending a wool sale in Launceston. 'You want to learn the game, do you, Nan?' he remembers asking her, although he was pretty sure of the answer. 'Righto, you've got a beautiful bit of wool in the sales, let's go.' A wily operator recognising the innate curiosity of his pupil, Davey organised things so she was sitting next to two experienced buyers. She spent the sale picking their brains. 'By crikey, she said to me afterwards, "Oh, I learnt a lot from them."'

Davey—or Mr Dave, as she often calls him in a reversal of the old-fashioned etiquette between boss and hired hand—is always very respectful, recognising it is Nan's farm and she is in charge. 'Davey, in his very careful and generous way, helped me to learn without making me feel like I was being bossed around. He never told me how to run things but I finally caught on,' she says.

She explains how she started to watch for the times when he would say to her, 'Nan?'

'Yes, Mr Dave?' she would reply.

'Would it be an idea . . .'

That thought-provoking phrase usually meant he had something to suggest, and that it was worth paying attention because it was likely to be insightful and important.

She can still remember the day when she finally had the opportunity to say, 'Mr Dave?'

'Yes, Nan?'

'Would it be an idea . . .'

The two of them look at each other and smile. 'Mind you, it probably took a good four or five years for it happen,' Nan says, laughing.

❖ ❖ ❖

What has happened in the past few years on the farm has Davey shaking his head in wonder. 'After a lifetime on the land it's got me, absolutely. I am just amazed at what we are doing and what we are achieving,' he says. 'I call it the experimental place—and it is.'

When Nan proposed her first major change to run sheep in family groups instead of dividing them into age classes, Davey recognised the approach was not so different to the way things used to be when his father looked after large mobs of sheep on enormous runs in isolated country. He could remember his father telling him as a young lad that the longer lambs were left on the ewes the better. 'I was quite willing to give it a go,' he says. But even Davey is amazed at how easy lambing has become.

For most of his 70 years as a shepherd, he has spent weeks in spring, going out in freezing cold weather, rescuing newborn lambs abandoned by their mothers and 'catching' ewes having difficulty lambing. Lambs on the edge of life have to be carried somewhere warm and revived. If they cannot be returned to their mothers, they have to be fed by bottle four or five times a day, gradually reducing the number of feeds until they are old enough to go back to the paddock. If the mothers are found but have disowned their lambs, efforts are made to 'mother up', which usually involves penning them together until the ewe reclaims her offspring and allows it to feed. Before Nan made the change to family groups, it wasn't unusual to pen about twenty ewes out of 1000. These days the hospital pens built in a shed for the contingency are so rarely needed they have become storage areas.

Lambing is now a favourite time of the year. Starting in early October, if the weather is reasonable, Nan fills a small backpack with morning tea—her favourite is homemade scones with Tasmanian honey and cream cheese—and sets off across the paddocks every morning on foot. Davey usually heads in the opposite direction on the bike, and they meet up somewhere in the middle to share the food and compare notes. If the weather is too cold and wet, Nan takes the ute and they both sit inside in the warm, hoping they don't have to get out to help a sheep in trouble. 'The last lambing I just couldn't fathom it,' says Davey. 'We were sitting back having our morning tea . . . and I said, "If this is lambing it'll do me, I'm good for a few more years." We never caught one sheep.'

What is even more fascinating to them both is the role nature is now starting to play in reducing lamb losses. Human intervention once meant all the lambs were weaned at exactly the same time. Once the lambs were weaned, the ewes tended to cycle at the same time, so they tended to get pregnant at the same time, with the bulk giving birth within about three weeks. Nan's lambing season is now spread fairly evenly over six weeks—a decided advantage because it means less lambs are at risk in those first few tenuous hours of life on any given night, if the weather turns nasty.

Now part of cohesive family groups, the sheep also seem to be keeping more of an eye on each other. 'I was moving sheep a few months ago in an area of very long grass, and I saw this small group away from the main mob. So I went over to them and there was a cast ewe lying on the ground. They weren't going to leave her,' says Nan. 'Normally you would see ewes go away from the mob to have their lambs, but in these family groups they don't tend to do that. You will see the mother, the daughters, the grandmother, the sisters all together, and the young sheep will babysit the lambs. It is absolutely fascinating.'

Lambing percentages on Lemon Hill have gone up too—that is, the number of lambs which are born and survive compared with the number of ewes mated. Farmers running sheep bred for prime-lamb production might aim for more than 130 per cent, given that many ewes successfully raise twins and sometimes even triplets. In merino flocks, anything above 80 per cent is considered pretty good. Nan's flock has increased from an average of 82 per cent to more than 100 per cent in less than three years, a rate of change that is virtually unheard of, especially compared with the slow, incremental changes that come from selective breeding alone.

But one of the changes that most delighted Davey was Nan's decision not to use superphosphate on her pastures. 'I never did like it, even way back,' he says. He believes it affects the worms and natural bacteria that break down organic matter in the soils and keep them healthy. Nan agrees and is using a seaweed concentrate to give her pastures a boost. 'My word, it's good,' Davey says, 'and we are getting all the worms and everything back in.'

He was even more pleased when she decided, right from the beginning, not to carry out mulesing, long before the controversial method of stripping skin from around the breech to prevent flystrike generated a major consumer crisis for Australian woolgrowers. Animal welfare groups started an international campaign against mulesing in 2004. Consumers were upset when they found out about a practice they consider to be cruel, and some very high profile international fashion houses refused to buy Australian wool until things changed. Midland growers were particularly upset in 2009 when an iconic Italian suit-maker withdrew its sponsorship for a prestigious trophy they had presented every year since 1963 at the Campbell Town Show—one of the biggest and most important sheep shows in the country.

Many woolgrowers argued they had no choice if they were to avoid losing sheep to flystrike, which they considered an even more painful end, but Davey has always disagreed. 'If there is one thing I have been against all my life, it's mulesing. Boy, did I cop some flack over the years,' he says.

As an alternative, he suggested a method to control flies he first used about 50 years ago on the Burbury properties, which didn't mules sheep either. Known as a Jim-Jet, it is a spraying unit which applies anti-fly chemicals via strategically placed spray jets mounted on a frame. Sheep step on a foot pad as they run through the frame, activating the jets. Nan uses a chemical with low toxicity and residues so it doesn't affect the European Union accreditation of her wool as eco-friendly. As a result, she has sold her fleeces for a premium direct to a Norwegian company that is prepared to pay extra for wool from non-mulesed sheep, grown by producers who actively work to farm sustainably.

Davey was initially a little less certain about Nan's most recent innovation—leaving the tails on the lambs. It is virtually unheard of in Australia for sheep to keep their tails. They are removed early in life to keep the rear of sheep clean and free of dags. After doing some research to develop a concise animal welfare policy for her farm and put it on paper, Nan found out codes of practice in Europe discouraged tail docking without good reason, and that it was an emerging welfare issue with animal rights groups.

Nan set up a trial with just a few ewe lambs and found they did better. They grew faster and weighed considerably more at the point when she sold them for meat. They seemed to use their tails to flick away flies, and there was no problem with dags because of the attention being paid to providing a balanced diet, which meant less diarrhoea. Davey has come to quite enjoy the sight of lambs trotting in front of the motorbike, swinging their tails in almost perfect synchronicity to the inaudible rhythm of nature.

The daylight hours are almost done on Lemon Hill and bedlam has broken out in the yard. Davey is giving the sheepdogs some exercise. Twice a day, every day, he lets all nine dogs loose at the same time so they can run together around the sheds and up along the stretch of pasture known as the Long Paddock. Rugged up to keep out the biting cold wind, Davey urges them on from his four-wheel motorbike. The younger dogs race ahead in a blur of movement, tongues lolling and ears flying as their strides lengthen. Within minutes they are distant black and white specks on the hillside. Even fifteen-year-old Pearl lives for these moments, defying age, arthritis and a limp to follow. She is aided by a special boot which Nan made to support a weak paw and reduce the limp, although the dog still has a distinctive 'rocking horse way' when she moves.

The matriarch of the group, Pearl was imported by Nan from America at the age of four, carrying six pups in utero. Nan bought the well-trained dog after she was put up for sale because she was too anxious when placed under pressure in working dog trials. However, Pearl's previous owners had given her two unusual skills. She had been taught to pull a small dog cart; and she had been part of a three-dog team trained to keep ducks and other migratory birds from settling on golf course greens and fowling them with manure. Pearl's job was to circle around water hazards. 'So even when she was out with me she would just go round and round waterholes, and the other dogs would all follow thinking there was something important going on. It was a great way to exercise all the dogs at once,' says Nan.

Nan is overseas in early June when Pearl dies in her sleep. Davey phones to tell her the sad news. 'She was probably the kindest, most gentle dog I have ever owned,' Nan says in tribute. 'She had a lovely personality. She was the top dog, but she never made a point of it. We got to be very good friends, and of course she just loved Davey. And she loved running with the other dogs, even though she did not have much left in the way of hips. She was doing that until the day before she died.'

The senior dogs in the pack are now thirteen-year-old brothers from the same litter, Bear and Russ. Nothing like each other in appearance or temperament, Russ is one of only two long-haired, or rough-coated, border collies in Nan's kennels, while Bear is short or slick-haired. Russ was the pup that Nan gave to Davey when they first met. Under Davey's experienced tutelage he became an excellent working dog, doing well in local trials. He still belongs to the stockman but he now lives with the rest of the dogs on Lemon Hill. 'He is just the most harmless dog imaginable, doesn't get into fights and is just generally happy to be alive,' says Nan.

Bear was the main working dog until he was about eight and arthritis slowed him down. He is particularly talented at finding sheep in rough, hilly country, where it is often useful to have a dog that will work effectively out of sight. Nan's favourite Bear story comes from the day she went out with him to look for a mob in a steep gully. She stood on one side and sent the dog searching for sheep on the other. 'He came back, no sheep, so I sent him again. He came back again, no sheep, so I sent him again. This time he disappeared for quite a while, and then he came back from a completely different direction with the sheep. They had been behind me, nowhere near where I sent him to look. He knew what needed to be done and that I had lost the plot so he just went and got them.' Bear is also the only one of Nan's dogs good at sorting sheep to create two specific mobs. Known as 'shedding', it is a key element in international sheepdog trials in the United Kingdom where dogs often have to work with their handlers to separate out five sheep wearing coloured collars from a mob of twenty.

The next generation of dogs are Pearl's pups from the litter conceived in America—Mac, Sis and Flash. Now ten years old, they are descendants from spectacularly successful trial dogs, including their grandmother, who was a British International Supreme Champion, three-time US Nationals champion, and one of only nine dogs in the US Border Collie Hall of Fame. Mac is a smart but forceful dog that doesn't take no for an answer from 'stroppy' sheep. Flash is wonderful with people and loves hunting mice in her spare time, but 'an absolute pain in the butt' with other dogs in her ambitions to be leader of the pack. She even takes on Mac, who is twice her size. Out in the paddock, she is a natural driving dog, pushing mobs in a straight line and holding it, whether there are 50 or 500 sheep. 'If I have to do a big long drive I will take her because I don't have to do anything,' says Nan. Sis is the softy of the siblings. The pick of the litter when she was a few months old, Sis stopped working until about four years ago and Nan had almost given up on her. 'Mac and Flash were having physical problems and in desperation I took her out. She just decided "I'm working again now" and she has worked ever since. In fact she has become quite a valuable member of the group.'

At seven years of age, the three youngest dogs are hardly a brat pack. Chance, Janie and Lucky were bred from Bear and Flash. Chance is a mischievous dog, a thinker who likes to push the boundaries of what he can get away with, but who quickly settles into doing the right thing if you catch him first. 'He is not bloody-minded like Mac,' says Nan. 'It is always a balance. You want them to think on their own and get the right answer, but you also want them to listen to you.'

Janie is the other long-haired border collie among Nan's dogs. She has had a sometimes troubled life, losing most of her confidence after she was given to someone who didn't know how to work her. She came back unable to push sheep that stood up to dogs, and Davey wasn't sure she would ever work properly again. 'It's been very interesting to see Davey work with her and bring her back to the point where she can move anything now,' says Nan.

Her sister Lucky had an equally rocky life, starting at birth when she fell out of the whelping box. It was early on a very cold morning when Nan discovered the tiny pup lying on the kennel floor. Too much longer and she would have died of hypothermia. 'It's why she was called Lucky,' Nan explains. The dog was sold when she was about three months old, and three years later her buyer rang Nan complaining she wouldn't work. Nan was appalled to discover he had being using an electric collar. An increasingly common practice often employed to train recalcitrant dogs, the collars are activated by remote control: when a dog does something wrong, it delivers a small electric shock. Davey and Nan are both strongly opposed to their use and Lucky's experiences only reinforced their views. 'She would be okay and then I would say something she would obviously associate with the electric collar and she would just go nuts,' Nan says. After twelve months of patient, hard work, Lucky was starting to settle down when she also died while Nan was overseas. Davey wasn't sure why but the dog had been off her food for a while and in the end deteriorated so quickly there wasn't even time to call the vet.

While Davey takes the dogs for a final run before they are bedded down in their kennels for the night, Nan moves the tractor into an undercover space that serves as a loading bay for her shearing shed. This is no ordinary shed. The main work area looks more like a community dance hall than a place used to harvest wool; it has, in fact, been used very successfully to host farm workshops and social events. Nan had it built after the original woolshed proved too small. 'I wanted it to feel like a working shed but have some elegance about it.'

The first time a local woman who is also a woolgrower walked into it, she stopped and exclaimed, 'It's a girl's shed!'

Clad with blue-grey metal sheeting on the outside, the building has large aluminium windows streaming natural light and a floor of golden Tasmanian oak. A raised platform at one end has stands for two shearers, backed by a solid wall of mini-orb corrugated iron the same shade as the external cladding. Double swing doors provide access to undercover yards where the sheep wait to be shorn. The traditional wool table used to skirt and class fleeces stands under a north-facing window, but there is no sign of any bins where the wool is usually stored before being pressed into bales. Nan designed collapsible bins which are put together like pieces of Lego just before shearing, and a hydraulic hoist runs across the room to collect the bales and swing them over to the storage area next to where the tractor is now parked. At the opposite end to the stage is an enormous wood heater, surrounded by a comfy sofa and chairs. Off to one side is a wooden table where the shearing team gathers for smoko and lunch breaks.

It takes a team of seven about five days to shear at Lemon Hill. Two shearers, a woolclasser and a roustabout usually arrive in the first week of September to shear all but the pregnant ewes, which are dealt with a few weeks earlier. The contracting team led by Murray Johnson are supported in the shed by Nan, who works the table with the woolclasser. Outside, Davey and the dogs are responsible for bringing the sheep up to the yards, while Nan's occasional stockperson and well-known local rodeo star, Karen Fish, takes care of penning up. For the past few years, Nan has also followed in the footsteps of her grandmother and fulfilled the demanding role of shearers' cook.

She took it on after abdominal surgery sidelined her from working in the shed one season. Rather than sitting around doing not much at all, Nan started preparing meals for the team, who had previously gone into Oatlands for lunch. 'It was such a hit I kept doing it. Now I have to work the table and cook, which is interesting. I really have to get organised.' The catering is not straightforward either. The woolclasser doesn't eat red meat and Nan is gluten-intolerant so she has to be inventive to keep everyone happy. Soups, curries and quiche are favourites, as well as cakes and biscuits made with gluten-free flour. Anything that can be is made ahead and frozen. To keep the more conventional eaters happy, she also buys in sausage rolls most mornings, although first time round she had to be told that serving them with tomato sauce was obligatory.

Nan always breathes a big sigh of relief when shearing is over, but she also takes great satisfaction from seeing the end result of a year's work. And she loves watching Davey's face when the clip meets his exacting standards for cleanliness—the most important criteria by which he judges all superfine wool. 'Every year, at some point or another, you will see Davey sitting by himself at the lunch table, looking back at the bins, just sitting there looking at them,' says Nan. He is admiring the beautiful white, luminous fleeces, with barely a trace of dust or dirt.

'I can assure you I really think that's great,' he says with genuine satisfaction.

The old bushman obviously feels immense pride for Nan and her achievements. Nothing gives him greater pleasure than when other woolgrowers from families that have been breeding sheep for generations drop in to admire her 'big fat' merinos, surprised at how healthy and well-grown they are compared with many others. 'She has beautiful quality sheep,' Davey says. 'Although I'm part of the show and get my few bob out of it, it's all about Nan Bray. It's her place and it comes back to her . . . As far as I'm concerned, after a lifetime on the land I'm learning something new.'

For Nan, there is pride in acquiring something of Davey's deep knowledge of farming the Midlands and an ability to observe the land and the signs nature offers up that only comes from long familiarity. 'I'm detecting change now in a way that horrifies the scientist in me because it's about having a feel for what is different, rather than quantitative measurement,' she admits.

Ten years after buying her first superfine merino and eight years after walking away from a high-powered career, Nan is content. Standing over a pot of boiling bagels in her kitchen, she contemplates the way life has changed. Darkness has swallowed up the view of Lemon Hill across the highway and the native garden around the house. The dogs are settled for the night in their kennels, savouring the warm bliss of underfloor heating. Skye, a black and white cat rescued from the paddock as a tiny kitten, is curled up in her favourite place inside the lounge room chimney. A British shorthaired cat named Gwendolyn is hiding under the bed, while another of the same breed, the openly friendly Oscar, is beside Nan on the floor, carefully flicking pellets from his food bowl with an elegantly curved paw.

'I could never ever go back to a desk job, I just couldn't do it. It's ironic, really, because with what I have learnt about myself and the world, and how to manage complex systems like farms, I could do my old job ten times better than I did,' Nan says. 'For me personally, success is about the level of enjoyment I have in what I do, and for me now that is directly proportional to the state of the animals and the landscape. I have come back to my *Sand County Almanac* roots and started to understand what a beautifully complex and intricate thing I am part of, and that is every bit as intellectually challenging and as satisfying as anything I have done in the past . . . This is what I care about, and getting it out there in the world.'

5

THE IRREPRESSIBLE FARMER

Susie Chisholm, Adelong, New South Wales

Susie Chisholm is in the shower, whistling. The mellifluous notes are floating out across the back verandah of the homestead and catching on the soft pink blossoms of a crepe myrtle tree sprawling over the garden path. She has returned from another long day in the paddock and is getting ready for a night out in nearby Gundagai. Emerging a few minutes later, dressed in black with long dangly earrings and a short, pixie haircut, this petite woman does not fit the image most people carry of an Australian cattle producer. In fact, Susie has extraordinary skill when it comes to handling cattle, and runs one of the best-bred commercial beef herds in Australia. If there is any doubt about the quality of her stock, the evening ahead will serve as an unlikely reinforcement.

Climbing into her trusty four-wheel-drive ute, Susie heads out along the relatively short driveway, dodging the erosion caused by flooding summer rains a few months before. A short distance down the road she pulls up in front of a small cottage and collects her part-time 'stockman', Carol Morris. The two women chat about the evening ahead as Susie negotiates a turn onto the Hume Highway and starts the final straight run into the town made famous by a dog sitting on a tuckerbox.

They are going to the opening of a special exhibition, organised by Susie's mate Peter Batey. The noted theatre producer and director, playwright and arts administrator moved to the area more than twenty years ago, and is an active force in local efforts to regenerate the town and build a thriving tourism and arts scene. Now retired from the world of theatre, he is applying skills and connections acquired in an extraordinary career stretching over 50 years, which included major collaborations with the likes of Barry Humphries and Reg Livermore. Peter directed Livermore in his record-breaking one-man extravaganza *Betty Blokk Buster*, in the 1970s, and is credited by Humphries with playing a part in the creation of his iconic character Dame Edna Everage.[9]

Tonight, though, he is hosting a retrospective of the Bald Archy Prize. He devised the competition eighteen years ago as a spoof on one of Australia's oldest and most prestigious art awards, the Archibald Prize. Like the Archibald, the focus is portrait painting. Unlike the Archibald, to make it in the Bald Archy paintings must be humorous and, preferably, deeply irreverent. The previous winners hanging on the walls of the old gaol complex do not disappoint. There is the notorious 1997 winner showing the then prime minister John Howard 'washing his hands' of a naked One Nation leader, Pauline Hanson, in homily to a famous Manet painting; Rupert Murdoch in media-mogul, taking-over-the-world mode, holding the earth in his hands, in a portrait titled *I'll Eat You in the End*; and the 2008 winner which took the prize's infamy to the world, showing Australia's own Crown Princess Mary of Denmark with her husband in his jocks, and Mary resplendent in red flannelette dressing gown, breastfeeding their baby daughter Isabella.

There are more than a few graziers at tonight's event, stumping up money as part of the fundraiser. A local councillor, Peter is also chairman of the Friends of Old Gundagai Gaol, and hoping the exhibition will raise money over the next month or so to help with efforts to establish it as a major tourist site. Only recently opened to the public, the heritage-listed buildings boast a dark and fascinating history that reverberates through the old stone walls. Captain Moonlite, the unlikely bushranger with a romantic name but violent tendencies, was kept here after his gang came to a sticky end.

Born Andrew George Scott, the Irishman worked briefly as a schoolteacher in New Zealand where he also served as an officer in the local militia before sailing to Australia and becoming a lay reader in the Anglican Church in Victoria. Scott reportedly began his career in major crime in 1869 when he attacked the Ballarat agent of the London Chartered Bank and stole the contents of his safe. The end came in November 1879, when he and his gang took control of Wantabadgery station near Wagga Wagga for two days, keeping children as hostages. A trooper and two gang members died in the ensuing gun battle. Scott was arrested and taken to Gundagai, where a local magistrate committed him for trial before he was sent to Sydney, found guilty of murder and hanged.[10] But Captain Moonlite wasn't done with Gundagai, nor Gundagai with him. Just before his execution, Scott asked to be buried beside his best friend and gang member James Nesbitt. Nesbitt had died in the shoot-out at Wantabadgery and been buried at Gundagai. The authorities ignored the request and Scott's body was interred at Rookwood Cemetery in Sydney. It remained there for more than 100 years before a campaign by Gundagai residents saw his wish finally fulfilled in 1995.

Among guests gathering in the heat on a humid autumn evening to toast the exhibition opening, there is little discussion of the notorious bushranger. As Susie circulates through the crowd, one by one, people stop to congratulate her on last week's cattle sale. The event was a newsmaker in rural media. She sold 200 pregnant heifers for a near Australian record-breaking price of $2330 each, topping the commercial female online sale organised by Te Mania Angus. Other cattle producers at the exhibition are genuinely pleased for her, and hopeful it is a sign of improving prices for them all in a season that is showing exceptional promise after several tough years.

The cattle sale was the culmination of more than twenty years hard work for Susie in an unpredictable story of intense love found and lost that stretches from the isolated Queensland outback to Sydney's comfortable eastern suburbs; from life as a lonely station brat to being the 'earth mother' of three children and a passionate participant in hippy-era protest movements, to eventually becoming a grandmother and a farmer raising elite black Angus cattle.

'Just plain' Susan Chambers (she has no middle name) was conceived in the outback and born on 22 January 1944 in Sydney. In her own words it was 'a bit of a dicky childhood', with her mother dying when Susie was only six, and her father not at all interested in his youngest daughter.

Vivian Chambers owned Bow Park station—32 000 hectares near Julia Creek, in north-west Queensland, where he ran shorthorn cattle. He was a descendant of a family well known in legal circles in New South Wales and Victoria. His great-uncle Charles Henry Chambers was a Sydney magistrate and first town clerk of the Sydney City Council, who came to Australia in the 1830s to work on a new constitution with then governor Sir Richard Bourke. Always 'mad about the land', Vivian turned his back on the family profession and studied agriculture at Dookie College in northern Victoria.

Susie's mother Jean was the daughter of a Macquarie Street dentist, William Morton, who moved his family from Sydney to the outback after successfully acquiring two parcels of land near Hughenden, in the same region of Queensland as Bow Park. To meet requirements that he build a house on each block and take up residence within a certain time to keep them, he built a single homestead over the joining boundary of what became Balcomo and Bundoran stations. Jean's brothers, Jack and Max Morton, were well-known identities in the area through their exploits as amateur pilots.

Susie suspects Jean and her mother Ida found life in outback Queensland a significant challenge. Jean had a burgeoning musical career as a concert pianist, having performed at the Sydney Conservatorium of Music and given concerts in London. 'It was very isolated and they must have nearly died from the shock,' says Susie. But local families welcomed Jean with open arms, often calling on her to play at social gatherings. It was at one of these occasions that she met Vivian.

They married and had three children in the 1930s—Margaret, Jean and John. Thirteen years older than Susie, Margaret married a Charleville pastoralist, Ben, and now lives on the Darling Downs. Jean looked after her father until he died, and then made a completely new start in life. She studied shorthand and typing, and found a job with the department of agriculture in Papua New Guinea, where she met her husband, Vic. They are retired and living on Queensland's Sunshine Coast. An epileptic who felt his illness was an insurmountable hurdle in life, John committed suicide as a young man. Susie remembers him as a 'wag' fond of practical jokes such as short-sheeting beds and lobbing frogs into the tub when she was having a bath.

Susie's father was 56 and her mother 47 when she finally arrived on the scene in 1944, very much an after-thought. She was always conscious that Vivian had not wanted another child, and he remained a remote and severe figure. 'I didn't know Dad at all,' she says.

Later in life she quizzed her sister Jean about why this might be. 'Oh, well, by the time you came along he felt that he had had his children, and he wasn't interested,' Jean explained.

'The saddest thing for me,' Susie reflects, 'is that I had no relationship with him and yet when I think about what I have done here with the cattle and horses, and with the dogs . . . I just wish he could walk down that path and I could show him.'

She was still a young child when her mother left her husband and returned to Sydney. 'My father was devastated,' Susie says. The heartbreak was compounded not long after when she died of bowel cancer at the age of 52. The rest of Susie's childhood was divided between living with her father at Bow Park and spending time with her loving grandmother, who had taken up residence in the eastern Sydney suburb of Bellevue Hill.

When she was about eight, Susie was sent to the exclusive Ascham School for girls at nearby Edgecliff, where her mother had been head girl. Initially she was a day girl but when her grandmother developed dementia, Susie became a boarder. Because her siblings were so much older, she was 'wildly excited' to find herself surrounded by children her own age. 'It was divine. I just loved it,' she says. But it is fair to say that Ascham didn't love her. 'I had a shocking reputation,' she admits. 'I got into the worst trouble for talking too much, and I am so allergic to authority you wouldn't believe.'

Students caught talking during designated quiet times were sent out of the room to stand in the hall. Boarders who persisted firstly had their Saturday leave revoked and then whole long weekends. The irrepressible Susie found herself standing in the hall a lot, where she would pass the time by making shadow puppets with her hands and, yes, talking, as she played out various scenes and characters. Inevitably, she would look over her shoulder during one of these renditions and find a teacher standing behind her.

An habitual prankster, on more than one occasion she also found herself threatened with expulsion. There was the incident where she convinced all her mates to take off their uniforms and go to chapel in their underwear, covered by just their raincoats. Then there was the day she and a few friends broke into the kindergarten building, where they helped themselves to the teachers' biscuits and coffee. They weren't caught but had to confess after the headmistress threatened to cancel leave for every boarder unless the culprits owned up. 'Anything I could do to be disruptive, belligerent and rude, that was how I spent my years at school,' Susie confesses. At one point her father threatened to take her out of Ascham and send her to a convent school at Charters Towers, but her mother's younger sister and an old Ascham scholar, Aunt Elaine, intervened, begging the headmistress, Miss Whitehead, to let her stay.

During these years she can only really remember her father writing to her twice, and he signed both letters 'V.J. Chambers', as if to a stranger. In fact one of the few happy memories she has of Vivian is a rainy afternoon when she was visiting Bow Park during school holidays. Everyone was stuck inside the basic homestead built of corrugated iron, and he was making puftaloons, a sort of fried scone. 'We had them with golden syrup and I just thought it was heaven,' Susie says. Rolled up in the memory is one of the stockmen, Tiddly Triffett, singing a well-known ditty about Mandrake the bucking horse, by Australian country music pioneer Tex Morton. 'He was yodelling and singing this great old song, and at the age of ten I fell in love with him,' she says, letting out one of her rich, hearty laughs.

Now in his 80s, Tiddly lives in Charters Towers, where he is something of a legend. Susie visited him two years ago during a sentimental return journey to Bow Park for the first time since she was a teenager and her father sold it. 'I didn't recognise him at first, but as the days went on things came back to me. Because of our shared past, it's like being blood relations,' she says. Susie got to meet his long-time partner Ollie, and now phones them both on a regular basis to see how they are doing and to reminisce about station life. 'When Tiddly gets on the phone it's like champagne in my blood,' she says. 'He is such a wag, and he has got the sharpest mind.'

At the age of seventeen, Susie finished what there was of her formal education and started taking commercial art lessons at the East Sydney technical college. By then she was living with Aunt Elaine and her daughter Ann, who became as close as a sister. Ever the rebel, Susie became a beatnik, revelling in the counterculture inspired by the Beat Generation of emerging American writers and poets such as Jack Kerouac and Alan Ginsberg. She would leave the house dressed respectably enough, and at the first available opportunity change into a black leotard and highlight her eyes with heavy black makeup.

The situation couldn't last. Increasingly appalled at her behaviour, her father insisted she train for a proper job, so Susie enrolled in a shorthand and typing course. Although she wasn't sure what she wanted to do with her life, she knew being a secretary wasn't it.

In 1964, at the age of twenty, she married Jonathon Bell, a solicitor from Sydney. 'We were too young, and as we grew up together we realised we were totally different. Our opinions were exactly the opposite. He was extremely conservative. I am an Aquarian and they love change and exotic things. Not that I hold much with astrology, but that describes me absolutely,' she confesses.

'I do not conform,' she reiterates later, as part of a wide-ranging conversation that skips from David Attenborough's skills in creating wonderful documentaries about nature, to life after death and being an agnostic, to the joys of reading the classic English novels of Thomas Hardy, her favourite writer of all time. 'I always have Thomas Hardy pretty close to me and I will go back and read him again and again. There is a terrible sadness to his books but that is what life is about. They are beautifully written,' she posits. The discussion provides a fascinating window into Susie's eclectic mind, hinting at the boundless energy, curiosity and joie de vivre she continues to display as a grandmother in her late 60s.

In the early days of marriage, Susie was oblivious to the differences between her and Jonathon and focused on being an 'earth mother' as she morphed from beatnik into hippy. Her oldest daughter, Dimity, was born when she was 21, followed by Melissa in 1967 and Hamish in 1975. In the mid-60s the family moved to a 122-hectare property just out of Queanbeyan, which Susie bought with her parents' money. 'I was the original earth person . . . and I spent probably the next fifteen years devoted to that style of life. We had our own vegetables, our own chickens, and I wouldn't let the children eat anything I hadn't made myself. We had some very happy times,' she says.

Melissa remembers a happy childhood with long family horse rides and picnics in the forest behind the property; and a 'relaxed, gorgeous mother' who was nurturing and never passed judgement. 'We all got into scrapes and it never fazed Mum,' she says. These days also hinted at the satisfaction her mother would find in later life as a full-time farmer. Apart from the chooks and the vegetable garden, they kept horses and ran Hereford cattle, with Susie taking the primary responsibility for managing them while Jonathon worked in Canberra. Reiterating that life was always fun and a little unpredictable around Susie, Melissa recalls some of the creative solutions applied to control the horehound weeds and briar roses that seemed to thrive on the relatively small acreage: 'At one stage she bought an old draught horse and used chains to pull out the briar rose with the horse. She has always loved horses. Then during the drought in the late 1970s and early 80s she heard that camels ate horehound, so she bought two—Myrtle and Sheba. The horses hated them, and unfortunately they ate everything else before they ate the horehound so then we had to get rid of them.'

Finding a buyer for the camels was not easy. Even a visiting circus rejected the opportunity. Eventually Myrtle and Sheba found a home with an animal farm just outside Canberra. It was the perfect solution, but delivering them proved a major challenge. Melissa clearly remembers Susie making her run ahead of the camels carrying a washing basket full of hay on her head in an effort to tempt them in the right direction, while Susie, Dimity and Hamish followed behind waving brooms. The two camels eventually deigned to enter the cattle yards, but there was no way to get them up the loading ramp onto the truck. They ended up being winched aboard, with the family car being used to raise them into the air.

Very much a part of the hippy generation, Susie also participated in the moratorium marches to end Australia's involvement in the Vietnam War, and was a supporter of feminist Germaine Greer and the emerging women's liberation movement of the early 1970s. She and a friend even took on the French government, protesting against nuclear bomb tests in the South Pacific. 'She had a Citroën car and we sticky-taped all over the front of it, "I am ashamed to be French!" We were the flower power children and demonstrating in the streets,' she says. Afterwards, Susie would sit down at dinner parties with some of their more conservative friends, and 'Holy smoke, the fighting that went on over the table.'

The writing was on the wall when Jonathon stood for the Liberal Party in the seat of Eden-Monaro during the 1974

Federal election that re-elected a Whitlam Labor government. 'I was thinking, "If this is going to be my life, I don't like it",' Susie says. It wasn't so much the political party her husband was supporting, as the idea of being a politician's wife that wore her down. But they were still together a few years later when Susie met the man of her dreams and fell instantly, irrevocably, madly in love.

David Anthony Chisholm was a Northern Territory cattleman with a flair for reciting bush poetry and a distinctive charm. Tony, known to his friends as Chissy or Chis, was born in Sydney on 3 October 1923, and spent most of his childhood in the city. His father, Roy Chisholm, was the son of a Sydney bloodstock agent well known in horseracing circles. Roy ran the business for a while after his father died and then headed to the Northern Territory in the 1930s, where he took over Roper Valley station in the Gulf Country. He later bought Bond Springs, one of the oldest cattle stations in central Australia, just north of Alice Springs. Tony went up there in 1943 to help him for six months, and ended up staying in the Territory for almost 40 years.

Tony's mother was formerly Miss Mollie Little, whose name appeared in the Sydney social pages when she became friends with Edward VIII, then the prince of Wales, during his visit to Australia in June 1920. According to a story published many years later in *The Australian Women's Weekly*, they were introduced through Mollie's childhood friend Sheila Chisholm, who had married into the English aristocracy and become Lady Loughborough.[11] A noted high-society beauty in London, Sheila was a member of the prince's set and Roy Chisholm's sister. Within days of Tony's birth in 1923, *The Sydney Morning Herald* announced that the future king, who abdicated in 1936 to marry Mrs Wallis Simpson, had agreed to be the baby's godfather.[12]

Roy and Mollie were estranged for many years before Roy died at Bond Springs in February 1944. She remarried about three years after his death and moved with her new husband, Jim Sargood, to the station, which was being managed by Tony with help from his younger brother Bruce. The family also bought into Anningie and Napperby stations, where Tony later lived with his first wife Judith. Napperby is still in Chisholm hands, the home of their son Roy and his wife Janet.

A frequent visitor to New South Wales, Tony first encountered Susie sometime in the 1970s, when he bumped into her at the Canberra picnic races. 'Everybody had to bring something to the tent for lunch and I had made some bread,' Susie recalls. 'I made this square of white dough, chopped up all these herbs, spread them over the top and then rolled it up. When it rose and you baked it, you got these swirls of herbs in it.'

Tony took one look at this creation and said, 'Oh my God, that's ropy bread,' using a popular Territory term for bread that has gone mouldy. The cook just happened to be standing nearby and took laughing offence. There was an instant 'electric' attraction between the two, but both were married and walked away from the encounter.

About three years later Susie attended a lavish party at a friend's property near Bungendore, combining celebrations for three significant birthdays and the 200th anniversary of their homestead. The elegant old house was decorated magnificently for the occasion. Guests dressed to the nines in honour of the event too, and Susie made a theatrical entrance in a stunning gown of tomato-red silk, dramatically offset by a black velvet throat band and a large fan of black ostrich feathers. The dress was hand-sewn in the 1940s for one of her elder sisters, and the fan had belonged to her great-aunt Madame Lucy Chambers, a noted opera singer who trained in Europe and was the first

Australian to sing at La Scala in Milan.[13] 'So I came out in this red dress with the ostrich fan, which I had to keep over it because the dress had press studs and every now and then pop, pop, pop . . . and I would have to breathe in. It was a divine dress, and I just felt there was something in the air.'

At some stage, Susie found herself dancing with Bedford Osborne, a Second World War naval hero who was a friend of her husband's. An older man, he was struggling with arthritis and found the music too loud, so he took Susie over to a group of chairs to sit down. 'He sat me next to Tony Chisholm, and Tony turned round to me very slowly and said, "Well, it takes one to know one". And I thought he could see into my soul. He was a beautiful looking man. He was pursuing and I was about 35, in my prime, and at that age you're pretty hot to trot,' she says, trying to explain the passionate obsession that swept over them both. 'We were mad about each other.' Within three years both had walked away from their marriages.

In 1984 they moved to southern New South Wales, where Tony bought Gwalia, a grazing property of about 800 hectares not far from the historic goldmining town of Adelong. There was no habitable house on the property, so they lived initially in a caravan parked behind a house across the road. Later they moved into an old timber cottage on the property, which was riddled with termites but a better option than the caravan, while they worked with an architect to build a new homestead.

Construction had only just started when Tony curled up in agony one evening with terrible pains in his abdomen. The next morning, Susie took him off to a doctor, who prescribed antibiotics and sent him home. But the pain got worse and at five o'clock the next morning she drove him to the nearest hospital at Tumut, about 40 kilometres away. In a cruel twist of fate an X-ray revealed he had bowel cancer, just like Susie's mother, which was causing a massive blockage. He was taken immediately by ambulance to the larger regional hospital at

Wagga Wagga, where they operated for more than five hours. 'I don't know how he survived,' Susie says.

Tony seemed to be in good health for the next twelve months; then he started experiencing high temperatures and profuse sweating. The cancer had returned. The fevers were being caused by abscesses forming around the necrotic tissue where the cancer was eating into his pelvis. Tony was in the Calvary Hospital in Wagga for some time with doctors debating the best form of treatment, when one of the nursing sisters advised him it was time to go to Sydney. 'I had been begging him for months to get a second opinion,' Susie says.

But Tony would always shake his head and say, 'Oh no, I'll be right, darling. Come here and give us a hug.'

Finally convinced, Tony contacted a friend with connections in the city who helped get an appointment with a top surgeon. He confirmed there was no time to delay—an air ambulance was booked to fly him to Sydney the next day for immediate surgery.

Susie and Tony had been contemplating marriage for some time before he became ill. He had proposed one day, while he was sitting at home in his singlet and long johns, mending a stockwhip. 'Let's get married,' he had said with deceptive casualness, looking up from the task in hand.

Concerned that he might not survive the operation, a Catholic sister at Calvary suggested they should get married that very night. They agreed it was an excellent idea but there were only a few hours to make it happen. Susie rushed to the courthouse, where a clerk recommended Dulcy, a local marriage celebrant. She raced straight to Dulcy, who confirmed she was happy to perform the ceremony at eight o'clock that evening as long as she had the required paperwork. The papers were in Sydney, but after a quick phone call to their lawyer they were rounded up and couriered off to the airport for delivery on the afternoon passenger flight.

With a few minutes to spare before she had to collect them, Susie rushed into a local jeweller and bought a gold wedding band. Across the road, she spotted a white cotton Indian-style dress in a shop window and decided it would make the perfect wedding dress. The woman in charge was more than a little bemused when the tiny whirlwind that was Susie on a mission rushed through the door and told her what she wanted, and why.

Amazed at how quickly the impromptu wedding was coming together, Susie climbed into the car and headed for the airport. Looking for some music to keep up her spirits, she grabbed the first cassette tape to hand and shoved it into the player without bothering to check what it was. To her complete astonishment up started the stirring anthem *Land of Hope and Glory*. 'You wouldn't believe it,' she says. Susie turned up the volume and drove along singing at the top of her lungs.

Papers in hand, she raced back to the house where she was staying to get ready. Joan and George Crouch were old friends of Tony's and had provided her with accommodation in Wagga so she could be nearby during his time in hospital. 'I stayed with them a lot. They had a room I could just sneak in and out of, so I could be at the hospital by eight in the morning, look after him all day and then leave at eight o'clock at night,' Susie explains. 'Anyway, I said to George as I was racing out of the shower, "Many people have tried to give me away, George, but will you do the honour?"' George was delighted.

Meanwhile, Tony had been making phone calls rounding up other friends and relatives. His brother Bruce was about 200 kilometres away at Khancoban and could make it along with his daughter Penny. The nurses decorated the hospital room with flowers, and even rounded up some champagne and glasses and a blue garter for the bride to wear. Eight o'clock arrived and with everyone crowded into the hospital room, the brief ceremony began.

MARY NAISBITT

Mary Naisbitt and her son Kevin out on the farm during the drought in early 2011. Behind them is the white salt pan of Lake Grace.

Mary and Joe Naisbitt on their wedding day—7 August 1971, at St Brigid's Catholic Church in Midland, WA (photograph provided by Mary Naisbitt).

RIGHT: Joe Naisbitt celebrating Diane's third birthday during a family holiday, just four days before he died, with baby son Kevin, and his three daughters (from left) Trish, Diane and Susan.

ABOVE: Mary's four children (from left) Diane, Susan, Trish and Kevin in 1984, with her favourite tractor, Butch the dog, and the picnic basket that accompanied the family whenever they worked out on the farm.

LEFT: Mary at the age of six with her parents, Bob and Teresa Starcevich.

ALL PHOTOGRAPHS ON THIS PAGE PROVIDED BY MARY NAISBITT.

LYNETTE RIDEOUT

RIGHT: Lynette Rideout trimming
Christmas trees—each tree is
pruned 16 times before it is ready
for discerning buyers.

BELOW: Lynette at work in her
orchard at Oakdale, NSW.

BELOW: Lynette and
Chris 'duelling' with
spanners over the bonnet
of Greasel—the little red
tractor which carried the
bride to her wedding at
Top Forty (photograph
by Valerie O'Brien
Photography).

RIGHT: Lynette's grandmother, Brenda Gapes, pulling swedes for the war effort at Wendyn Orchard in the early 1940s, with help from Brenda's son Roger and her father-in-law, William Alfred Gapes.

BELOW: Lynette, aged three, riding on her favourite tractor with her mum, Audrey.

BELOW: Leo Rideout preparing a patch of ground to plant fruit trees in the late 1950s.

ALL PHOTOGRAPHS ON THIS PAGE PROVIDED BY LYNETTE RIDEOUT.

JAN RALEIGH

Timboon dairy farmer Jan Raleigh.

Jan watches Timboon veterinarian Liz Coghlan treat a sick cow.

ABOVE: Jan takes in her favourite view on the farm at Timboon in western Victoria.

LEFT: The dairy herd makes its way to an overnight pasture.

BELOW: Jan loads a bale of silage ready to feed her cows.

NAN BRAY

LEFT: Tasmanian wool producer Nan Bray with one of her superfine merino fleeces.

RIGHT: Nan's father, Don Bray, as a young man in Idaho, c 1934 (photograph provided by Nan Bray).

BELOW: Nan and her irrepressible border collie Mac move a mob of sheep on Lemon Hill.

ABOVE: Nan's dogs Bear and Lucky take a run in the snow on Lemon Hill (photograph provided by Nan Bray).

LEFT: Nan when she was working at the Scripps Institution of Oceanography in California, c 1994 (photograph provided by Nan Bray).

RIGHT: Nan's right-hand man, third-generation stockman, 84-year-old Davey Carnes.

SUSIE CHISHOLM

ABOVE: Susie Chisholm and her New Zealand Heading dog, Poi.

LEFT: Susie as a young girl on Bow Park station near Julia Creek, in north-west Queensland (photograph provided by Susie Chisholm).

BELOW: Susie drafts some of her elite Angus cattle herd in the yards on Gwalia that she redesigned.

RIGHT: Susie and the love of her life, Tony Chisholm (photograph provided by Susie Chisholm).

LEFT: Susie's son-in-law Nicholas Clancy, her daughters Dimity Bell (centre) and Melissa Clancy, and her grandchildren (from left) Ireland, Indigo and Willow (photograph provided by Susie Chisholm).

RIGHT: Susie's son, Hamish (photograph by Jane Apthorpe).

CECILY CORNISH

ABOVE: Cecily Cornish and her daughter Edwina who is Senior Deputy Vice Chancellor at Monash University (photograph by Katrina Cornish).

LEFT: Cecily Cornish in the kitchen at Barnoolut with the much loved Aga cooking range (photograph provided by the Cornish family).

ABOVE: Cecily (centre) in the family governess cart being pulled by Queenie, c 1934.

LEFT: Cecily on her pony Zeb, with her parents Edwin and Nancy Crozier.

BELOW: Cecily feeding lambs in front of Barnoolut homestead.

ALL PHOTOGRAPHS ON THIS PAGE PROVIDED BY THE CORNISH FAMILY.

CATHERINE BIRD

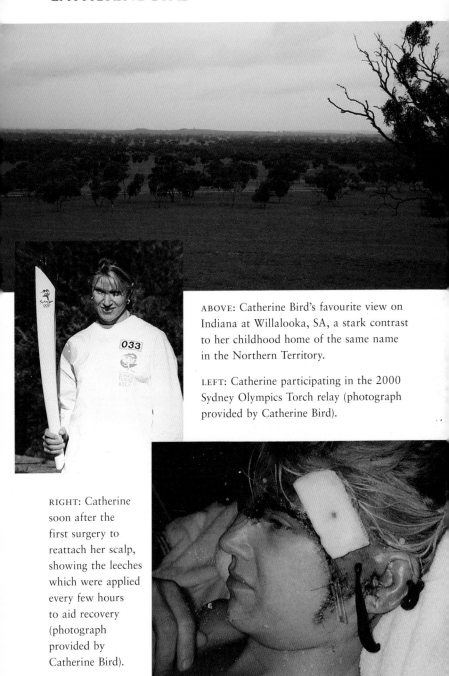

ABOVE: Catherine Bird's favourite view on Indiana at Willalooka, SA, a stark contrast to her childhood home of the same name in the Northern Territory.

LEFT: Catherine participating in the 2000 Sydney Olympics Torch relay (photograph provided by Catherine Bird).

RIGHT: Catherine soon after the first surgery to reattach her scalp, showing the leeches which were applied every few hours to aid recovery (photograph provided by Catherine Bird).

ABOVE: Catherine as a young girl, riding in an event at the annual Harts Range picnic race meeting (photograph provided by Catherine Bird).

LEFT: A view of the ranges on Indiana station, east of Alice Springs, where Catherine grew up (photograph provided by Catherine Bird).

RIGHT: Catherine with her oldest children, Brett and Renee, her partner Simon (far right) and their two children, Summer and Scarlett (photograph by Michelle Gilbertson Photography).

KEELEN MAILMAN

ABOVE: Mt Tabor station manager
Keelen Mailman.

RIGHT: Keelen walks through part of
Lost City, one of the Bidjara cultural
sites for which she cares.

BELOW: Some of the extraordinary
Indigenous hand paintings created
thousands of years ago on Mt Tabor.

ABOVE: Burning off long grass in the house paddock at Mt Tabor to reduce fire danger and encourage fresh feed.

LEFT: Keelen tops up a trough during one of the regular stock lick runs which keep her busy.

BELOW: Keelen with Maggie (left), one of five children she took into foster care, and her youngest daughter Charlee.

'We all kept the tears away, which was the biggest battle,' Susie says softly, thinking back on the day that should have been one of the happiest in her life. 'It was a really poignant experience, but I was excited too. And they let me stay the night with him, so he and I slept in the same bed. Then the next morning Chissy flew out at seven o'clock and I got in the car and drove to Sydney. He'd had the operation by the time I got there.'

The outcome was not what the bride of a few hours wanted to hear. The surgeon emerged from the operating theatre and told her the cancer was too far gone. He estimated Tony had only six months or so to live.

Despite the clear-cut prognosis, Susie says they never really accepted the inevitable. 'We didn't think he was going to die. We thought that our love was going to push away the cancer. But no, it doesn't actually. Cancer is cancer. I found out later he had been passing blood for two years and did nothing about it,' she says, clearly exasperated at just how recalcitrant men can be when it comes to looking after their health.

A determined man, Tony lived for another two years. He got to enjoy their completed house on Gwalia, sitting peacefully on the spacious verandah or lying in bed in a light, airy room designed to capture the first rays of the rising sun. He would encourage Susie to lie with him and watch television westerns; his favourites were *Davy Crockett* and *Bonanza*, or any movie starring John Wayne. 'I got the videos and we watched them until they were coming out of our ears, but we still loved them,' Susie says. Having spent much of his time on isolated stations in the Territory, Tony in particular enjoyed the luxury of television.

And he was an excellent patient. 'He never complained. Not once can I remember him saying he was in pain. Never, never,' says Susie. Often, as she walked past, he would grab hold of her shirt and pull her to him for a quick cuddle; Susie still thinks of him whenever her shirt catches on something. She also finds herself obsessively straightening objects. 'All his tools and possessions were immaculate and very organised,' she says. 'I used to wipe the table beside him and put his things back in the wrong place, and I would come back and he had rearranged them all in rows. I think that is why I can't stand things being skew-whiff,' she says after pausing to reflect.

Tony died on 23 July 1987. A week before he had a total renal collapse and was taken to Gundagai Hospital. Knowing the time had come Susie insisted on taking him home, where she nursed him with help from Cecily Mitchell, a nursing sister who had looked after Tony in Wagga. Susie remembers that it poured with rain the entire time, adding to tensions in the house, which was filled with the grown-up children from both their previous marriages. She spent every hour possible lying beside him, until he slipped into a coma a few days before his death.

There was a large turnout for Tony's funeral, where Susie summoned up all her courage and read one of his favourite poems, 'Where the Pelican Builds Her Nest'. A classic bush poem from the 1880s, it begins:

> *The horses were ready, the rails were down,*
> *But the riders lingered still*
> *One had a parting word to say,*
> *And one had his pipe to fill.*

> *Then they mounted, one with a granted prayer,*
> *And one with a grief unguessed.*
> *'We are going,' they said, as they rode away*
> *'Where the Pelican builds her nest!'*[14]

It is seven o'clock on a beautiful, mild autumn morning and Susie is getting ready to head to the cattle yards, sustained for the hard work ahead by a bowl of thick, steaming porridge. She has been awake since about four o'clock, following her usual routine of making tea and toast and taking it back to bed, where she wallows in the luxury of reading a good book while the sun creeps up over the hills. It is Susie's favourite part of the day, a quiet pause before hours of physical exertion, a time when she is refreshed from an early night and less likely to fall asleep over the pages.

Susie walks out to the back verandah and balances on one foot at a time to pull on a pair of well-worn elastic-sided boots. She dons a large, cream-coloured western-style Akubra, which sits snugly on her short locks, the wide brim casting a protective shadow over her face. Apart from the hat, she is dressed all in black today. Her promotional T-shirt was a gift from Hamish, who works in New Zealand for one of the international film industry's most highly regarded visual effects studios, where he was part of the team that created the Hollywood blockbuster *Avatar* and is now lending his skills to Steven Spielberg's movie version of *The Adventures of Tintin*.

Crossing the backyard, Susie heads for the shed to collect Poi, one of two dogs she has trained to help move cattle. As always, the striking black and white New Zealand heading dog is eager to work. She jumps up behind her mistress, balancing on the back of the red four-wheel motorbike that is Susie's main workhorse these days. Waiting in the yard is Carol Morris, who has just arrived on a similar bike with her own dog, a black and tan kelpie called Idaho.

The two women head up the driveway with a rattling roar. Instead of turning onto the road, they follow the track as it veers past the old cottage, now derelict. The track winds across a large paddock to the Adelong Creek, where they carefully negotiate banks torn apart by floods last summer. There is still plenty of water flowing across the shallow crossing—nothing too deep for the bikes to manage although the ground is treacherously muddy on either side.

With the main track virtually unusable from this point, Susie and Carol head across the paddock. They pause on a hilltop overlooking the yards and talk about how to approach bringing in a mob of cows and calves that need to be drafted so the cows can be pregnancy tested and the calves weaned. One mob of 44 cows, with calves at foot, was rounded up the day before and put in a holding paddock alongside the stockyards. Susie wanted to have a 'jump start' so they were sure of being ready for the veterinarian, who has a long list of calls and needs to finish as quickly as possible. Now, the two women have to bring in a second mob so they can be drafted and tested too. In no time at all, with the help of Poi and Idaho, the cattle are down at the yards in a separate holding area, bellowing at their mates over the fence.

The two women confer again over the lowing of both mobs, talking through the best way to configure the yards which Susie has just redesigned. Today is the first time they have been used since she realigned the panels and gates to make it easier to work cattle, and Susie is excited and a bit anxious about how it will go. Clear on what needs to be done, the women head off to their agreed positions and start to bring the first mob in from the holding paddock. Susie's piercing whistle directs Poi behind the mob, and the cattle find their way easily enough along the fence and into the first enclosure. So far, so good.

After pausing again to set up some internal gates, the two women start separating the cows from their calves. This time the dogs are kept on the sidelines, while Carol and Susie move quietly among the cattle. The drafting is finished in what seems like a matter of a few minutes, with minimal fuss and no raised voices, a rare achievement during a job that often has even the mildest mannered stock handlers yelling in frustration at either the cattle or each other. Instead, Susie walks quietly through the mob, placing herself carefully in relation to the livestock and the gates, raising her hand gently on occasion as if to shepherd them along, and whistling intermittently in sing-song tones that differ considerably to the whistle she uses for the dogs. Before long all 200 animals have been drafted and everything is ready for the veterinarian. It is a bravura performance, and a remarkable demonstration of Susie's skills handling cattle, not to mention the initial success of the yards she has redesigned.

Susie loves learning about the psychology of cattle, their herd instincts and how to manipulate them to reduce stress for the livestock and the handlers. This morning was an illustration of how much she has learnt over the years, both from practical experience and a revelatory stock-handling course she attended in Adelong. She was encouraged to go along by Andrew Gubbins from the Te Mania Angus Stud. 'It was phenomenal,' she says. 'We learnt that it is all about where you place yourself with the herd.' She explains about approaching the herd from a particular angle, moving forward to apply pressure and then moving back to release it, so the cattle head in the desired direction.

'I am a great believer in not hitting them and not roaring at them,' she says. 'You might think this is odd, but when they are weaners I whistle them through the gate, and surprisingly enough they know something is happening and they walk forward. I have a whistle for my dogs to work but the whistle for my cattle to move through a gate is different.' She demonstrates the gentle tones employed during today's drafting. 'I honestly believe those cattle today knew that whistle. They knew when we were drafting them out. They know that you want them to move. That is the music that makes them draft out. You will always get one old pill that won't do it, but mostly if I use that sing-song whistle they go forward.'

Out in the paddocks, Susie likes her dogs to keep well back from the mob, letting the cattle follow the animals that naturally take the lead rather than distracting them by getting too close.

'When we're mustering I stay way out,' she says. 'Let them walk along, let the lead cow go and the mob follow, and just tickle them up. When you get to a gate, hang back. Stop your dog. It drives me nuts when I see a dog fly in when they are at the gate because what do the cattle do? They watch you and the dog, not where the rest of the mob is going, which would draw them through the gate.'

It is one of the reasons she uses New Zealand heading dogs. Relatives of border collies, they have a natural instinct to circle out widely from the mob and work silently to bring it towards their handler. 'I like a dog that casts out and comes in slowly,' Susie explains. 'Someone told me it's not about commanding the dog. Let the work bring their instincts out. If it sees a job that needs doing, let it do it, don't command it, and that is a pearl of advice. So I will go along on the bike and Poi knows which way to go. She is soft but strong so I can say, "Here, Poi," and she will go around and bring them up to me. I just adore working with Poi.'

Susie and Poi also put in a fair amount of time in between yard work getting the mobs used to their presence and encouraging them to move cohesively at a steady pace, so they stay calm during mustering. The education process starts at weaning, when the young stock are left together in a holding paddock at the yards for about a week, establishing bonds with their peer group. This means they are more likely to stay together out in the larger paddocks, and makes it a lot easier for Susie to move mobs without assistance. She also spends time getting them used to moving through gateways. By preference this would be done on horseback, which she believes is much better for the cattle, but horses have not been used as much on Gwalia in the last few years because of the extra work involved.

With time to spare, Susie and Carol sit down for a quick morning tea. Susie has packed a thermos of hot, brewed coffee, fresh bread, and a jar of her special fig and ginger jam, made with figs she received from a neighbour in exchange for homegrown cucumbers. Flavoured with fresh air, sunshine and the satisfaction of a job well done, the simple snack is particularly enjoyable.

Shortly afterwards, a white four-wheel drive pulls up alongside the yard and Bill Graham climbs out. The Coolac vet specialises in cattle reproduction and gives the impression of being a man in a hurry. The usual pleasantries quickly dealt with, he encourages Susie to start moving cows into the raceway, which leads to the cattle crush where he will examine each cow and take blood samples. The crush incorporates a set of scales which Carol has hooked into an electronic scanner and data collection unit. The scanner is a thick, black wand that Carol will wave over the head of each animal so it reads an electronic ear tag that carries the cow's identification number. The data collector notes the number and automatically records the cow's weight. Using a simplified and robust keyboard encased in heavy-duty green plastic, Carol can then key in any extra information they want to record about the animal.

As each cow steps up into the crush, Carol pulls a lever that shuts the gate behind it and scans the ear tag. Once a red light goes off, indicating the weight has been recorded, Bill steps up behind the cow and pushes his latex-covered hand and arm deep into the rectum so he can reach the back of her uterus and feel gently with his fingers in search of the foetus. At this stage, about four months after mating, it is very easy to detect.

The three work quickly, with little discussion, not that it would be easy anyway over the bellowing of the cattle and the crash of the gate as it closes behind each cow. Most of the cows don't seem to mind the procedure too much, but once the front gate is released they lose no time skipping out of the crush and into a yard adjoining their calves. Susie is doing a good job keeping up a steady supply of cows, finding it much easier to move them by herself with the new design. In less than an hour the job is finished and they know only one cow is empty out of 100—a very pleasing result given the disruptions caused this year by floods.

❖ ❖ ❖

The cattle being tested today bear absolutely no resemblance to the small mob of 160 fat cows Susie inherited almost 25 years ago from Tony. The red and white Herefords would scatter in all directions as soon as she appeared in the paddock, and were impossible to drove. 'They were dreadful,' she says. 'They were the most stinking cows you have ever come across.' She shared the horrible experience with Jeffrey and Jill Luther, who had been doing contract work on the property for Tony and stayed on to help manage Gwalia for the first few years after his death. 'Gee, Jeffrey and I had some fun with those cattle. They used to split up and go in about ten directions . . . and we had these mesh yards that had been stapled together on the outside, so when anything hit them, the panels fell off. We were working like slaves and getting nowhere.'

Managing the cattle and gradually improving the herd was not the only challenge Susie faced in the first years after Tony's death. Under the provision of his will she did not inherit Gwalia so she had to earn enough money to pay off a lease in order to stay there. She had inherited some money from her parents, but on advice she invested it in Lloyd's of London, losing everything when the insurance underwriting business collapsed in the early 1990s after a series of disasters hit the world's insurance market. She also had to battle the crippling grief of losing her husband. According to her oldest daughter Dimity, 'She was pretty shell-shocked. She walked around like she had been hit with a shovel for the next ten years or so.'

Anxious about her mother, Dimity found a job in nearby Tumut and moved to Gwalia from Canberra for the next five years or so, to keep her company and lend a hand. Dimity loved life on the property and spending time with Susie, who she considers 'a very precious person'. 'She has an amazing relationship with her kids. Very few of my friends have the relationship that I have with my mum. She is much more a friend than a mother, really.' Dimity says that while there is rarely a serious moment, Susie is also very hard working. 'She is from bloody tough hard-working stock—the hardest working woman in Australia. She just won't stop. She cannot sit and relax—it may not be physically hard work, but she is always occupied.'

Despite the enormous financial pressures and her lack of experience, Susie's children were not at all surprised when she decided to become a farmer in her own right. 'I think Chis thought she would go back to Sydney after he died, but Mum is too much of a bushie to do that,' Dimity says.

'Her interest was cattle anyway, and she was very actively involved in the property with him,' adds Melissa. 'It was all very difficult but it was just another chapter of her life and she pulled herself through it. I know she was shell-shocked but she just kept going.'

As far as Susie was concerned there wasn't another option. 'I married at twenty and had no qualifications. What would I have done? Served in David Jones? I would have died,' she says.

On the other hand, Susie was good with stockhorses and had the experience of working alongside Tony with the cattle for a while, as well as childhood memories of Bow Park. But she was hopeless at the business side of running a farm enterprise. 'I had only ever produced cakes, vegetable gardens and kids,' she says.

Dimity agrees. 'Her bookkeeping skills consisted of knowing how to put a stamp on an envelope,' she jokes. Then, more seriously, she explains, 'Chis didn't want to admit he was dying and training her up to run the farm would have meant acknowledging that.'

Susie finally had enough one day when she found herself sitting at home with the 'tears dripping off my chin' as she struggled to make sense of some financial figures. Picking up the phone, she called a friend and fellow grazier, asking if he knew a good accountant. He told her: 'You don't need an accountant, you need Ian McMichael.' An experienced farm management adviser, Ian was a partner in an agricultural consulting business based in southern New South Wales and more than willing to meet Susie and talk about what could be done. 'When he came down that path, it was just unction to an open wound,' says Susie. 'He is a great bloke.'

Ian advised her to start crossing her Hereford cows with good quality Angus bulls, to produce what are known as 'black baldies' for the beef market. The cross would produce cattle with greater hybrid vigour, capable of growing faster, producing more meat and therefore generating more money. To get her started, he took her to visit the Hazeldene stud near Cooma, part of a pastoral and seedstock breeding enterprise that has been operated by the Litchfield family since the 1860s and is highly regarded for the quality of both its cattle and sheep.

Over the next eight years or so, Susie built up a substantial herd of black cattle as well as her own knowledge of farming. She continued to buy in Hazeldene genetics and work with Ian until one day she was faced with a very tough decision. She could stay with the stud, or become part of an exciting new progeny-testing program being set up by Te Mania Angus. Another highly regarded cattle stud, it was established in western Victoria 40 years ago by Andrew Gubbins and his wife Mary, based on imported livestock bred by her father in New Zealand. Since then it has set every sales record for Australian Angus cattle. Susie was well aware of their reputation and had been following their approach to marketing with great interest. 'Who hadn't heard of them?' she says. 'I used to look at *The Land* and think, "Oh my God, I would love to go down and look at their cattle." They were great marketers.'

The people behind Te Mania had heard of Susie too, through her involvement with Hazeldene. Looking for more participants for the program, which had only just been established, they arranged a visit. Dimity has a favourite story which she loves to tell about what happened when Andrew and Mary's son, Tom, and his brother-in-law, Hamish McFarlane, who both now manage the business, showed up to check out Gwalia and convince Susie to come on board. After taking them around the property she offered them dinner, but there were no green vegetables in the garden, so she decided to steam some rocket instead. Although Susie is an excellent cook, it was terrible—'the worst dinner ever', says Dimity. The men ate every mouthful anyway, apparently determined to win her over.

Whether it was the rocket-eating effort or not, Susie decided to join the program but it meant walking away from Ian McMichael and Hazeldene. She decided to go and tell them in person. 'I walked through the door and Ian said, "Is there anything wrong, Susie? You look terrible." I was ashen. They had been my backstops and guided me through those first ten years or so, and I had made this amazing decision to draw away from them.'

Difficult though it was, it is fair to say that decision in 1995 opened up a whole new world for Susie, who has become incredibly passionate about recording the performance of her cattle and understanding the genetics and management principles involved in breeding livestock that produce quality meat. These are top priorities for the progeny-testing program, which was a new concept at the time for the Australian beef industry. Known as Team Te Mania, it brings together like-minded cattle producers, who are given access to the best bulls from the Te Mania stud. Te Mania helps select the bulls and then leases them to team members for three years. The stud also provides ongoing technical advice and support, and helps market the cattle produced, leveraging what has become a nationally recognised brand to get the best prices.

In return, Susie and the other team members collect information about their cattle and provide it to a performance recording scheme run by the Angus Society of Australia. The scheme keeps track of the pedigree of every individual and how they perform when it comes to traits important to commercial beef producers, such as fertility, growth rates and carcase quality. Producers can then use the database as a guide to help select breeding stock that offer the best potential to improve their herds.

Joining the program meant Susie had to make a serious commitment to keeping a careful record of which bulls are mated to which cows, and when; tagging every cow and calf so that they can be easily identified and their performance traced; noting down the birth date of every calf; and recording the calves' weights when they are weaned from their mothers. A special research and development fund set up by Team Te Mania even goes to the extent of having all the progeny scanned while they are alive, using special ultrasound equipment to check the amount of fat and red meat, or 'muscle', they are carrying. The feedlot Susie sells them to then provides her with information from their 'kill sheets' which record things like how much meat each carcase yielded, and the amount of marbling or fat that streaks the meat, a major indicator of eating quality, particularly for the valuable Japanese export market.

According to Andrew Gubbins, Susie threw herself into the challenge right from the beginning, soaking up the information she was provided and taking an active interest in the latest science and technology available to make her a better cattle producer. 'She is a very enthusiastic person about all things in life,' he says. 'It was quite a struggle to set up Team Te Mania because it had never been done before. Susie wasn't a founding member, but she was in the first six or eight of about 30 people.

Since then she has probably been the leading enthusiast and driver of the whole thing in terms of getting new members. That is her greatest attribute—her unbridled enthusiasm . . . It makes nations, that sort of enthusiasm.'

Andrew also rates her very highly as a cattle producer, ranking her among the best he knows: 'She handles cattle well, and of course she loves them. She is pretty smart, and she uses her brains. She might have done any particular thing, but luckily she decided on Angus cattle. She has had some great successes and she knows precisely what she is doing.'

Apart from topping the 2011 sale of commercial females, those successes include taking out four awards for outstanding performance in the Certified Australian Angus Beef Quality Awards, and coming second in the carcase quality section of a major competition run as part of Beef Spectacular, a major industry event held every year at Dubbo in New South Wales. Today Gwalia runs up to 600 breeding cows, as well as heifers, steers and calves, and seventeen Te Mania bulls.

The cattle work finished earlier than expected, Susie is back at the homestead in good time to enjoy a relatively relaxed lunch. A 'BLT' is quickly pulled together, with bacon fried on a large barbecue kept ready for action near the back door. Taking the sandwich out to the front verandah, she sits down in one of the brightly coloured chairs that bring splashes of dramatic colour to what was once a 'bland' palette for both the house and the garden.

'My colour tastes have changed so dramatically. Twenty-four years ago it was all pale pink. All the garden was pale pink, all the house was pale pink. And now at this glorious time in my life I love red and orange and purple,' she says in wonder at the change. While the weatherboard walls of the house are still a conservative cream, the verandah posts and French doors are the brilliant blue-green of vert-de-gris. The only remaining sign of pink is the poor man's pipe shrub growing on the edge of the verandah, but it is offset by the intense red of old-fashioned geraniums and deep purple salvia.

With the appearance of a classic colonial homestead that has been settling into the landscape for decades, the house was designed by renowned architect Espie Dods. He was also responsible for an impressive new homestead built at Newcastle Waters in the Northern Territory, when Tony owned the station in partnership with Ken Warriner and Peter Baillieu. 'He came down and looked at the site. I wanted our bedroom to be on the north-east side and the house to be facing north, and the kitchen to be a big French-style kitchen,' Susie says. 'Chis picked the site. I would have had it a bit further off the road, but it's really practical to be closer, and Chis was all for practicality.'

The house is also well placed to catch cooling breezes and take in sweeping views of the south-west slopes of the Great Dividing Range. Surrounding paddocks drop away to Adelong Creek, which carves a deep scar through Gwalia's paddocks as it continues its journey towards the mighty Murrumbidgee River. A short distance upstream lies an historic goldfield which drew thousands of prospectors from around the world in the 1850s. Remnants of a battery complex built to extract reef gold perch in a steep gorge, where the first lot of floods that swept through Susie's property last spring also tore apart some of the old workings.

Susie's stretch of the creek was dredged for gold too, many years ago, leaving behind deep holes which are now full of water. She finds enormous joy in the sight, after six years of drought almost brought the farm to its knees a few years ago. With all the feed reserves gone she had to ramp up the overdraft to buy in semitrailer loads of straw at a staggering $4000 each, and put out bins of stock lick which had to be cleaned out regularly because it turned rock hard when the cattle slobbered on it. 'I couldn't do it again. I know I will have to at some point, but it makes me feel faint at the thought,' Susie says.

Thanks to the floods and ongoing rains that have soaked deep into the soil and tipped the annual rainfall closer to the historic average of 800 millimetres, last season's calves know nothing of such deprivations. A group of them is hovering around a hay feeder placed about 100 metres outside the garden fence, chewing contentedly. Nearby stands a lone gum tree where the galahs love to roost in the evening. At the moment a family of magpies is in residence, carolling to each other over the occasional distant bellow of cattle back at the stockyards.

On the homestead verandah, the industrious buzz of insects is creating a soporific effect that seems to wash right over Susie as she munches the sandwich and contemplates a to-do list that will keep her busy until sunset. She has to drive into Tumut on a series of errands, accumulated over a week or so to make the most of the twenty-minute journey. Then there is the usual round of animals to check and feed and the lawn to mow. But first there is a fence to fix. Lunch is only just finished when the contractor who helps her with fencing arrives to check an electric fence that is losing current. Susie heads out into the paddock with him, eager to solve the problem so there is no danger that separate mobs of cattle will intermingle. In the process, they discover the tester she has been using to check the voltage being carried by the wires is not working properly.

It is another item to add to the list of errands in Tumut, and means she needs to make a start straight away so there is plenty of time to get everything done before businesses close for the day. Climbing into the ute, she makes a small detour to the horse yards across the road, where a five-month-old foal is being weaned. The young quarter horse is being kept company by an older mare so she doesn't fret too badly in the first days away from her mother. Susie gives them each a biscuit of lucerne hay and checks on their water supply.

Taking the winding bitumen road through Adelong, she drives to the beautiful little town of Tumut, once a gateway to the famous Snowy Mountains Scheme that brought thousands of workers from more than 30 countries after the Second World War to build an ambitious series of dams and hydropower stations. Set in a picturesque valley at the foot of the Snowy Mountains, the town is today the centre of a softwood timber industry and draws large numbers of visitors in the autumn months, when extensive plantings of exotic trees bring extraordinary colour to the streets and surrounding river plain.

The first stop for Susie is a rural merchandising business on the outskirts of town that can provide her with a new electric fence tester. Mission accomplished she moves on to a small side street where she pops into her favourite butcher, not for meat but for the prized olive oil he also sells. In the same street she pulls up beside a refrigerated van and exchanges banter with the visiting fishmonger, who drives down every week from Sydney. Susie is a regular customer and has timed her visit to Tumut so she can treat herself to fresh fish for dinner.

Next stop is the supermarket to pick up a few essentials. Pausing at the dairy section, she frowns at the generic label milk being sold at a discount price of $1 per litre. Like many farmers, Susie is highly critical of the sales campaign which she fears will undermine the already low prices dairy farmers receive for their produce and put even more power into the hands of the supermarkets. As it is Australians pay less for milk than they do for bottled water, despite all the work and costs involved in producing it. Heading to the check-out, she bumps into some neighbours and makes arrangements to catch up properly another day. The final stop is a small engineering business at the back of the town, which has been redesigning a metal plate for the stockyards.

Back at home there is no rest for Susie after unloading the ute. Not stopping even for a cup of tea, she heads back out into the paddock on the four-wheel motorbike to do some more work on an electric fence and check the cattle; then she has the chooks and more horses to feed. It is 6.30 before she gets back to the house, and there is more than enough daylight to climb aboard the ride-on mower and cut the lawn. It has been a long day of physically active work, but she is not done yet. Before preparing dinner, there is enough energy left to check her emails and the results of a carcase competition in which she entered some steers.

Finally, Susie takes time for a quick shower and a glass of wine in front of her favourite television show—*Australia's Funniest Home Videos*. She roars with laughter at every agonising misadventure captured on camera, recognising in the hapless victims her own tendencies towards being accident-prone. Susie has countless stories of things that have gone wrong and the unfortunate repercussions of mistakes she has made over the years as she tackled the challenge of learning to become a farmer and run Gwalia on her own. She compares herself to the bumbling television character Frank Spencer, created so memorably in the 1970s British sitcom *Some Mothers Do 'Ave 'Em*, by actor Michael Crawford.

'People make mistakes and that's what I do on a daily basis,' she says, frankly. 'That is what I love about working on my own. I haven't got someone there to see . . .' She laughs and recounts a few misadventures with tractors, motorbikes and handling feed, and then points to the flipside—moments like this morning in the cattle yards when the new design worked well, or yesterday's performance by Poi, when the dog followed Susie's instructions brilliantly to reunite and bring back a mob of cattle that had split along a creek bed. 'They gave her a hell of a time, but she brought them back. I was so proud of her, she is such a good dog,' Susie says.

Listening to Susie, it also becomes clear that she is a great networker, openly embracing the opportunity to learn from people and accept advice from those willing to teach her. There are a whole series of individuals like Tiddly Triffett and the Gubbins family who have shared their knowledge and taught her things she values, not to mention all the contractors and rural advisers she has called on over the years. 'I have some divine people who help, and people who have been huge influences on my life,' she says. 'I love learning, and I love people who can teach me things.'

Then there was the horsebreaker she fell for, years after Tony died, who taught her a lot about stockhorses and introduced her to New Zealand heading dogs, and how to train them. He even encouraged her to take up the guitar—something with which she continues to persevere, with help from a guitarist in Gundagai who has put together some music for her and a CD that she can play along to. A guitar stands in the corner of her lounge room ready for the next practice session when she has a spare moment.

A few weeks later and Susie has made a very exciting discovery. She not only has direct connections to Australia's first 'overlander', but it is highly likely he passed through her favourite place during his famous pioneering cattle trek. Wyuntha is a block of 122 hectares which takes in 4.5 kilometres of beautiful river frontage along the Murrumbidgee near Gundagai. Susie loves this spot with a passion. The first land she has bought and owned in her own right, it has a timeless quality which touches something deep in her soul. 'The minute I saw it I knew that I would fight through hell or high water to get it,' she says.

Years later, she wonders about the strange serendipity that may have drawn her to Wyuntha. Back on her father's side of the family, her great-grandfather Hugh John Chambers, a solicitor based in Melbourne, married Margaret, the eldest daughter of John Hawdon. The ceremony happened by special licence on 19 July 1849 at Banyule Estate at Heidelberg on what is now Melbourne's eastern outskirts. Long since buried under subdivisions, the farm was the 'seat' of John's more famous brother, Joseph.[15]

The two men made an indelible mark on colonial Australia. John immigrated to Australia from England in 1828 with his wife and two sons. He rented a property at Elderslie, south-west of Sydney, where Margaret was born in 1830, and later held numerous land grants across New South Wales and Victoria, becoming well known for his cattle. Joseph sailed for Australia in 1834 at his brother's suggestion.[16] Two years later he made headlines with two other men when they drove some 300 cattle overland from Jugiong, about 40 kilometres north-east of Gundagai, to Port Phillip Bay and the tenuous new settlement that became Melbourne. It was the first expedition of its kind from New South Wales and blazed a trail which others soon followed.[17]

In 1838 Joseph cemented his reputation as a daring cattleman when he and Charles Bonney drove another mob from John's station at Howlong on the banks of the River Murray in New South Wales to Adelaide, in what was described as 'an epoch in the annals of early exploration, droving and bushcraft'.[18] John shared the expenses for the drove, which provided much needed meat and livestock to the fledgling South Australian colony.[19] At about this time, the brothers also helped establish the first overland postal service connecting Sydney and Melbourne.[20] For a contract of £1200 covering the first year of the service, they employed one of their stockmen, John Conway Bourke, recognised as Victoria's first mailman, to ride between Melbourne and Yass, where the post was handed over to a rider from Sydney.

Susie is delighted with her connection to the Hawdons, not only because they were obviously very capable cattlemen, but because it is highly likely Joseph's first overland drive to Victoria crossed the Murrumbidgee somewhere near Wyuntha. This only occurred to her quite recently when she read a book about Joseph Hawdon and his pioneering efforts. 'My eyes nearly fell out of my head,' she says. 'He would have crossed the river very close to me. It's really amazing to think that I am here now.'

Susie bought Wyuntha in 2007. For some time she had been thinking it would be a good idea to have a small piece of grazing country where she could fatten her steers. At a farmer seminar one night, an adviser told her there was a block of land on the river for sale that might suit perfectly. Susie went to have a look. He was right, but she was worried about finding enough money to cover the deposit. As she drove home from inspecting the land, she pulled up at a turn-off and spotted a smiley face painted on the wall of a schoolbus shelter alongside the words, 'Happyness to all' [sic]. 'That's an omen!' she thought. Omen or not, after several financial institutions refused to loan her the money, Susie was becoming desperate. Then, 'as fate would have it', she was contacted by an old friend who offered to use his not-inconsiderable influence with his own bankers. 'So I got Wyuntha,' she says with simple satisfaction. 'I think I'm still celebrating.'

On the practical side, the property takes in river flats where she can grow lucerne pastures and crops of fodder oats to fatten her cattle. Just a few weeks here can add $300 a head to their value when they are sold direct to the award-winning Rangers Valley feedlot, owned by a Japanese corporation near Glen Innes. A rocky hill provides sweeping views of the river lined with majestic gums as it swings through the flats in a huge horseshoe curve. Across the bottom of the curve is a broad expanse of bare sand that covers with water when the river floods, effectively creating an island.

Susie had 119 steers, worth about $1000 each, stuck there when the river peaked at more than 10 metres at Gundagai in December 2010. Concerned about their welfare, and the financial disaster their loss would spell, she monitored the rising waters with the help of a neighbour. But there was not enough time to get them off the property. She spent several anxious days worrying the water would rise high enough to cover the island and sweep them away. In the end that didn't happen and they all survived, although she lost an oat crop and is still trying to clean up the debris.

Even when there are no cattle on the block, Susie will drive over to spend time sitting on the rocky hill top where she has dreams of building a cabin in her retirement. And in the summer she loves to come here with friends and family for picnics on the riverbank. During the holidays this summer she drove down every day with her daughters and granddaughters to go skinny-dipping in a safe pool of water they found out of the main current. Susie laughs at the memory of 'wobbly old granny' dashing into the water alongside her daughters and the screaming laughter of Melissa's three children, Island, Willow and Indigo. 'You can imagine what I looked like when I was going in,' Susies says. 'We had a great time, and those memories are probably the most precious you will have in your life.'

Susie's granddaughters—who she describes as 'the most gorgeous girls who drive their grandmother batty'—spend at least a week with her every holidays, travelling down from their home between Gunning and Yass, where Melissa and her husband Nicholas have a small property and a contract fencing business. Reflecting on the close relationship her mother has with them all, Melissa says: 'She is a great inspiration as a mum and as a grandmother. I feel very privileged that she has been my mum, and my kids idolise her. She has always got time for them.'

The past summer's frolics were the latest incarnation of a family tradition that began back at Queanbeyan, where Jonathon used to joke that pilots flying into Canberra would make a detour over their farm just to catch a glimpse of Susie swimming nude in the family pool. At Wyuntha the only concern is the odd boat or two. 'We treated it as a beach holiday,' says

Melissa. 'We would get down there at about 10 a.m. and go for this fabulous swim then spend the whole day there. Sometimes people would surprise us by coming up the river in a boat, but we have always skinny-dipped at Wyuntha . . . It is a very special place, and a very big part of who Mum is now. She is very much at peace there.'

Having a place like Wyuntha where her descendants can create happy memories and share family experiences is the driving force behind everything Susie does, and not just as a farmer. 'I want to leave something on this earth for my grandchildren's grandchildren,' she says. 'Somewhere they can go that is pristine and full of nature, where they can swim in the nuddy, and see the sunrise and the moonrise. I'm not religious, but it will be vital to their wellbeing, to their spirit.'

Feisty by nature, Susie says the toughest moments in her life have made her 'put up my dukes and come out fighting'. It took her many years to start enjoying living on her own, and she still misses Tony every day, but she recognises she has reached one of the happiest times of life, surrounded by loving friends and family, and with a certain amount of hard-won freedom.

'For a long time I just wanted to have that feeling back, that divine happiness I had with Chis. If you are mad about someone it is a total obsession. You can't think about anything else and everything falls by the wayside,' she says. 'People may think, "Why hasn't she got someone?" But I don't want anyone. I have got my children, who are my very best friends, and the most wonderful granddaughters.' Pausing, she adds with a grin: 'I have stopped chasing men. It's a total waste of time. If only I had discovered these cattle years ago, my reputation would be much better!'

Susie fiercely hopes her family will keep Wyuntha, and expand on it as she herself would like to do in her remaining years as an active farmer if the seasons are kind and cattle prices buoyant. Well past the age when most city professionals retire, she has no immediate plans to stop yet, although the physical demands are increasingly limiting. 'I have to keep thinking like a 40-year-old,' she says. 'People my age seem to be obsessed with looking young. I'm quite happy to accept myself looking crinkly. Why shouldn't I be? But I am terrified of not getting to where I want to get to before I go . . . The thing that is difficult for me is losing my physical strength as I get older. My body is not really enjoying it. My back aches, my knees ache, although I guess that happens to everyone my age. I just want to keep active, which is what the doctors say—keep going, don't stop . . . And there is no way I want to end up in an old folks' home. I don't want to leave the kids with a batty old woman who is costing them a fortune.'

When the time comes she wants to die with dignity, and have her ashes buried on the banks of the Murrumbidgee. She has kept Tony's ashes so they can be placed there together 'for eternity'. In the meantime she takes great comfort from one of the best-known verses penned by Australian poet Adam Lindsay Gordon. She discovered it while Tony was sick, and it has provided inspiration ever since:

> *Question not, but live and labour*
> *Till yon goal be won,*
> *Helping every feeble neighbour,*
> *Seeking help from none;*
> *Life is mostly froth and bubble,*
> *Two things stand like stone,*
> *Kindness in another's trouble,*
> *Courage in your own.*[21]

6

A HORSE NAMED RIFFAYAL

Cecily Cornish, Wando Bridge, Victoria

For many Londoners the towering elegance of St Paul's Cathedral and its impressive dome is a symbol of hope and resilience. To Cecily Crozier it seemed little short of miraculous when she first saw the famous landmark as an excited teenager embarking on the adventure of a lifetime. Although London was the city of her birth, her family had left when she was only a few months old. She was returning just four years after the end of the Second World War and the relentless bombing campaigns that had torn the city apart, destroying more than a million buildings and killing thousands. Despite being the specific target of enemy bombers because of its symbolic importance to the people of Great Britain, astoundingly St Paul's had survived. 'It was both the most beautiful and the most dreadful sight really.

There was this huge great building and everything around it was flattened,' she says, picturing clearly in her mind's eye Christopher Wren's masterpiece surrounded by empty space; foundations were the only evidence of all the buildings that had once crowded in upon it.

Cecily was sent to England to find and buy a horse. Not just any horse, but an Arabian stallion that would become the founding sire of a new stud destined to make an important contribution to the breed in Australia. Travelling to the other side of a world still recovering from war, the eighteen-year-old was given the daunting responsibility by her parents of choosing the right animal. They were quietly hopeful the trip would also give a little social polish to their tomboy daughter, who was mad about horses and becoming a farmer. As was to be expected, Cecily wasn't on her own. Acting as chaperone was her aunt, Mary 'Molly' Legoe, from Callendale station near Lucindale in the South East of South Australia, who had already established her own well-respected Arabian horse stud and imported stallions from a top breeder in England.

The two women travelled to London by liner in an era when the journey was enjoyed as much as the destination. They boarded P&O's *Stratheden* at Outer Harbour in Adelaide on 24 March 1949, for the second of three voyages the ship made between London and Sydney that year under the care of Captain SWS Dickson.[22] The *Stratheden* had returned to the company's passenger fleet about two years before, after almost six years of war service as a troopship and an extensive refit. One of the famous 'Strath' liners built for P&O during the 1930s, the ship had made its maiden voyage to Australia in 1937, newspapers marvelling at the modern design wonders of a single funnel and air-conditioning in the first-class saloon.[23]

Passengers joining the vessel in Adelaide for the autumn cruise of 1949 had to be on board by 8.30 the evening before departure. They could choose to travel to Outer Harbour by special train from the city centre or make their own way. Molly and Cecily arrived by car with an 'unbelievable' thirteen pieces of luggage, most of which were stowed away in the hold. Lady Kitty's regular social column in *The Advertiser* informed readers they were seen on board by Cecily's parents, Edwin and Nancy Crozier, of Barnoolut, Casterton, Victoria.[24] The liner set sail at six o'clock the next morning and the two travellers settled in for the 29 days it would take to reach the port of Tilbury.[25]

Cecily found the voyage very glamorous although she was appalled at seeing beggars in the streets when the ship called in at the Indian city of Bombay, now known as Mumbai. 'I had never seen a beggar before, and that was a shock. I have never forgotten it,' she says. It made the whole experience even more surreal for the young country girl, who was very conscious of the stark contrast to life on the *Stratheden* where she had her own cabin and dressed for dinner every evening. 'You wore long dresses and the fellows wore dinner suits, and there was a fancy dress party at some stage,' she recalls. 'It's a world that's gone. I'm glad I did it but it sort of seems like a dream—not real.'

Also on board was Posy Grimwade from Lismore, New South Wales, who was to remain a close friend until she died of cancer more than 60 years later. 'Gosh, I still miss her,' says Cecily. 'There are things I want to ring her up and talk to her about, but I can't.' Posy was the first of several lifelong friends about the same age made during the trip, which turned it into a life-changing experience. They included twins, Jan and Sue, from Adelaide who were staying in the same apartment building in Kensington when Molly and Cecily took up residence after arriving in London.

Despite the excitement of being in one of the world's great cities, Cecily was shocked by evidence of extensive bomb damage, and not just around St Paul's. While a great deal had been done to clear up the rubble, there was no getting away from the large numbers of bare blocks and damaged buildings. She and Molly also had to cope with the strict rationing that applied in England until the 1950s, making it a challenge to buy many basic foods, although restrictions on purchasing clothes had ended the year before. Petrol rationing was still in force too, but they bought a small, economical Morris Minor, which they dubbed 'Little Pet', so they could attend the season's horse shows and visit stables.

In June they travelled to Cambridge for the famous 'May Week' balls with Cecily's brother Digby and Molly's son Christopher, who were both studying at the famous university. The balls were a series of formal events celebrating the end of the academic year. Although they usually fell sometime in June, they kept their name from the early days of the tradition which was originally held in May. Looking back at those heady few days, Cecily admits she didn't really appreciate the experience as much as she should.

More importantly to their mission, the two women travelled to Hertfordshire and one of the top Arabian horse studs in Britain. Hanstead was run by Miss Gladys Yule, the only child of Sir David Yule, who made his fortune as a merchant in India. 'I remember we walked round all the stallions and she did have some for sale but they were over what my father wanted to pay,' says Cecily, admitting in an aside: 'I had a budget and this time I stuck to it—I haven't done it since. As my eldest son says to me, "Mum, have you ever heard of the B word?" Anyhow, she didn't have anything in my price range but she told me about this horse and she said he had improved so much in the past twelve months he would be worthwhile looking at.'

Riffayal was a seven-year-old stallion whose sire, Fayal, came from the Crabbet Stud in Sussex. One of the most famous Arabian studs in the world, it was run by the eccentric Lady Wentworth and established by her parents, Wilfred and Lady Anne Blunt, who travelled the Middle East in the nineteenth century buying the best horses they could and bringing them back to England. The stud became an extraordinary repository of Arabian bloodlines, influencing the breed worldwide.

A strong horse bred for practical riding as much as the show ring, Riffayal won a highly commended at the International Horse Show at White City in the summer of 1949 after being ridden 240 kilometres to compete. The feat was recorded briefly in a special double-page spread about the event, published in the *London Illustrated News*. Both the horse and his owner were going to be at the annual Arabian horse show at Roehampton, on the south-western outskirts of London, and Gladys Yule advised Cecily to go there and take a look.

It is fair to say that when Cecily saw Riffayal it was love at first sight. The beautiful, dappled-grey horse standing 15 hands high not only had the breeding and conformation she was looking for, but personality as well. 'I fell in love with him. He was very quiet with a lovely temperament but he was a real character,' Cecily says simply. She was not so sure about the owner, who apparently made his fortune selling used cars in the years immediately after the war and came across as a bit of a 'wheeler dealer'. Much to the amusement of Cecily and Posy, who joined them on the mission, he insisted on calling Molly 'Aunty'. 'He would keep saying, "Cum an' 'ave a cup o' tea, Aunty,"' she recalls, mimicking a northern accent. 'We would be hysterical, as you would expect at eighteen, and Aunt Molly was "Aunty" for ever, ever more.' The deal was sealed and the owner invited the women to come and stay at his beautiful Georgian manor house to make the final arrangements.

At another stage during the trip, Cecily and Posy decided to seize the opportunity and attend the pioneering Porlock Vale Riding School in Somerset for a week or two. On its way to establishing a reputation as one of the world's finest riding schools, Porlock Vale boasted one of the first indoor riding facilities in the country and supplied horses for the pentathlon event at the 1948 Olympic Games held in London. It was run by the highly respected horseman Captain Tony Collings, who helped organise the first Badminton Horse Trials just days before Cecily arrived in England. At Porlock Vale, his goal was to teach the art of 'happy riding' and provide the highest possible standard of instruction to young riders from around the world.[26]

Cecily was so inspired by the experience she signed up for a more comprehensive horse master's course, which took about thirteen weeks to complete. During that time students boarded at the Collings family house in the hills of Exmoor. Each pupil was responsible for looking after one horse, and participated in lessons covering a range of subjects such as equitation, stable management and treating minor horse ailments. Cecily found it 'hard work, but the greatest of fun'. Students who successfully completed an examination at the end of the program received a preliminary instructor's certificate issued by the British Horse Society, but much to her regret she didn't get that far. Her parents sent word that she must leave before the course finished and return to Australia in time for Christmas. 'I didn't want to come home, but I did,' she says with obvious regret.

As instructed, Cecily set sail for Adelaide in November. Arrangements were made for Riffayal to follow on another ship, which docked in Melbourne in January 1950. Edwin and Nancy Crozier were very happy when they saw the horse their daughter had selected, and it wasn't too long before Edwin fell in love with Riffayal too. 'My father adored him,' says Cecily. 'I think he was the best horse we ever had, which was probably a fluke, but there wasn't much wrong with him. He was a beautiful horse to manage and ride.'

A year after he arrived in Australia, Riffayal competed in the 1951 Royal Melbourne Show and was named Champion Arabian Stallion. Among Cecily's most treasured possessions is a beautiful certificate featuring a delicately coloured drawing of a bygone era, with horsedrawn wagons in a field being loaded with sheaves of hay. It was presented to her in honour of the championship on behalf of the Victorian Minister of Agriculture. 'It was the first time I had won anything like that. It was a great thing,' she says.

Also precious is a cream-covered album in which Cecily keeps a photo of her and Riffayal competing at the 1954 Royal Melbourne Show when she was able to ride him into the show ring for the first time. 'Up to then you weren't allowed to ride a stallion at events because it was considered dangerous, but I used to ride him everywhere, he was so quiet,' Cecily says. 'The first year we went down to Melbourne we were only allowed to exercise on the trotting track and we had to be off by eight o'clock. I kept lobbying for a ridden class of stallions but I wasn't getting anywhere.'

Then one of the society councillors suggested she donate a trophy. 'They can't resist a trophy,' he told her.

So she provided the Cecily Crozier Perpetual Trophy for the best ridden Arabian stallion. It was the first ridden class for stallions of any breed at the show—ironically, Riffayal only came second that year—and continues to this day, with Cecily's contribution noted in the event schedule.

Known affectionately as Riffy, the handsome grey stallion went on to produce more than his share of top performing offspring in Australia and New Zealand. He sired his last foal when he was 30, and died in December 1973, a few paragraphs in a local newspaper paying tribute to him as a 'member of the family'.

It's eight o'clock in the morning at Barnoolut and a blustery winter southerly is blowing across the property, flattening the rich, green pasture and tearing at the gnarled beauty of the old red gums. The meteorological bureau has put out a 'sheep weather alert'—a warning to all livestock producers in western Victoria that rough weather lies ahead. It usually means a combination of rain, hail, gale-force winds and freezing temperatures that chills people to the bone and whips away the lives of newborn lambs. It is the sort of weather that has most people pulling the covers over their heads and refusing to get out of bed.

Now aged 80 and far from retired, Cecily is preparing to go outside and complete her morning chores. She is making a bit of a late start after a sleepless night, but that is no excuse when there are animals to be fed. First to greet her are two rambunctious lambs on the back verandah. Desperate for the first of four feeds for the day, they climb up the railings of their portable steel pen to get her attention. Cecily has mixed up a jug of special powdered milk formula and poured it into two plastic bottles capped with rubber teats. The lambs tug fiercely at the surrogate udders, draining them in a moment. Normally they would now be let out into a small paddock near the house for the day, but this needs to be reconsidered given the forecast.

Rugged up in a light blue waterproof jacket, cream wool beanie and black rubber boots, Cecily picks up her shepherd's crook and heads out to the horse yard, a hundred metres or so from the house. An extremely useful aid which she applies to everything from guiding sheep through gateways to ushering chickens out of their coop, the crook is one of two she purchased in Scotland during her 1949 trip. She is not exactly sure why the idea of owning one appealed to her, but family research has revealed her maiden name is derived from the Latin word 'crocia' and the old French word 'crosier', both terms for a bishop's crook or pastoral staff.

There are only seven horses left on Barnoolut now, compared with its heyday as an Arabian stud when there were as many as 30 and the Croziers held their own on-property sale. Cecily is no longer breeding horses because the work involved is too physically demanding. 'I'm just keeping the old ones going, and as they go that's it, unless one of the children decides they want to take it on,' she says. She also gave up riding in her late 60s following hip surgery. After being told it would 'make a hell of a mess' if she fell off, she concluded that wouldn't be fair to the rest of the family, who would have to look after her.

The horses being fed today are three veterans who are kept close to the house so they can receive special treatment. All descendants of the remarkable Riffayal, they move up to feed bins hung from the post and rail fence, and whicker softly as their carer approaches. Barnoolut Triton belongs to Cecily's daughter Edwina. The chestnut gelding was kept for her to ride during visits, but now aged 25 is long retired. Barnoolut Carina is a 27-year-old grey mare who was once fleet of foot and won a race for Arabian horses held at Ballarat. Barnoolut Catalina is another grey mare of the same age. She had quite a successful show career and produced the last foal bred by Cecily, a sweet-natured grey named Barnoolut Rimini.

Rimini has been competing with considerable success for the past few years under the capable guidance of experienced show rider Rebecca Farran. When Rimini was old enough to ride, Cecily wasn't too sure what to do with him. He wasn't particularly exotic or pretty looking and it was unlikely anyone would buy him as a stallion, so she had him gelded and broken in, and then looked for someone prepared to ride him on her behalf. 'Arabs are starting to get such a bad name with the riding people and it's a shame,' she says. She eventually tracked down Rebecca, who had reservations on learning he was an Arabian but agreed to give him a go.

Preparing for his first show, Rebecca told Cecily: 'I'm not going to ride him because he is still too green, but I will put him in the novice led class and get him used to it.' Rimini won the class before taking out an open led class and being named champion galloway (in between a pony and a horse). Since then, he has won the ridden gelding class for purebred Arabians at the 2008 Royal Melbourne Show and the best novice show hunter award for galloways of any breed at the 2009 show. In 2010 he took out a novice event at the Australian Sports Pony Register Pony Dressage Challenge.

'He is a superb moving horse,' Cecily says. 'I don't get to see him very often but, gosh, he has done well. I wanted to prove you could breed Arabs that could compete in open company and hold their own. He is doing it, and not only in the open show ring.'

Horses fed, it's time to let the chickens out for the day. Watching closely as Cecily ushers them out with the crook is Pepper, a twelve-year-old black Labrador who had one front leg amputated last year because of bone cancer. The dog has adapted well to the handicap and it slows her down very little as she heads back to the house. Smart enough to know the best place on a day like this is inside, Pepper tucks herself under the kitchen table where her bed is made up, while Cecily sits down to a bowl of porridge. A blend of traditional and quick oats cooked slowly overnight in the traditional Scottish method, this constitutes breakfast most days, even in the summer.

Cecily is almost done when a young stockwoman from down the road, who checks the sheep and cattle every morning, pops in with good and bad news. Kimberley has found two new sets of twin lambs that were born overnight and seem to be doing well, but a sheep that was poorly after giving birth to dead lambs a few weeks ago has died.

Breakfast over and the dirty dishes packed away in the dishwasher, Cecily prepares to 'saddle up' once again and feed the cattle. Twice a week during winter she and Ivan Naylor run out some baled hay so the stock are better able to ward off the cold. A spritely 85-year-old, Ivan lives with his wife Pat in a weatherboard cottage tucked behind a cypress windbreak a short distance from the main house. They have become dearest friends over the 25 years or so they have lived there, with Ivan more than happy to help with anything mechanical, as well as maintaining things like the electric fences and watering troughs. 'I am very lucky to have him,' Cecily says. He and John, Cecily's husband, got on very well too. 'They weren't great talkers but they understood each other. When John died the Naylors were away, and they didn't have to but they came straight back, and Ivan came in and put his arms around me and said, "I'm going to look after you," and he has.'

Cecily picks up Ivan in the ute and takes him to where the tractor and hay feeder are stored. He backs them out and heads down the central laneway that connects most paddocks on Barnoolut, Cecily following behind. They are heading to a small enclosure where large, round bales of hay are kept. Ivan uses the tractor to pick one up and place it in the feeder, which will slowly rotate the bale and feed out the hay as he drives across the paddock. Cecily helps to remove the string mesh holding the bale in shape and sets up the gates so he can get into the paddock where the cattle are waiting.

Stirred up by the wind, some of the younger stock break into a canter and kick their heels in the air in happy anticipation. They are a beautiful lot of Poll Hereford cattle, in excellent condition following a mild summer and wet autumn that has produced bountiful feed. Looking at their red coats and white faces, Cecily is pleased with the herd of about 100 breeding cows and the quality of this year's calves. She attributes much of this to the livestock agent from Hamilton who helps select the bulls from James Russell's Russlyn Poll Hereford Stud at Balmoral, less than an hour's drive to the north-east. 'I have always liked Herefords. Of course they are not fashionable now but they are coming back and James is so enthusiastic about his cattle,' she says.

The tractor back in its shed, Cecily returns Ivan to his house and heads down the long driveway to collect the mail from what her late husband humorously called the Barnoolut Mail Exchange. It is a big white box with a hinged lid, set on the roadside close to the front gate. Cecily pulls up the ute, trying not to focus too hard on the view immediately in front of her. In the distance, a pale, grey-green tide of blue gums is creeping across the landscape. She hates the large-scale plantations gradually covering thousands of hectares of what was once prime farmland, and the flow-on effects on rural communities as families move out to make way for the trees. 'I cannot believe that such beautiful red gum country is going into these horrible trees,' she says.

To her right is Wando Bridge and the beautiful valley of Wando Vale, which lies in the heart of some of Australia's most fertile grazing country. Majestic red gums dot rolling hillsides which are kept green most of the year by a relatively high average rainfall when the seasons do the right thing. The first Europeans to reach the area in the 1830s recognised its potential immediately, with early pastoralists competing for large runs and populating them with sheep, displacing the Indigenous people of the Konongwootong Gundidj clan, who occupied the area for thousands of years.[27]

Twelve kilometres to the south-west is Casterton, the district's main service centre and a relatively small but thriving town famous as the birthplace of the kelpie breed of Australian working dog. The original 'kelpie' was a black and tan female with floppy ears born on Warrock station, next door to Barnoolut, in about 1872. She was bought by a stockman named Jack Gleeson, who christened the dog after the mythological water creature of Celtic folklore. He trained her to work sheep and took her to New South Wales, where one of her pups performed so impressively in the first sheepdog trials held at the Forbes Show that it eventually sparked the recognition and naming of a new breed.[28]

These days, thousands of people descend on Casterton during the long weekend in June to celebrate kelpies in all shapes and forms at the Australian Kelpie Muster, where they pay extraordinary prices for the best dogs at a special auction and watch kelpies perform in everything from sprints and high jump events to a more conventional mustering challenge. Ironically, given its location, there are no working dogs on her property, but like every sheep producer in the district Cecily was brought up on the story of Jack Gleeson and his amazing dog.

When Cecily bought Riffayal she was following a strong Crozier tradition. Her great-grandfather, John Crozier, imported an Arabian stallion from India in the late nineteenth century to improve the endurance and strength of his station horses. The first member of the family to immigrate to Australia from Scotland, John arrived in New South Wales with his new wife, Jessie, in 1838. An experienced drover with good references, he found work as overseer on a property near Braidwood and later managed Sandhills station at Bungendore, not far from the future site of Canberra. Having raised enough money to purchase the nucleus of his own sheep flock and a bullock dray, John and his family set out to the south-west of the colony where they squatted on land without clear title in the Deniliquin area. In conjunction with a partner, he finally took possession of his own lease in 1849 at the confluence of the Darling and Murray rivers, on what was to become Kulnine station. The purchase was the first of many for the emerging pastoralist, whose holdings covered more than 285 000 hectares by the time he 'retired' to Adelaide in the late 1860s.

This time the Crozier home was Oaklands Estate, in what is now the suburb of Marion. Far from retiring, John threw himself into public life and was immediately elected to the state's upper house of parliament, with a ball being held to celebrate his unequivocal victory. He remained a parliamentarian until his death in 1887, and in between many public duties he indulged a passion for horses. He bred successful racehorses, was elected the first steward of the South Australian Jockey Club, and was a strong supporter of the Adelaide Hunt Club. In 1874 he drew favourable comment in the press when he exhibited the Arabian stallion Rustoon at the Royal Adelaide Show.

A down-to-earth woman more interested in the welfare of the Indigenous and the poor, his wife Jessie was not always completely supportive of John's social activities. Cecily loves the story of her great-grandmother deliberately bringing her husband down a peg or two by wandering through his high-society guests with a bucket of pig swill as they gathered at Oaklands for a garden party. She even turned down the opportunity to hear John make his maiden speech in parliament. When he asked her to go, she apparently replied, in her broad Scottish accent, 'Noo, John, I would die o'vera shame.' The phrase became a family favourite.

During her time at Kulnine, Jessie made friends among the Indigenous women, who apparently lined the riverbanks wailing the day she left. In Adelaide, she insisted that a paddock be set aside so Indigenous people could camp if they wanted. She also made a point of providing baskets of food to homeless women and children in the area. 'I love Jessie,' says Cecily, who like her ancestor has an aversion to 'putting on side'. When Jessie died ten years before her husband, the funeral was attended by 'a large assembly of persons of all ranks of life'.[29]

Among John and Jessie's seven surviving sons was Cecily's grandfather, Edwin Crozier. The second youngest in the family, he was born in 1859 and grew up mainly at Oaklands. Of slight build and introspective nature, he was a keen amateur jockey with several notable wins to his credit. Like his father before him Edwin also loved Arabian horses, purchasing stallions from former South Australian premier and supreme court judge Sir James Penn Boucaut, who was one of the first to import breeding stock from England to Australia. Boucaut established the highly influential Quambi stud at Mount Barker in the 1890s with horses purchased from Crabbet.

Keenly interested in medicine, Edwin wanted to become a doctor but ended up working in an Adelaide bank, where he developed sound financial and business management skills. When two of his elder brothers ran into financial difficulty at Bimbowrie station, west of Broken Hill, their creditors insisted Edwin take an active role in straightening things out. He succeeded, after spending much of the rest of his life at Bimbowrie. In 1898 he married Ethyl Trew, the younger sister of one of his brother's wives. Their first child died, but in January 1900 John Edwin Digby Crozier, Cecily's father, was born in Adelaide. Also known as Edwin, he grew up at the station under the care of a retired Afghan camel driver and learnt to ride at about the age of five, going on rounds with his father, but their time together was short-lived.

Edwin senior died tragically when the boy was only six years old. He fell asleep in an armchair sitting before an open window. A candle was blown over by the curtain, falling between Edwin and the chair. After rallying for a day or so, he succumbed to extensive burns and complications associated with the fact he had only one kidney. The other had been removed during what the family believes was the first operation of its kind successfully performed in South Australia. Cecily's father told her the kidney was kept in a jar at the University of Adelaide for years afterwards. 'You could go and look at it,' she says.

On his death, two-thirds of Edwin's estate was placed in trust for his son, with the remaining third given to Ethyl, who was strongly advised to sell up and move to Adelaide. She refused to go, deciding instead to keep the property until more of its debts could be paid off. She ran it with help from members of both her own family and the Croziers until 1911, when Bimbowrie was sold in eight lots and she retired to Adelaide and remarried.

Two years later, with money now available, Ethyl decided it was time Edwin should fulfil his father's ambitions by going to school in England and studying to become a doctor. Mother and son sailed to Great Britain, where Edwin was duly delivered to Rugby, the prestigious school that invented rugby football. When the First World War broke out a year later, Edwin found himself stuck in England. After graduating from Rugby, he remained there and served as a junior officer with the Coldstream Guards, but he did not end up facing battle; Armistice was declared just before he was due to go to France. 'That was a good thing. He was a subaltern and he said the average life of a subaltern at the front was twenty minutes. Unbelievable,' Cecily reflects, considering the horrors of the Western Front and the enormous number of lives lost.

With the war over, Edwin decided to stay in England, where he studied medicine at Cambridge University and St Thomas's Hospital in London before taking up a career in medical research. In 1926 he married Nancy Legoe, another South Australian who he had known off and on since childhood. The wedding was held in a small historic church in the village of Hurley, west of London. The newlyweds set up house in the fashionable suburb of Kensington, where their two children were born. Digby Glen Crozier arrived on 16 May 1927, followed by his sister, Cecily Anthea, on 11 November 1930. Not long after, Edwin came home one day and said, 'I can't stand not seeing the sun any more. We are going back to Australia.'

Cecily was only a few months old when the family returned. Her parents were keen to buy a property and take up farming, but after about twelve months or so they had failed to find a place they both liked. With his family's extensive pastoral interests in previous generations, Edwin may have been interested in heading north, but Nancy refused to consider anything above Goyder's Line because she disliked the heat. Just as they had given up the search and were contemplating returning to England, the Croziers heard of Barnoolut and decided to take a look. 'And the rest, as they say, is history,' reflects Cecily, who quickly established a strong spiritual connection to the place.

When the Croziers bought Barnoolut it covered about 1650 hectares, about twice the area it does now, and had developed a reputation for lush pastures producing prime cattle and stand-out Corriedale sheep. Cecily is not sure of the early history of the property, but in 1925 a local newspaper reported the then owners, Messrs Harris and Dunn, had treated 1200 acres (490 hectares) with superphosphate fertiliser, achieving impressive results. Pasture growth on the best land had practically doubled while on the poorer soils it had still increased up to 70 per cent:

> The maximum number of stock which Barnoolut carried prior to this treatment was 5000 sheep and probably 120 cattle. From last November to June 6850 sheep were maintained, while 240 cattle were kept on it until April, since which the number has been 120, besides horses. Hitherto sheep fat in January have gone off in condition after that month, but for the first time in local experience they not only kept their condition but many of them improved, so that frequent sales of fats were made up till June, in which month 250 were sold at big prices.[30]

At some stage in the next few years Barnoolut was acquired by one of Australia's more colourful political figures, Senator James Guthrie. A passionate sheep and wool man originally from central Victoria, Guthrie lost a leg in his early 30s after contracting anthrax. Although his bosses found him 'unpredictable' and 'insubordinate', he held senior wool-broking and management positions within the big pastoral house of Dalgety and Co for many years, continuing even after taking up his seat in the senate in 1920. He founded the Australian Corriedale Sheep-breeders' Association in 1914 and won international recognition for his own flock, helping to build the breed's profile.[31]

Guthrie's significant pastoral holdings included Barnoolut, where his manager at one stage was a member of the Wettenhall family, who were among the first to develop dual-purpose types of crossbred sheep in Australia. However, cattle were also intended to be a major focus at the property. Guthrie told the annual meeting of the Red Poll Cattle Breeders Association of Australia in Melbourne, in September 1929, that he had bought it specifically to breed red polls because they were excellent dual-purpose animals which produced plenty of milk for their calves and matured early.[32] The view resonates with Cecily, who is also a fan of red cattle.

Guthrie had apparently intended to hand Barnoolut over to his son Jim, but in 1931 he put it on the market. The decision may have had something to do with the serious accident Jim suffered in late 1929. A keen aviator, he was acting as observer in a plane which crashed during the final stages of an air race from one side of the continent to the other. Jim survived after making a miraculous recovery, only to be killed six years later in a car accident on the Hume Highway.

In 1932 Guthrie sold the property to the Croziers.

❖ ❖ ❖

Cecily's earliest memories of Barnoolut are walking into the nursery, finding her toys and having a sense this was going to be home. Originally a fairly small house, it was extended soon after purchase by Edwin and Nancy to better accommodate their family and allow plenty of space for entertaining guests. The sprawling series of rooms and wings connecting old and new has changed little since then. A weathered slate roof with a moderately steep pitch sits over white walls and elegant sash windows divided into square panes, creating a look that is more English than rural Australian.

At the front of the house a flight of six shallow steps leads up to the archway of a small front porch. Inside there is a cavernous wood box running along one wall, making it convenient both to deliver firewood and to carry small lots straight through the wide front door into the sitting room. More of a vestibule than a conventional room, this space connects the bedroom wing, the formal lounge and dining rooms, and the 'working' part of the house. A large wood heater and soft, plump sofa upholstered in pale, sage green make it an inviting place to relax. Cecily's Abyssinian cat, Cinnamon, thinks so too; he is stretched 'a yard and a half long' on the rug in front of the fire, absorbing the heat. A long passageway lined with bedrooms runs off one side of the sitting room, ending in the nursery area Cecily remembers from her childhood, which was later converted into a flat for her and her husband. The main bedrooms have views from the front of the house across a broad expanse of lawn that drops away to a white post and rail fence.

While there is only one formal front door, people arriving at the back of the house are faced with a plethora of choices, creating some confusion for first-time visitors. An original wing houses what used to be staff quarters. Its doors open on to a verandah paved with red bricks, which provides a sheltered spot to hang washing on damp days. In winter, it's not unusual to find a pen of motherless lambs here too, snuggled into a warm bed of straw and bleating imperiously to be fed. A concrete path runs around the corner to a small courtyard with yet more doors. One leads to what used to be the boiler room, another to the old milk room where butter was once made, another to the nursery area, and yet another to the original kitchen, still relatively intact and now a useful utility space. From here you step into the current kitchen, and the true heart of the house.

A light and airy space despite the fact it is relatively small and narrow, the kitchen is a pleasant, well-used room lined with white cupboards and traditional, square white tiles. In the afternoon, sunshine streams through a wide window above the kitchen sink, glancing off the gorgeous, enamelled wonderment of the classic Aga cooker that takes up most of one wall.

Forged out of cast iron to an external design that has changed little since the original Aga was designed in 1929, the cooker works on a 'heat storage' principle. It is permanently switched on, with the cast iron radiating gentle warmth and acting as a magnet for anyone who visits Cecily, not to mention Cinnamon and Pepper.

The first Aga at Barnoolut was a traditional cream model run on coke. It was installed by Edwin before he joined the army so his wife didn't have to worry about chopping and bringing in wood. It was later converted, first to oil then gas then electricity, and kept running for 70 years, almost every day, apart from the hottest months of summer, before being replaced with a new model painted deep British racing green. Cecily's version incorporates four ovens and three hobs, and a smaller extension model which gives her a gas cooking top and another two ovens that can be switched on and off. There are two covered hobs—one for boiling and one for simmering—and a very gentle warming plate where her old-fashioned kettle usually stands.

The ovens each have a different purpose too. There is one for roasting that is large enough to take a 13-kilogram turkey, one for baking, a simmering oven perfect for slow cooking, and a warming oven. The latter was designed for keeping food warm, but Cecily knows it is also the perfect place to revive sick lambs. She has saved two that way in the past few weeks of winter after finding them out in the paddock almost dead from the cold, having been abandoned by their mothers. One of them is the last surviving lamb of quintuplets, a relatively rare phenomenon in the sheep world. 'I gave her a slug of brandy and put her in the bottom oven wrapped in a towel. It is unbelievable what warmth does for them but she did take a long time to recover. She is going to be a beautiful ewe.'

Watching Cecily use her Aga is a study in time and motion efficiency. At breakfast, she reaches down into the warming oven to bring out a saucepan of porridge that has been gently cooking all night. The kettle is moved from the warming plate to the boiling plate, where it quickly reaches the right temperature to make a pot of coffee. This part of the stove can also double as a toaster, while the hob next door is the perfect place to dry damp clothes. In the evening, preparing a simple meal of savoury chicken and tarragon stew, she places a pot of vegetables on the hottest plate to bring it to the boil within minutes, and then moves the saucepan to the simmering oven where they continue to cook perfectly. Cecily knows the best use for every part of this wonderful contraption, although she hasn't been able to produce biscuits as crisp as they should be in the new model, and is still experimenting.

Aside from anything else, the cooker warms the room, a definite plus in a part of the country notorious for its cold winters. 'I don't know how people get on without one. I couldn't,' she says matter-of-factly. 'For two winters when the old one was playing up, I had to have a radiator in the kitchen. It wasn't funny . . . When I'm on my own and I come home after being away, walking into this kitchen and this range—it's like having another person here.'

In her younger days, people were lucky to find Cecily inside at all. Even as a very small child she was drawn to whatever was happening outside, running away from the house to explore the shearing shed and the stables quite some distance away. 'I just loved it from the word go,' she says. 'It was a very good upbringing.'

Her love of horses and riding started early too. 'When I was about four my father had a little pony and he would take me out on a leading rein, and we would go round the ewes and lambs. I only ever wanted to be a farmer right from that moment,' she confesses. When they weren't doing stockwork, the family would ride together just for the pleasure of it, sometimes taking a picnic. One of their favourite spots was Deadman's Gorge, overlooking the Glenelg River, which marks the eastern boundary of the property.

At the age of seven, Cecily was introduced to the joys of competing at shows. She rode her Shetland pony at the annual spring agricultural show in nearby Hamilton, won a ribbon and 'that was that'. She also remembers very clearly the excitement when mobs of mares returned home after spending a season at the Legoe's Callendale station about 150 kilometres away. They would be mated with one of Aunt Molly's Arabian stallions, and then a drover would walk them all the way back with foals at foot, once the young ones were old enough to tackle the journey.

Life for Cecily changed very little in those early years. Unlike many other children in the district, she didn't go to the local primary school. She and her brother were placed in the care of a series of governesses and, by preference, seen and not heard. 'I didn't really have much education, which in a way is a pity,' Cecily reveals. 'But I have always read a lot. I learnt to read when I was very young and that has been a great solace. As long as I have a good book I'm quite happy.'

Digby went off to Geelong Grammar School at the age of about seven, and Cecily stayed home until she was twelve, taking on more responsibility for helping to run the farm after her father enlisted in August 1941. He joined the medical corps of the Australian Imperial Forces, was made a captain and assigned to care for men in the 1st Armoured Division. Intended for deployment to the Middle East, the division was retained in Australia after the outbreak of the Pacific War to help defend the country in the event of Japanese invasion. They spent most of their time in Western Australia, waiting for something that never happened.

Edwin later told his family the wait, and a sense they were not contributing usefully, placed the highly trained men under enormous strain, leading to problems with depression. He also wrote home to Nancy of his encounters in the Northern Territory with refugees who had escaped islands to the north of Australia that had been invaded by the Japanese. 'They had horrific stories, and he wrote to Mum and said if the Japanese land you are to shoot the children and shoot yourself. That was a nice thing for her to live with, wasn't it? You just can't imagine it.'

Sheltered from the worst fears generated by the conflict, Cecily enjoyed the first year or two when her father was away because she was encouraged to play a more active part in running the farm. Although a few men too old or unfit for war service were around to help, labour was short and everyone was expected to 'muck in'. She recalls, 'We had a ball because we were treated like responsible adults. We were given jobs to do and told to get on with it, and we did.'

The bulk of responsibility for managing Barnoolut and making daily decisions fell on Nancy. It was not always easy to know the best thing to do, and sometimes there were challenges to her authority. The most memorable came when she unwittingly ran fowl of a contract shearing team because of a Land Army girl called Jean, who was assigned to work on the farm. The Australian Women's Land Army was a voluntary group set up in 1942 to help overcome the labour shortage. Nancy's long-serving cook took exception to Jean, accusing her of 'entertaining' a shearer in her bedroom.

One night the cook pounded on Nancy's door, yelling: 'He's in there now, he's in her room. You have to do something about it. Either she goes, or I'll go.'

So Nancy walked down to the old harness room that had been converted to accommodation and knocked on the door. 'Jean, do you have a man in your room?' she asked. Sure enough, the shearer emerged, claiming he had just dropped in to borrow a book.

Hearing the story later, Edwin laughed: 'Well, I've never heard it called that before!'

In danger of losing a cook who had served her faithfully for thirteen years, Nancy sacked Jean on the spot. The next morning she was faced with mutiny. The shearers were going on strike unless Jean was reinstated. With her heart in her mouth, Nancy stood her ground. Jean packed her bags and so did the shearers. Left with pens of unshorn sheep but undaunted, Nancy picked up the telephone and contacted a local bloke called Les Anderson and asked if he could help find replacements. 'I'll be there tomorrow, Mrs Crozier,' he said without hesitation. Anderson and his team sheared for Barnoolut for years to come, followed by his son.

Ever practical and determined, Nancy thought carefully about what might be needed when she was asked by the authorities to accommodate evacuees if bombs started falling on Australian cities and ports. Realising sanitation was likely to be a major issue, she rang the local hardware store and bought their entire stock of dunny cans and a large supply of chamber pots. They were never needed but after the war, when chamber pots were apparently in short supply, she came to the rescue of more than a few families wanting them to toilet train their children.

Despite the war, and much against her will, Cecily was eventually sent off to boarding school. She found the experience frustrating in the extreme. 'Having been given a whole lot of responsibility and treated like an adult, you were suddenly confined and had to obey rules. It was terrible,' she says. 'I used to weep buckets every time I had to go back to school.'

For the first couple of years, she went to Woodlands in Adelaide, travelling by train from Binnum, a tiny community just over the border. 'One time I remember coming back from school and there must have been an accident or a derailment or something. It took thirteen hours to get from Adelaide to Binnum and the train was packed because it was full of soldiers,' she recalls.

With the war making interstate travel increasingly difficult, Cecily switched schools and was sent to Melbourne, where she boarded at Toorak College near Frankston. The school proved a much better match, even having its own riding mistress and an annual gymkhana. Cecily was named best novice girl rider at the event in March 1947, scoring a mention in the junior section of *The Argus* newspaper in a story espousing the benefits of animals at boarding schools in helping students to overcome the wrench of leaving their own pets after the holidays. Cecily recalls loving the school for the friends she made there. 'There were a lot of like-minded rebels. We learnt to be everything but ladies I think, but everybody in my year did something interesting with their lives.' She adds with a twinkle in her eye: 'One of them became Melbourne's top madam. For a while she was a dancer at the Folies Bergere in Paris, where she brought them all out on strike for more pay. She was a real character.'

After toying briefly with the idea of becoming either a veterinarian or a doctor, Cecily came back to Barnoolut. 'When I finished school, I just wanted to come home. I was going to be a farmer,' she says. Then came the adventurous trip to England. When she returned, Cecily worked with her father to establish the Barnoolut Arab Stud, building Riffayal's reputation by competing in shows. But her days of living at Wando Bridge and spending most of her time with horses were about to be interrupted—for 25 years.

❖ ❖ ❖

Towards the end of 1953, Cecily was contacted by one of her best friends, Bunty McConnan, who had some exciting news. Bunty was going to marry Hamilton Morton at the Presbyterian Church in the inner Melbourne suburb of Toorak on 19 February 1954 and she wanted Cecily to be chief bridesmaid. Cecily was delighted to accept. She had met the groom, but she had no idea who would be best man and therefore her partner for the occasion. When someone asked her, she replied, 'I don't know, some old man.' The 'old man' in question was John, ten years her senior and a workmate of the groom.

Christened with given names coincidentally in line with Crozier family traditions, John Edwin Cornish was born in Crystal Brook, in South Australia's Mid North, on 2 May 1921, the eldest child of Ross and Stella. Described by his co-author in a published family history as 'an uncomplicated and private man whose strong sense of honour and responsibility was his memorable feature', young John proved to be an excellent scholar.[33] After a period commuting by train to secondary school in Port Pirie, he won a scholarship to study at Adelaide High School and moved to the city to live with his grandmother, Mary Ann Robinson.

John was only twenty and studying science at Adelaide University when his father died. In need of money to support himself, his mother and two younger sisters, he found night work as an industrial chemist and made do on just three hours sleep a night so he could continue his final studies, albeit at a slower pace. His job also prevented him from joining the Royal Australian Navy. Although it was wartime and he made several attempts to enlist, the applications were rejected because it was classified a reserved occupation essential to the war effort.

After the war John headed overseas, working for the Anglo Iranian Oil Company (later to become British Petroleum), first in the Middle East for a brief period, and then England, where he was offered a prestigious research scholarship by the Leverhulme Trust. In an unprecedented response, he turned it down, telling people with his characteristic dry humour that he was planning to return to Australia because 'the price of gin was too high'. The real reason, says Cecily, was that he had been away from home for several years and was ready to go back. He also felt he could make a worthwhile contribution to Australia's industrial sector, which was entering a post-war boom period. John made the trip back home aboard an Anglo Iranian Oil Company tanker, technically serving as a member of the crew because passengers were not allowed. When he arrived he borrowed some money from his mother to buy a suit and headed to Melbourne for a job interview with the chemical and manufacturing giant ICI.

Cecily and John were instantly drawn to each other when they met. Within four months they were engaged, and in less than a year they were married. 'That was quick, wasn't it? No mucking around,' she states with satisfaction. 'You can just get lucky and he fitted in so well.' John followed protocol and formally asked her father for his daughter's hand in marriage during a visit to Barnoolut. While the two men were having this important discussion, the generator which provided electricity to the house failed and the lights went out. Another man well-known for his dry sense of humour, Edwin Crozier apparently readily agreed because Cecily was 'costing him a fortune in harness', and hurried John out to help restore the power.

The wedding ceremony was held at the red-bricked Anglican church in Casterton's main street on 18 December 1954, a 'most beautiful day'. Cecily walked down the short aisle in a dress of white silk organza with a wide fichu neckline and a full skirt dipping into a long train. As was only proper given the role she had played in bringing the bridal couple together, Bunty served as matron of honour, along with Jan, one of the twins Cecily met in England, now Mrs Alastair Angas and living in Clare in South Australia. After the morning ceremony, guests adjourned to Barnoolut for a reception in the garden. A passionate gardener, Nancy had overseen efforts to make sure it was looking its best. 'The Korean War was on and the price of wool was a pound a pound so no expense was spared,' Cecily admits.

After a very brief honeymoon, the newlyweds settled into life in Melbourne, although Cecily missed Barnoolut and the horses terribly. Their first child Edwina was born in November 1955, followed by John in October 1958. In 1962 the family packed up and moved across the Tasman for eight years, when John was appointed director of ICI's New Zealand operations. A third child, David, was born there in May 1964.

Edwina remembers her mother hated being even further away from Barnoolut, with visits restricted to once a year at Christmas. As compensation, Cecily rented a small property about an hour's drive from their home in Wellington and kept a few horses. 'She just couldn't cope without a farm,' says Edwina. 'She would be out in the garden and a plane would go over, and she would say, "There goes a plane load of happy people going to Australia".'

Smiling at the shared memory, Cecily concedes: 'I didn't mind it too much in the end. In fact it did me a lot of good, I think.'

The tables were turned in 1970 when the family returned to Melbourne, with fifteen-year-old Edwina distraught at leaving behind her friends. Knowing that it would only upset her, John forbade her friends from coming to the airport to say goodbye, but they came anyway, sobbing their hearts out. Edwina didn't stop crying until they were about halfway across the Tasman and a wise airline steward offered 'the young lady' a glass of champagne to drown her sorrows. 'That cheered her up considerably,' says Cecily.

❖ ❖ ❖

Like her brothers, Edwina grew up with 'two lives running parallel'. Their home was in inner-city Melbourne, but every holiday plus occasional weekends were spent at Wando Bridge. 'It was fabulous,' she says. Earliest memories revolve around a trip made without her parents at the age of three, while Cecily and John were coping with the arrival of her baby brother. On that occasion, Edwina travelled with her grandmother and stayed with the overseer Les Brant and his wife Peg in the small weatherboard cottage where they lived on the property with their children, Sally, Merrilyn and, later, Trudy.

Following family tradition, Edwina learnt to ride at a very early age. She was barely two the first time she sat on a horse. A prized family photo shows her on a large pony sitting snugly in a small cane chair-like contraption designed specifically to be strapped onto its back. She laughs looking at the black and white image, remarking that it is hard to find any photos in her mother's albums that do not include horses. When Edwina was older and able to sit on horseback by herself, she graduated to the family's Shetland pony, Banjo, or she would climb aboard a larger mount called Primrose, hugging closely to the Brant sisters. 'We would all get on the horse together,' Edwina recalls.

At other times, Sally would take charge of a horse and cart and gather them all up for trips around the property, dropping over to visit Digby and his wife Jill, who lived on the northern side of Barnoolut. 'We would go out and pick up the Crozier kids and we would go round in this cart, with my baby cousin William in a pram in the back. It was fantastic.'

Like Cecily, Edwina resented spending too much time indoors, although she doubts her mother would have given her the chance even if she had wanted it. Recalling the frustration of entertaining guests on Sundays, Edwina describes a way of living from a bygone era, providing an insight into her grandparents and family life at Barnoolut as Cecily must have experienced it too: 'When there was a lunch party we would have it in the dining room and it would take all day—first there was preparing the lunch, then we had the lunch, then we would go for a bit of a walk around the garden, and after that we would come back in and the trolley would come into the sitting room with a silver tea service, and we would sit around having tea and sponge cake. So it wiped the whole day off.'

A great homemaker, Nancy Crozier focused her energies on a well-run house and a well-kept garden, with the grandchildren roped in to help when they were visiting. 'She used to make me do the dusting and clean the silver . . . and during marmalade season we would make a batch every night. We would sit around the kitchen table chopping up the fruit. We seemed to have hundreds of jars of marmalade—it went on for months.'

Most afternoons were spent in the garden if the weather was fine. Aside from the formal ornamental beds and lawn, there were fruit trees and a large vegetable patch. Nancy didn't like any fruit going to waste so she collected whatever was ripe every day in a bucket and took it inside to preserve or make into jam. When Edwina was staying, she would join her grandmother dead-heading the roses or picking bunches of violets from the masses that grew in the extensive flowerbeds.

'She was a woman of routine; there was a sort of rhythm to the house,' Edwina explains. 'In those days the hot meal was always at lunchtime. So Poppa and I would be out working in the vegetable garden, and she would ring a big bell and we would come in.' Lunch was always served before one o'clock so the family could join the rest of rural Australia and listen to 'Blue Hills'. The legendary radio serial ran every weekday on the ABC for an extraordinary 27 years, its theme tune halting conversation for the next fifteen minutes. Countless farm families regulated their mealtimes so they could take in the latest instalment in the lives of a country doctor and his neighbours and friends. '"Blue Hills" was part of the routine,' says Edwina.

A fabulous cook who was always putting the Aga to good use, at supper time Nancy often served French-inspired culinary treats such as soufflés and fricassee. Afterwards there was a bowl of homegrown walnuts and fresh oranges. 'She ate her orange by cutting a lid on the top and then scooping out the flesh with a spoon. Poppa ate his orange by peeling it, cutting it up, and eating it with olive oil and salt. And then he would make percolated coffee . . . and we would drink it from little espresso cups. It was all very elegant, and I don't know how they had time to do it,' reflects Edwina.

Some of Edwina's favourite times were spent with her grandfather, who she loved enormously. 'He was very good with kids,' she says. 'We would sit out there in the courtyard on a Sunday. He would always clean all his boots and shoes and his wife's. They would all be lined up on the table and I would sit there with him, and we would chat away about all sorts of things.' Prominent in pony club circles as an instructor and judge, he was also Edwina's preferred riding instructor. 'He didn't yell at me as much as Mum did,' she says mischievously, looking sideways at her mother.

A man 'who never made a fuss about anything', Edwin Crozier died the way he had lived one afternoon in early 1979. Father and daughter were sitting together on the terrace at the front of the house, enjoying the sunshine and the view. They had just come back from the vegetable garden, where Edwin wanted her to pull some weeds out because he couldn't manage it any more. 'So I fixed all that up, and we were sitting outside, and it was a lovely day,' Cecily says. 'He was having a brandy and dry. "Oh," he said, "we must get your mother into a small car, she is dangerous." And I was laughing and all of a sudden his glass dropped. He was dead.' It was a shock for his family but a marvellous way to die, and Cecily feels lucky to have been with him when it happened. Her husband said Edwin must have had 'a hotline to God'.

Although he was responsible for running the property at the time her father died, her brother Digby was spending much of his time in Melbourne in those years, fulfilling his duties as a minister in the Liberal state government led by Sir Rupert Hamer. Passionate about politics from an early age, Digby served in the upper house for sixteen years, representing the local electorate until 1989. Edwin made his children equal partners in Barnoolut, arranging things so that the property would be divided equally between the two of them. Digby chose the northern half, which he named Kalabity, leaving Cecily with the section containing the main house. John decided to retire a few years ahead of schedule and in late 1979 they moved permanently to their half of the farm, with Nancy still in residence. She lived with them until the last few years of her life, when she broke her hip and moved into the aged care home in Casterton, where she died at the age of 96.

John instantly took to his new life as a farmer and member of a country community. He joined the local fire brigade, serving as its secretary and treasurer for some eighteen years and keeping meticulous records. A frugal man who was an excellent manager of money, he worked hard with the other volunteers to create a solid financial base for the brigade, and he kept a tight rein on farm expenditure too. 'Dad was very careful with money and if you could make do, you did,' Edwina says. 'For example, when we were back in Melbourne we had a very old television set which had lost its knob to change channels so we had a pair of pliers hanging off it. And we had a bit of four-by-two to keep the oven door closed.'

'He was very good at fixing things so if he could fix it he didn't replace it,' defends Cecily.

On the other hand, admits Edwina, after retiring he was more than happy to indulge Cecily's expensive love of horses and to encourage her to live the life at Barnoolut that she had always wanted.

Apart from breeding horses, that included her long-term commitment to judging at horse shows. 'I am not a competitive person, but I love comparing animals,' Cecily explains. Her mentor in judging for many years was the late Jean Luckock, who founded the Ennerdale Stud at Darlington in Victoria at about the same time the Barnoolut stud was created, and made a considerable contribution to Arabian horses being accepted in hunter and jumping events. Jean talked Cecily into judging at a children's gymkhana soon after returning from England. In 1956 both women became founding members of the Arab Horse Society of Australasia, now known as the Arabian Horse Society of Australia. Cecily later served for many years as a director on the society's board. She was made an honorary life member in 2001, and is now the official patron. According to Jean's granddaughter, Kate Luckock, who joined the board when Cecily retired and has since served as chairman, the honour was bestowed in recognition of her long-standing contribution to the society and as a judge at the highest level of competition. In a system which is strictly regulated to ensure judges are properly qualified, Cecily was part of a national panel of individuals permitted to judge at Australasian championships, capital city royal shows and international events. 'Her appointment as patron reflects the general respect for her integrity,' says Kate. 'She is much loved and admired among people who have been involved with Arabians for some time.'

Cecily retired from judging in 2000 when she was 70, but not before achieving one of the highlights of her career—judging at the Arabian horse show at Kempton Park in England in

1988. 'It was a terrific honour, really, and they treated me like a queen,' she recalls. 'All the stewards wore suits and bowler hats, and they called me Ma'am.'

Her son David went too, telling his mum, 'This I must see!'

Meanwhile, John didn't want to take on too much physical work, so they leased most of their share of Barnoolut and concentrated on running sheep and cattle on just a few acres. While her father favoured Corriedales and her brother merinos, Cecily wanted to run Suffolk sheep, a traditional English breed with striking black faces and legs. 'They are just so decorative, and they produce beautiful meat,' she explains.

A local livestock agent gave her the name of a farmer who could provide some ewes to get started. Cecily opened the negotiations when she ran into him at Les Brant's wake. Les had died suddenly from a heart attack, much to the devastation of the entire Crozier family. 'We were terribly upset about it, and I suppose I had a little bit too much to drink, as you do on those occasions, and I met this fellow and said, "I understand you can get me some Suffolk sheep".'

The deal was done and Cecily took delivery of a load of large-framed ewes. Some time later when she and John were struggling to handle them in the yards, John took great delight in teasing her: 'Do you mind next time you are buying sheep not to get drunk and buy the biggest sheep you can possibly find!'

John had his foibles too. He developed a reputation with the family for driving around the property 'like a bat out of hell' on a little grey Ferguson tractor, which was the farm's only form of transport. Cecily would usually ride behind in a trailer, bouncing over the paddocks. 'There was one occasion where the trailer came off the tractor, leaving Mum in the middle of the paddock while he was charging off,' recounts Edwina.

❖ ❖ ❖

John and Cecily farmed Barnoolut together for almost twenty years before he died from an aneurysm one night in 1999 at the age of 78. Cecily was bereft but in many ways at that point she came into her own as a farmer. 'She was able to run the place the way she wanted to and she has transformed it,' says Edwina. Asked where her mother started, she smiles and quickly replies: 'I will tell you exactly what she did. She spent a lot of money!'

Completely unashamed, Cecily nods slowly in affirmation.

Without John restricting the cash flow, she invested in much-needed infrastructure such as new fences and a new roof on the woolshed, and began renovating the pastures. Her children decided she needed a four-wheel-drive ute, which was the first purchase, although it was not made going home from the funeral as one apocryphal story would have it.

Edwina pointed out early on that the property needed to be set up so it was 'female friendly', so they designed new raceways that made it possible for one person to move livestock easily from one paddock to the other, and Cecily bought a Lyco Loader, a device fitted to the tailgate of the ute which allowed her to lift as much as 300 kilograms just by turning a handle. Interested in the latest ideas in farm management, she also engaged a farm adviser and agronomist to help her return the pastures to the quality for which Barnoolut was once known.

'My father was always very innovative, and being a scientist he would take on anything new he thought was worthwhile in the way of things like drench or fertilisers,' Cecily says. 'He was an early pioneer of pasture improvement and got pretty well round the whole place before the war broke out. I remember he said the first thing he did when he got here was to put on a hell of a lot of super. All the neighbours said he would go broke but he didn't. He ran sheep. He hated cattle, partly I think because where his family were up north they reckoned cattle would wreck the soil. I often cringe a bit when I think what he would say.'

John and Cecily had introduced cattle to the enterprise because they were easier to manage than sheep. They started with a herd of old shorthorn dairy cows and crossed them with Poll Hereford bulls to produce vealers for the beef market. Despite recent trends towards the black Angus cattle favoured by supermarkets, Cecily has stuck with the red Hereford breed. But she has switched from Suffolk sheep to White Suffolks, a relatively new all-white breed developed in Australia to suit local conditions. Cecily has 800 purebred ewes and her own stud but she hates the paperwork involved, especially these days when producers are looking for comprehensive data recording how animals perform before they are willing to buy them. 'I am not good on the figures,' she admits. 'I can look at a sheep and say if it's good or not, but the figures bamboozle me a little, and it's a lot of work.'

The admission highlights one of the few things she dislikes about being a farmer—the extraordinary amount of paperwork involved. Her husband, who was very good at it, used to say to her, 'I don't know what you're going to do when I die.'

'Well, I have found out,' she says. 'I put it off until I absolutely have to. I am only interested in the animals—the paperwork I think is just a total waste of time. I have somebody to do the books for me and they go to an accountant, but the amount of paper that comes across my desk! I am inclined to look at it and chuck it in the bin, and I chuck out things I shouldn't . . .'

The sheep and cattle take no notice when Cecily drives across Barnoolut in the middle of the afternoon making her usual daily rounds. She likes to check on things for herself every day, taking considerable pleasure from monitoring the progress of the livestock and pastures. 'I have had an awful lot of help,' she says, considering how much the farm has improved in recent years. Pepper usually joins her on these drives. Cecily has to lift her up into the front seat of the ute but the old dog still gets excited at the prospect of these expeditions, revealing flashes of puppy-hood as she skips ahead. Cecily inherited Pepper, or 'Pep' as she calls her, from her former son-in-law John Pettitt, who remains close to the family despite being divorced from Edwina.

Cecily peers through the rain that is now beating down steadily as she drives along the wide laneway connecting most of the farm. She notes with satisfaction that every dam on the place is full for the first time in more than ten years. It's something she did not expect to see again in her lifetime given the run of dry seasons in recent years. Unbelievably, one dam broke its banks in January. It has been dubbed 'Little Eildon', after one of Victoria's largest public dams. 'Water limits how much stock you can carry even in this area,' she says.

Taking a detour, Cecily drives through a wide double gate that separates the part of Barnoolut she is managing from the area leased to her neighbours, Scott Farquharson and his partner Penny. They bought Kalabity about four years ago when Digby and his wife retired to the coast. It is easy enough to tell where Cecily's boundary ends—Scott favours Angus cattle and there is a large mob just inside the gate.

Despite the weather, Cecily is heading to her favourite part of Barnoolut. She comes to the edge of a wide plateau and looks out across the valley and down along the meandering line of the Wando River. They can't authenticate it, but as her family understands it this is the very spot where Major Thomas Mitchell paused on his famous expedition across Victoria in 1836, and was so impressed by the landscape and its pastoral potential that he christened the region Australia Felix—Fortunate Australia. His subsequent reports led to the rapid occupation of south-western Victoria, with squatters quickly moving in and establishing 'some of the richest grazing land in the world'.[34]

On the way back to the house, Cecily stops to check on some heifers that have just delivered their first calves. She does a quick head count and notices a steel gate that is giving off a faint tingle of electricity. Obviously current is escaping from the electric fence somewhere along the line, and some repair work is needed. She also takes in with satisfaction a mob of ewes, many of them nursing twins and triplets. 'They are very good mothers,' she says. They are big sheep too. Cecily has been forbidden by her children to climb into the yards with them now during shearing in spring, or when they are drafting out the wether lambs to send them to the Hamilton saleyards before Christmas.

Parking the muddy ute undercover, Cecily settles into the final chores of the day. Well used to working in cold and wet conditions, she ignores the rain which is getting heavier and heads back out to the horse yard to give her three retired charges another small feed. On the way back, she collects some eggs from the chicken run, feeds the chooks and locks them up for the night. As the early winter dark begins to gather, she prepares the lambs' evening bottles. Cinnamon sits on the windowsill above the sink watching her whisk the powdered formula.

She pays particular attention as Cecily begins to sort out two large bottles of thick, yellow colostrum which her farm adviser, Andrew Speirs, dropped off earlier. He managed to source the precious liquid from a nearby dairy farmer so she would have it handy to give to motherless lambs during the first few days of their lives. A potent mix of antibodies, colostrum is crucial to the survival of newborn animals and the first thing they would normally drink from their mothers to build up their immune systems. When she was younger, Cecily milked some of her stud ewes soon after they gave birth to collect an emergency supply, which was poured into ice-cube trays and stored in the freezer. These days she is not able to get down low enough to milk a sheep, so substitute colostrum from a cow will have to do.

Having fed the horses, the chooks and the lambs, and put some extra pellets in a bowl for Cinnamon, Cecily now thinks about feeding herself and sitting down beside the Aga for 'a little nip of something' before dinner. She has had a busy weekend with visitors, and missed her usual afternoon nap today, so an early night is on the agenda. 'It sounds pathetic, I know,' she says, in defiance of her age, 'but I usually have an hour's rest after lunch.'

Recognising that their mother is starting to slow down a little, all three of Cecily's children are now playing an active part in helping her to manage the farm, dividing responsibilities to match their personal areas of expertise and inclination. They are equal partners in the enterprise, and none of them take it for granted. Their father lined them up when they were still at school and told them: 'Don't any of you think that you are going to come straight back to the farm and run it. You are all going to go and get a profession. I will put you through tertiary education and after that you are on your own.'

John is a civil engineer who is now living and working in Melbourne after travelling the globe with his career. Logically enough, he is in charge of infrastructure. In recent times, that has meant improving the farm's approach to managing water, renovating dams, installing new pumps and setting up reticulation systems that cover the whole property more efficiently so it is better able to withstand the dry seasons that hit even this temperate part of the world. Now the father of two grown-up children, John met his wife Cathy while he was working in England and they married in 1987, in the same church as his grandparents.

David, the youngest in the family, focuses his efforts on financial management, and is taking over responsibility for the sheep stud and its associated record keeping. He has a degree in agricultural economics from the University of New England at Armidale in New South Wales, topped up with qualifications in business accounting and financial planning. Over the years he has worked for banks and farm consultancies, and is in the process of establishing his own consulting business so he can work from home at Mount Buninyong, near Ballarat, where he lives with his wife Libby and their two children.

Edwina is the scientist of the family and has notched up an extraordinary career in both the commercial sector and the academic world. She can't remember consciously deciding to become a scientist. 'It was never really a burning ambition. I just did it and liked it, but it was also accepted in the family that science was a good thing to do,' she says. Although her father was a highly qualified industrial chemist, it was Edwina's grandfather who encouraged her the most to take an interest in something he was enthusiastic about all his life. At one stage she considered becoming a doctor, but in her final year of high school she became fascinated with genetics, the structure of DNA and how it carries inheritable traits. So she enrolled at the University of Melbourne in a bachelor of science degree, graduating with honours in biochemistry before moving on to a doctorate in microbiology.

While she loved the discipline of pure research, Edwina found herself drawn more towards research that could be applied and in 1988 she left academia to join one of Australia's first biotechnology companies. Over the next eleven years she played a key role in building Florigene Limited into a global commercial organisation recognised internationally for its pioneering work manipulating genes to create novel flower colours for the cut-flower market, most famously creating a blue carnation.

From entering the business as a research scientist, Edwina eventually became managing director, playing an important role in marketing Florigene and its products to the world, securing funding and managing an enterprise that contracted growers across six continents. The job carried enormous pressure and involved a great deal of travel, but she gained considerable satisfaction from working with excellent researchers and finding ways to capture the commercial value of their discoveries.

When the company was eventually sold, Edwina decided it was time for a change of direction. Perhaps inevitably she found herself returning to the academic world, where she was offered the position of deputy vice chancellor of research at the University of Adelaide. 'God knows why I answered the ad. I didn't even really know what a deputy vice chancellor of research was,' she jokes.

Despite her background, it took Edwina a while to settle back into university life, its protocols and decision-making processes. 'When you're running a small company you talk to people and you make decisions on the spot. At universities you have to write a dissertation,' she says. 'At one stage I abolished a committee. It was a year before anyone realised it was one of those committees universities had to have but no-one had noticed!'

After four years in Adelaide, Edwina was appointed to the same position at Monash in 2004 and returned to Melbourne. She still wonders at times what the job is really about, although someone once described it by saying, 'She goes to a lot of meetings'. In fact, Edwina is second in charge of the largest university in the country, with a budget of tens of millions of dollars. She is responsible for the research performance of the university, which in itself is quite a task. One of the most prestigious universities in the country, with 15 000 staff and 62 000 students, Monash has an extensive program embracing 150 fields of study and 100 research centres. As well as Victoria, there are campuses in Malaysia and South Africa, a research and teaching centre in Italy and a graduate research school in India.

A former member of the Australian Research Council, at one stage Edwina also served on the board of one of the world's most remarkable agricultural research facilities, the International Maize and Wheat Improvement Centre, commonly known by its Spanish acronym, CIMMYT, in Mexico. A virtual 'United Nations' of scientists, it was founded by the father of the Green Revolution, Dr Norman Borlaug.

Shrugging off the pressures of a demanding career, Edwina points out that her work has become easier with experience and help from a lot of very good people. Yes, there are a lot of meetings and long hours, but there have been some unexpected bonuses along the way. Like the ritzy pyjamas decorated with diamantes that she scored after being upgraded to first class on a recent flight to Chicago. Mind you, it was one of the few bright spots in a rushed trip that had her flying to America and back in just four days for a one-day meeting.

With no people to manage and no meetings to attend, at Barnoolut Edwina can relax and spend time with her mother, sitting at the kitchen table, or getting out onto the farm and doing some physically satisfying work. Down-to-earth like Cecily and with the same ready laugh, for all her seniority on weekdays Edwina is happy to serve as general factotum at Barnoolut, taking on anything that needs doing during her frequent weekend visits, from cleaning out the chook shed to pulling weeds in the garden. Far from being a passionate gardener like her grandmother, she is none-the-less committed to restoring the garden and the house to their 'former glory'.

At this stage her plan is to move to Wando Bridge within the next five years. 'The question is when. I don't want to cramp Mum's style,' she says wryly. Until then she intends to keep working and earn as much money as she can to contribute to the cost of renovating the big rambling house, which has changed little in her lifetime. 'In one way it's a very badly designed house, but we love it and we don't want to wreck the character of it, so we keep dithering about what to do,' Edwina says.

Inevitably, Cecily's thoughts are turning more and more to the time she might have to retire completely from active involvement in running the land she loves so much. She dreads the thought of ending her days in a nursing home, and would dearly love to 'go out with her boots on'. She and John worked hard to create a sanctuary that their children and grandchildren could retreat to when they were ready, and she is delighted the family seems to love Barnoolut too. 'It has always been here to come back to. I couldn't have borne for it not to be here,' she says. 'I had a charmed growing-up and I suppose it catches up with you sometime, but I am very lucky to still be here.'

7

THE FIGHT FOR LIFE

Catherine Bird, Willalooka, South Australia

Driving into Keith early on a warm Tuesday night, it's clear something unusual is happening in the quiet country town. The roadsides are crammed with cars, farm utes and hefty four-wheel drives. Two minibuses are disgorging passengers outside the town's main community hall, which is the focal point of activity. People are walking purposefully towards it like ants drawn compulsively to their nest. Inside the foyer, they line up at a table to sign forms or pause to chat with friends and neighbours before making their way into the large auditorium, which is filling steadily. There is a low-key buzz of anticipation in the air as a small group of officials starts to gather on the stage and sit at a long table angled slightly to the crowd.

The people of Keith and surrounding districts in the South East of South Australia are gathering for an event that reflects the cohesiveness and determination of a country community under siege. Over the coming two hours, in what proves to be an inspiring example of grass-roots activism, local citizens conduct themselves with dignity and good humour as they consider an issue of fundamental importance to rural communities across the nation. Like many other country towns, Keith is fighting desperately to hang on to its health services. While city dwellers lobby for extra beds at their hospitals, Keith is struggling to keep any hospital at all. While doctors compete to make a living in suburban clinics oversupplied with practitioners, residents in the Keith area often wait for days to see one of two overworked GPs, grateful they at least have resident doctors when many smaller regional towns do not.

Now the state government has announced it is cutting funds to the small community-run hospital, which residents fear will not only lead to the facility closing, but jeopardise the viability of the town's medical centre. Aged-care patients resident in the hospital will have to move away from family and friends, more than 50 jobs will be lost, and there will be no emergency care close at hand for people injured in the road accidents that frequently occur along the two major highways passing through the town. An even bigger fear is that once the hospital and the jobs go, the very fabric of the town itself will begin to pull apart. All this lost to save the state government about $370 000 a year.

Sitting quietly among the 800 or so people who have packed the hall to learn more about recent negotiations with the government is a slightly built blonde, dressed in a stylish white shirt and jeans, long hair pulled back from her face. Although everyone in the hall is keenly interested in the proceedings, it is fair to say that Catherine Bird has more reason than most to want to see the hospital remain open. Fourteen years ago it saved her life.

❖ ❖ ❖

Catherine Bird was a station brat. She grew up on Indiana, a cattle property covering almost 3000 square kilometres east of Alice Springs on the edge of the Simpson Desert, where she ran wild and free like the brumbies that her father occasionally rounded up, trained and sold for extra income. The middle of five children, she has two older sisters, Rebecca and Tricia, and a younger brother and sister, David and Melanie.

Their father Fred Bird came from remarkable stock. His father, Jim 'Squire' Bird, was originally from Mount Gambier in South Australia. Like many boys of the era, Squire started work at the age of thirteen, chopping wood for 5 shillings a week. At nineteen he headed for Western Australia and worked as a drover, some years later ending up in Darwin where he turned his hand to anything going 'except piano tuning' and became known as a champion amateur boxer.[35] In 1926, after several stints droving and trading sheep, cattle and horses in Queensland and the Territory, he bought Bushy Park, north of Alice Springs. It was unimproved at the time and thought to lack water, but he sank a bore and struck a good supply.

Squire met his future wife when he called into a neighbouring station while droving cattle. Pearl was the youngest daughter of Fred Price, who served as postmaster at the Alice Springs Telegraph Station for about eight years, and Isabelle Hesketh, a young woman from Nottingham in England whose extraordinary 'pluck' won her considerable respect across central Australia and provided daily inspiration for Catherine's mother. After her husband died in 1924, leaving her with four children, Isabelle decided to go ahead and realise an ambition the couple had shared to take up station life. With help from a stockman and her children, she drove 200 sheep about a thousand kilometres through central Australia, from the Oodnadatta railhead to Harper Springs, north-east of Alice. One of two properties her husband had leased before his death, it was virtually undeveloped when they arrived, with only a well and a trough to get them started and no buildings. Isabelle soon decided to move further west to the second block because it was more suited to sheep. She named it Woola Downs.[36]

By the time Squire and Pearl were married in October 1927, Isabelle was running a thousand sheep, as well as cattle and goats. Reporting on her achievements, Darwin's *Northern Standard* newspaper wondered at the courage and abilities of the Price women, who tackled all the stockwork themselves, including branding and shearing. Pearl's sister Molly was recognised as 'one of the best riders in the Northern Territory and in the opinion of outback pastoralists . . . as accomplished and as useful as any skilled stationhand' and all three women were considered excellent trackers who could 'tell in an instant the tracks of animals and reptiles'.[37] The report was quick to point out that, although doing the work of men, the daughters were also 'accomplished in the art of housecraft, and have learnt from their mother how to cook, to make their own dresses, and be skilled pianists'.

Squire returned to his birthplace with Pearl for their wedding. They were married at the tiny Rosaville Church in Mount Gambier, only two hours drive from where Catherine farms today, although she did not know of the regional connection until very recently. The groom was more than twenty years older than his bride, who was only eighteen. In the autobiography she wrote many years later with help from her daughter, Pearl explains it was far from a love match.[38] She only agreed to marry the much older man because Isabelle thought he would look after her.

The couple had four children, including Catherine's father, who was the oldest and born at Bushy Park in 1928. They stayed together until the 1940s, when Squire sold the property without telling Pearl, who was sick and visiting a specialist in Adelaide.

After spending some time at Kapunda in South Australia, Squire returned to Alice Springs and in 1952 helped his oldest son secure the lease for Indiana, an undeveloped station at the eastern end of the MacDonnell Ranges, where they were joined for a while by Fred's younger brother Tom, who helped drill bores, put up fences and clear tracks.

Now 83 and living in Keith, Catherine's mother Margaret was a city girl from what became the northern Adelaide suburb of Salisbury. A trained bookkeeper, she was in her mid-twenties when she headed to Alice Springs to work in the office of Loutit's Emporium. The general store was a major source of supplies for station people and it did not take her long to meet Fred Bird. They looked at each other with a strong sense of recognition, and realised they had often caught the same train during a period when Fred lived at Gawler and was studying engineering in the city and Margaret was employed as a bookkeeper at Harris Scarfes department store.

The couple married in 1957 and Margaret found herself having to adapt quite quickly to an isolated life without any of the frills she had taken for granted while growing up. After a honeymoon to the eastern states of Australia looking at bulls, they returned to Alice Springs where Fred left her to organise enough food supplies for three months while he went off to see the livestock agent. Margaret had no idea where to start, but luckily a friend, who had been her bridesmaid, worked in Loutit's grocery department and was able to offer advice.

Piling everything into the back of a ute, the newlyweds headed out of town on the four-hour journey to Indiana, following what was then only a track winding around the hills of the MacDonnell Ranges, which stretch for more than 600 kilometres either side of Alice. Just like Isabelle and Pearl had experienced before her, there was no homestead waiting for Margaret. For the next few weeks she lived in the back of the ute, while Fred built a small tin shelter under a big gum tree. 'There was a tent but that was for the stores, and I didn't go in there very often because my husband kept a python there to keep the mice down,' says Margaret, who found coping with snakes, harmless or not, the worst part of station life.

After a few weeks, Fred bought Margaret a small caravan, which offered some privacy from the communal camp life they shared with stationhands and Squire, who lived with them at Indiana until he died in the late 1960s. Catherine remembers the caravan being round and little. Years later she and her sisters used it as a cubbyhouse. 'It was revolting,' she says. 'It was so small Mum ironed the pillowcases and sheets and things so they were as flat as possible and would fit in the cupboards.'

Meanwhile, Margaret had to learn how to cook over a campfire and get used to an endless diet of beef, which the men insisted on having even for breakfast. They would kill one of the cattle every now and then, and fit as much of it as they could into a small kerosene-powered fridge. 'But you only had fresh meat for a week or so. We had to salt the rest of it,' Margaret says. Kitchen facilities improved significantly when a bloke visiting the station sold the Birds an old, green Meters wood oven, which they set up at the campsite. It wasn't in very good condition but Margaret loved the 'beautiful old stove', which baked wonderful bread.

She didn't particularly enjoy the wretched flies that hovered around in swirling blankets while food was being prepared, or the scorpions that emerged after it rained, but it was the snakes that worried her most, particularly after the children were born. She still has the horrors thinking about one that forced its way in through the homestead back door. By the time she found the spade kept handy to despatch such unwanted visitors, the snake had disappeared under a cupboard in the kitchen. What worried her most was that it must have come straight past her youngest child, who had just run out the door into the darkness with bare feet.

Despite the lack of creature comforts, especially in the early years, Margaret loved her life with Fred. 'Every day was an adventure because everything was so new to me,' she says. 'I thought it would be a rather wonderful life and he was a wonderful person, and it turned out very well. We had a wonderful time together building it up from nothing, and I was lucky. We didn't have children for three years or so and that gave me time to learn about life on a station.' She was never lonely despite the isolation, even when Fred was out at the camps. 'There was always something to do, and I was used to it.'

With a family on the way, the Birds moved into their first proper home. Although it was only a tin shed, it had a lovely view of the rocky hills of Harts Range and was a significant improvement on the caravan and campsite. 'My dad and mum used to come up in the wintertime,' Margaret says. 'Dad was a carpenter, and one year Fred had all the materials teed up and Dad lined the shed for us, and put in a ceiling and bigger windows so it looked like a real house.'

The homestead gradually expanded to accommodate the five children who arrived in ten years, although it still had an outside toilet and bathroom until Catherine was about eight, relying for hot water on a 'donkey boiler', basically a drum mounted above a fire. 'When we lit the fire too hot, the pipes used to burst and the water would spray everywhere so we couldn't have a hot bath,' she recalls.

A considerate husband and father, Fred bought additional 'luxuries' for his family as soon as he sold some cattle and money became available. Perhaps his greatest triumph was installing a stove fuelled with gas from a cylinder—believed to be the first in the Northern Territory. Margaret even had a washing machine powered by a small petrol engine that had to be kick-started, to help clean the endless stream of dirty nappies and grimy work clothes. As soon as a generator was installed to provide electricity to the homestead, her husband replaced it with an electric washing machine. 'Fred heard about these washing machines before I did and went and bought one. I was wonderfully looked after,' Margaret says.

But he wasn't necessarily all that helpful when it came to encouraging the children in their studies. 'They were all horse mad and trying to keep them in the schoolroom at mustering time was impossible,' she says. 'Fred would put his head around the schoolroom door and say he was going to do a bit of mustering, and they were gone.' Most of the children learnt to ride on an old horse called Jimmy or a big black mare named Black Beauty before graduating to their own horses, which were usually brumbies caught on the station and broken in by Fred and the stockmen. The brumbies were beautiful animals bred from some of the best horses in the area, thanks to the well-known tendency of a bloke who camped on Indiana before the Birds arrived and used to 'borrow' horses from neighbouring stations. He had a good eye for horse flesh, and so did Fred, who made sure a quality stallion or two was mixed with the wild horses to continually improve the strain. One brumby sold at auction after leaving Indiana went on to become one of Australia's top showjumpers; it was such a classy horse the owner never suspected its background. Years later she identified the station brand and wrote to the Birds looking for another with the same breeding. 'We couldn't tell her it was some brumby brought in from the Simpson Desert,' says Catherine.

Like her siblings, Catherine learnt to ride at a very early age. Born on 26 November 1965, she was only four when she set out with her father for a week of mustering, bouncing around on Black Beauty in an adult-sized stocksaddle with no stirrups and her legs sticking out to the sides. Fred admired his daughter's determination and bought a more suitable saddle for her fifth birthday. Catherine loved the stockwork and staying out in the mustering camps, particularly as she got older and started noticing some of the stockmen were 'pretty hot'. Even before then, mustering was much preferable to staying at home and doing schoolwork.

All five children began their education through School of the Air, a correspondence school for isolated children which combined written work with sessions over the radio several times a week, led by teachers based in Alice Springs. They were supervised by a governess, when their mother could find one willing to live in such an isolated location, but more often than not Margaret was on her own and had to take charge. She 'tried to keep a routine', and says that one advantage of School of the Air was if the children missed out for a few days they could always catch up because the schoolwork was sent off fortnightly on the mail plane.

Catherine remembers a few governesses fondly, but she and her siblings questioned some of their mother's recruits. At one stage Margaret packed up the younger children and took them to Adelaide, where they stayed at the Grosvenor Hotel on North Terrace, a traditional favourite for many years with country families visiting the city, while she interviewed prospective candidates. One showed up in rolled-up jeans, bright red socks, desert boots with bright yellow shoelaces, and wearing her hair in pigtails sticking out either side of her head. While the children were not impressed with her fashion sense, even though it was the 1970s and vaguely in vogue, it was the fact she exhibited 'no warm and fuzzy' interest in them at all that really turned them off. Another candidate who came across as nice and friendly was their preferred choice. They were mystified when Margaret picked the first prospect, who proved a disaster and left the station within weeks. Meanwhile, a neighbouring station employed the children's choice, one of the best governesses that station ever had.

The highlight of the year for the whole family was the picnic race meeting held at Harts Range about 100 kilometres away. Station people travelled in from huge distances for three days of racing and all the associated social events. For the Bird children it was a rare opportunity to leave the station and play with others their own age. Apart from the mail plane which flew in every Saturday to deliver and collect mail, they led an extremely isolated existence, usually only heading into Alice twice a year or so on a shopping trip. Visitors to the station were rare too, if you discounted the occasional lost tourist or passengers that stopped briefly on the way through in the mail plane.

Treating it as an annual holiday, the Birds camped at the Harts Range track for an entire week, putting up their tent alongside families from neighbouring stations who had become good friends because they were about the same age and shared similar experiences. Several men in the area had married town girls at about the same time. 'We all met once a year at Harts Range and we all camped together in what was called Pregnant Alley, because one or two of us were always pregnant,' recalls Margaret. When managing five young children in tents became too much, Fred put up a large shed; it is still standing and being used by David and his family, who now run Indiana.

Fred and the children all competed in the various races and gymkhana events held as part of the gathering. For Catherine, a highlight was the mile-long foot race run around the track used by the horses and ending at the finishing post in front of the crowd. A 'skinny little rabbit of a thing', she loved to run, and still does. At the age of about eight she beat a mixed field of children and adults of all ages to take out the event, although it was not without cost. 'I had bare feet because I didn't have any runners and I wasn't going to do it in my riding boots. When I finished the race I had actually run the soles off my feet and my feet were bleeding,' she says.

Catherine was taken to the first-aid tent, where a volunteer provided treatment. Mistaking his patient for a boy, he called her 'matey'. Outraged, she told him: 'I am not a matey, I am a girl!' Vowing quietly to herself that from then on she would make a bit of an effort to dress more like a girl, she hobbled outside. In reality, Catherine says, little changed. As a child, she was never interested in being a 'girlie girl' and was always considered a tomboy. 'We were feral little station kids. We really were,' she confesses. 'I had a boy's haircut, we wore nothing but boy's clothes and I had bare feet 90 per cent of the time.'

Margaret remembers her daughter as an indomitable spirit always up to mischief. 'She was game for anything,' she says. 'You couldn't scare her with horses, or push bikes, or the four-wheel motorbikes we had to use when it was too wet to get around on anything else. All the children had to have a try at anything, but Catherine was the one I worried about later on when she went to work in Alice Springs. She used to get into a bit of strife.'

While Margaret says the children were all pretty 'straight-forward' and didn't attempt to hide any misdeeds from their parents, none of them forgave her for sending them off to boarding school. 'They hated me for it,' she admits. Now a parent herself, Catherine says she could never imagine sending her own children away even though it was a pretty typical experience for most station children in those days. It was inevitable in central Australia if you wanted your children to have a sound education and the opportunity to socialise with others the same age.

There is no doubt boarding school came as a tremendous shock to Catherine. She was only nine and her brother seven when their mother took them both to St Philip's College in Alice

Springs one day, and—as it seemed to them at the time—left without explanation. Looking back at that day, Catherine recollects: 'It was bloody horrendous. I will never forget it. I can still remember sitting in this office. My mum was talking to the principal, but I had no idea who he was. She was just talking to this man over the other side of the desk, and they were having this good old yackety yackety yack. My brother and I just sat there and thought, "Where are we? What are we doing here?" We had no idea what this place was, and the conversation didn't seem to involve us in any way.'

Now a fully fledged boarding school, at the time St Philip's was only a residential college set up by the Presbyterian, Methodist and Congregational churches to provide accommodation for children from across central Australia so they could attend the government schools in Alice Springs. Catherine was assigned a bed in the girl's dormitory, where she shared a room with about half a dozen other girls of similar age. While she later made some good friends, there didn't seem to be much of an induction process. 'I was beside myself because I didn't get lunch for two weeks because I had no idea where to get lunch from. No-one told me, no-one explained a bloody thing, not even the house mistresses. I was starving, and the meals were disgusting. Everything was boiled and just so foul.'

It could have been worse. Rebecca and Tricia were sent all the way to Adelaide, where they attended Wilderness school, and had to wear ties, jackets, hats and gloves. Catherine and David at least got to spend occasional Sundays with their father's brother Tom and his wife Pat, who lived in Alice. They would collect the two children, take them to church at the local Salvation Army, and then provide a substantial home-cooked meal. 'We hated church, but Uncle Tom and Aunty Pat were good value, and the food was better than boarding school, and we could eat more,' Catherine says frankly. All the children went home to Indiana for school holidays, desperate to get back to the station, the family and the horses.

For Catherine, the saving grace of her primary school years was sports. She turned out to be very athletic, playing softball with the seniors after an older girl offered to teach her the game. She ran with the older students too. 'I love running,' she reiterates, explaining that she still jogs 8.5 kilometres around the farm three or four times a week and is about to tackle her first half-marathon in Melbourne. 'I could run from here to Darwin if you asked me to,' she says. At one stage, she was selected to compete in the 800-metre race at Tennant Creek during the Northern Territory trials for primary school students. She flogged the rest of the field by half a lap.

Conscious that none of the children were enjoying boarding school, Fred and Margaret decided to bring them all home until they were a bit older. So after a little more than two years at St Philip's, Catherine returned to the station and studied via School of the Air. The respite lasted until she was fourteen, when she made the mistake of falling in love with one of the stationhands and her parents found out. 'He was nineteen and gorgeous—really hot, like Johnny Depp hot, and a really nice bloke, but it was a very forbidden relationship. He got the sack and I was sent to boarding school—again,' she says, laughing.

This time the school was even further away, at Charters Towers in Queensland. The Birds chose St Gabriel's because it had a good reputation with station families and was set in an outback country town, with most of the students coming from similar backgrounds. Margaret figured this would make adjusting easier and she was right. The downside was the amount of travel involved. 'It took us a day to drive into Alice Springs, and then all the next day to get there. We had to fly to Mount Isa, then to Cairns and down to Townsville, then we had to travel by bus from Townsville,' says Catherine. 'It was so far we couldn't go home for weekends or anything.' And it was the early 80s, long before social media, mobile phones and email made it easy for students to stay in touch with their families and lessen the feelings of homesickness. 'We had to get permission to use the phone. It was like prison. We had to write letters home every week but other than that we didn't have any contact with our parents at all.'

The whole experience of leaving home to go to school fundamentally changed how Catherine wanted to live her life. 'There was no way I was going to live that life again where you had to be sent away to do anything. And also I didn't want to have children in that sort of situation either, much as I loved station life,' she says. 'I missed the station, but I wanted to work in Alice Springs.'

Thinking that hairdressing might be 'funky', at the age of seventeen she decided to apply for an apprenticeship at the biggest salon in town. 'It was the best option to get out of school,' she confesses.

Catherine was one of sixteen girls employed by the highly successful business, which served regular clients from across the Territory as well as visiting tourists. The salon also had a contract to look after employees at the nearby Pine Gap defence facility, jointly operated by the Australian and United States governments. 'It was great fun. The social life was amazing. The best thing was on Saturdays if we had a wedding, we used to serve champagne and biscuits, and we could share it with the bridal party. It was great. We did lots of weddings and fashion parades—I loved all that sort of stuff.'

Although they partied hard the staff also worked hard, starting at eight in the morning and continuing until six o'clock every weekday except Mondays, when they finished early in compensation for working Saturdays too. 'By the time we were finished we were exhausted, and the wages were crap so I used to do waitressing as well. We all had two or three extra jobs when we were apprentices.'

Catherine loved the creative side of her work, and proved particularly talented at men's haircuts and women's cuts and colouring. She and another apprentice also entered quite a few competitions, and ended up winning one that offered an all-expenses paid trip to the new Cable Beach resort at Broome. Much to the girls' surprise the bosses claimed the prize and went without either of them. 'Do you think we were spewing? We were disgusted. We had stayed behind every night to prepare for the competition and done all the work.'

After she finished her four-year apprenticeship, Catherine was lured away by another salon in town. Her original boss didn't want her to leave, but she was starting a new phase in her personal life and thought a change in scene at work might be a good idea too. She had just married.

Catherine met Les one night at the Alice Springs Casino when she was out with some friends. A year or so later they were engaged, and in 1987 they married. Meanwhile, Les trained as a constable in the Northern Territory police force. Not long after the wedding, he was transferred to Yuendumu, about 300 kilometres and six hours drive north-west of Alice Springs on the Tanami Track. It was a big change for them both and a tough gig for a young policeman more or less straight out of the academy. Recognised as one of the larger remote communities in central Australia, Yuendumu had a population of a few hundred, mostly Indigenous people from the Walpiri tribe, when they arrived. Like many remote communities it was battling problems relating to alcohol abuse, health, education and childcare. 'It was certainly interesting,' says Catherine with brief understatement.

Catherine found herself being accepted relatively easily because some of the older members of the Walpiri tribe knew her father, or had known and worked for her grandfather. 'They were interesting characters and had a lot of respect for Dad,' she says. She and Les also earnt respect because they helped cook and prepare hot meals for local families to make sure the children had some decent food to eat at least once a week. Up to 100 packs of meals like roast chicken and vegetables with gravy were prepared on Thursdays, Fridays and Saturdays.

Catherine and Les were still living in Yuendumu when both their children were born, not without drama. Catherine was eight and a half months pregnant when she rolled the car while travelling back from Alice Springs on the Tanami Track, which has a reputation as one of the worst roads in Australia. She was okay, but ended up in hospital the next night giving birth to Renee. She was born in September 1989. Brett followed almost two years later in July 1991.

Somewhere in between, Catherine began to realise her marriage was going 'pear-shaped'. 'Basically, within a week of Renee being born, for some reason Les became really control-ling and quite unfriendly and demanding. To make it worse, Renee was colicky for six months, so I had a screaming baby and an arsehole of a husband, and I found it pretty hard,' she says bluntly. Catherine's family were too far away to help, but luckily she had a neighbour who came over and lent a hand as often as possible, while she found her feet as a new mother. Eventually she became more confident and Renee started to cry less too, which also helped to reduce tensions with Les. But the problems flared up again when Brett was about six months old and developed tonsillitis and a perforated eardrum. He was crying frequently in pain and distress, and Les started becoming even more aggressive and controlling than before.

'Brett had been the most amazing, perfect baby in the world. He didn't cry. It was feed, sleep, be happy—that was it . . . But from six to eight months old, he had tonsillitis nonstop for about a year. The doctors said they wouldn't take his tonsils out because they didn't do that any more, and they wanted us to wait until he grew out of it. Eventually I took him to a specialist and stood in the doorway until he would see me. He agreed to take the tonsils out straight away and basically Brett hasn't been sick since.'

By this time, Les had left the police force and they were living at Mildura in northern Victoria. When he couldn't find work, he bought a bakery but it proved to be an unwise investment and they lost their house as well as the business. After leaving the Alice, they moved five times in two years and lived in three different states before ending up in Queensland. 'It was bloody terrible, it really was,' Catherine says.

When her father died of cancer in December 1994, she decided she'd had enough. Brooking no discussion, she told Les she was moving with the children to a property her parents had bought at Willalooka in the south-east region of South Australia. The Birds had purchased it about ten years before during a run of bad years on the station, to provide a reliable backup for fattening cattle. Catherine says, 'When I came here I said, "That's it, I belong here."'

Named Indiana after its 'parent' property in the Northern Territory, the farm at Willalooka is tucked away off the Riddoch Highway, south-west of Keith. Dense smatterings of scrubby gum trees cover most of the paddocks, which are green and saturated after a thankfully wet winter. While this is normally a reliable area when it comes to rainfall, the past few years have been relatively dry and the property seemed to miss out on most of the autumn rain that inundated areas further south. Now the lower-lying sections of some paddocks are flooded. Black swans and wild ducks paddle on sheets of grey water that reflect a leaden southern sky promising more rain to come, and the cattle are huddling together to ward off the cold.

The contrast to the place where Catherine grew up could not be greater. Not only is the climate cooler, but the colours, tones and textures of the landscape, the scale of farming, and the sense of isolation are vastly different too. This Indiana lies only fifteen minutes drive from the nearest rural township and less than three hours easy drive from the city of Adelaide, which Catherine visits regularly. While Indiana station sprawls across 3000 square kilometres, its namesake covers less than 10 square kilometres—966 hectares, to be precise. A well-maintained bitumen road reaches to within a short distance of the front gate and a driveway lined with desert ash trees. The rugged stony outcrops of the MacDonnell Ranges have been exchanged for smooth, low-lying hills, and gentle dips and hollows that provide shelter for the cattle. Instead of the tough native tussock grasses that find a foothold in the station's dry, ochre sands, pale sandy loam soils nurture dense pastures of introduced grasses and clovers.

This wasn't always the case. The area around Keith is part of the Ninety Mile Desert, which was once considered of very little use for grazing, although at first sight it did not look like a desert at all, especially compared with the unmistakable sands of the Simpson. But despite a reasonably high rainfall, pastures and livestock failed to thrive here until scientists in the 1940s uncovered serious trace element deficiencies in the ancient soils. The AMP Society set up a famous agricultural development scheme, which included part of Indiana, to bring life to the desert. Over the next few years thousands of hectares were cleared, sown to pasture and spread with modern fertilisers containing the missing trace elements. Hundreds of farmers and soldier settlers came to the region to take up new land.

When Catherine arrived at Willalooka in January 1995 with Les, Renee and Brett in tow, the property was a fairly conventional beef operation running a few hundred *Bos indicus* cattle brought down from the station. For most of the past ten years, it had been managed by Catherine's elder sister Tricia and her husband Lance, but they had left the year before to return to the Territory. A new manager had been employed to look after things, and recognising they had a lot to learn, Catherine and Les decided to keep him on for the first year at least while they found their feet. By then Margaret was also living on the farm in a small house close to the main homestead, and so was Melanie, who had moved into another house on the property with her husband Vince. For the next two years Catherine, Les and Melanie worked alongside each other. Catherine was not happy in her marriage, but she found reasonable contentment focusing on her children and the farm work until one fateful Tuesday afternoon in 1997.

The New Year was not quite 21 days old when Catherine headed out into the paddock with her younger sister Melanie. After three days of incredibly hot weather, climbing to almost 42 degrees, a cool change was blowing in and Catherine was keen to get started on replacing a short strip of fence on the other side of the farm. The two sisters loaded some new treated pine posts into a small trailer attached to the farm's four-wheel motorbike, and set off. Dressed in workboots, jeans and a long-sleeved, heavy-duty work shirt, Catherine rode the quad bike, with her two children on the back. Melanie followed on the old tractor, which had a post-hole digger mounted to the left of its engine, just in front of the big rear tyre.

Out in the paddock Melanie sat on the tractor and oper-ated the post-hole digger, while Catherine worked alongside, measuring distances between posts and making sure the augur was in the right place. Five-year-old Brett stood behind her, determined to help place the new posts despite his small stature. Renee was perched beside her aunty Melanie singing a favourite song: 'Daddy's taking us to the zoo tomorrow, the zoo tomorrow, the zoo tomorrow. Daddy's taking us to the zoo tomorrow. We can stay all day . . .'

They had only completed a couple of holes when Catherine noticed some timber was coming up out of the ground and was caught in the augur. Without intention, they were drilling in the exact same place as an old gum post from the original fence; the augur was bringing up part of the post which had rotted off at ground level. Her hands protected by thick work gloves, Catherine took a step closer to the machinery and bent down to grab the timber and pull it out of the way. In bending down she slipped a little and her baseball cap came off, releasing the ponytail always worn out on the farm to keep her hair out of the way. 'I have never been able to work out how the cap came off but it could have been because I had really long and such thick hair that my caps would never sit down properly, or it could have been because it was a really windy day,' she says with a quiet calm that belies the horror to come.

Catherine remembers with absolute clarity every detail of what happened next. As the cap came off, her ponytail blew forward and the ends of her long, blond hair stuck to the black grease on the augur. 'Oh shit, this isn't going to be good,' she thought, scrabbling desperately through the clumsiness of the gloves to free her hair, while she yelled to get Melanie's attention. In hindsight she wonders if she managed to make any noise at all in her terror, or whether the screams were trapped silently in her throat.

As the augur continued to turn slowly, tunnelling into the soil below, her hair became inextricably tangled, pulling her face closer and closer to the sharp, curved blades. 'So I hang on to my face and start pulling back, and that is when I felt my scalp coming off. It felt like a Chinese burn, or a serrated knife going across your skin, and it burnt like shit. And then I could actually feel the warm blood coming down. My heart was going a thousand miles an hour and the blood was pouring down my chest,' describes Catherine, the pace of her words speeding up as if to mirror the increasing rate of her heartbeat.

Although in reality it must only have been seconds since her hair first caught, at the time Catherine had the sensation everything was unfolding in slow motion. She remembers with film-like quality every single turn of the augur just centimetres from her face. She remembers wondering why Melanie wasn't listening to her and switching off the machinery. She remembers very clearly thinking, 'Oh my God, the kids are seeing this.' And just as she could feel the blade start to cut into the side of her face, she remembers realising that if the augur didn't stop now, she was going to die.

With that thought everything seemed to stop. Instead of the noise of the engine there was total silence. The smell of the warm earth coming up through the augur disappeared. The wind no longer blew. She even stopped seeing the ugly blades in front of her. Instead she was looking at the faces of her mother, Melanie and Les. In what she later came to realise was a near-death experience, she started saying goodbye to the important people in her life, but not her children; books she has since read about the subject reveal that for some reason people rarely say goodbye to loved ones who still need them.

A sense of perfect, comforting nothingness enveloped Catherine. 'I can feel the sensation now as I'm talking about it,' she says, struggling to find the words that will accurately convey her experience. 'It's the hardest thing to explain to someone who hasn't been there. If I was to say I had a thumping headache, people would know what I was talking about because they have probably had one . . . Try to imagine a sensation that covers your whole body, and you can feel nothing else apart from knowing that you are one hundred per cent fine, at peace and secure . . . Like a baby wrapped up in a bunny rug—that sensation of being so secure and totally safe. That is what it feels like, but there is also this physical sensation covering your whole body surface that sort of feels like energy, a fuzzy type of warm.' She pauses, searching for another way to explain it. 'Have you ever put your finger in water when there is electricity around? It's not painful, but a little zingy. It actually gives you a shiver of energy.'

At the same time, Catherine felt the welcoming presence of her father. Fred had died without an opportunity to say their final goodbyes. As she looked up towards where she sensed her father was waiting, Catherine saw a bright light. It was blue, not white—the intense vibrating blue of light bouncing off a diamond or a crystal. 'I could feel him picking me up,' she says.

Then *bang!* Without warning, Catherine was yanked back to the real world. Thoughts of Renee and Brett flashed through her mind, and she felt a slamming jolt as if someone had hit her body. Melanie had realised what was going on and managed to stop the augur.

Catherine was alive but the danger was far from over. To extricate her sister, Melanie had to put the augur into reverse. She had four choices when it came to moving the lever that controlled it and reverse was not always easy to find on the cranky old machinery. Only one of the settings would save her sister. Any of the others and her head would be crushed. 'Luckily, the machine we had stopped instantly—some of them just wind down gradually—but it only needed to go a nanosecond more and I would be dead because my head was actually right in there at this point,' Catherine says.

'Melanie, reverse this fucking thing right now,' she remembers yelling.

'I am, I am,' Melanie replied, trying not to panic. Focusing on the controls, she eliminated the options one by one. Forward and down was wrong, and so was forward and up, but was reverse back and down, or back and up? Melanie selected back and up.

'Thank God for her wits. She got it right,' says Catherine, the gratitude and pride in her sister evident. 'She did an amazing job. She obviously beat herself up over the whole thing for ages, but I said to her, "Melanie, you had a one-in-four decision. You made the right one, just think of it that way. I'm still alive."'

Catherine recalls staying relatively calm and collected throughout the next 30 minutes or so as the drama continued to unfold around her. Released from the machine, she fell backwards to sit on the ground, hands holding her forehead and the dangling strip of scalp and hair. 'I actually tried to pull the scalp open but the skin had gone into shock. It was really hard. It wasn't pliable at all and it was all stuck together. It looked like a cap. I was going to put it back on but it wouldn't do it, so there I was hanging on to it.' At the same time she was thinking, 'I have to keep it warm, I have to keep alive.'

As soon as she could Melanie jumped off the tractor. Thinking of her children first, Catherine told her to gather up the kids, put them on the bike, take them away from the horrible scene and get some help as fast as she could. Melanie wanted to move her sister into the shade of a big gum tree nearby, but Catherine refused so she turned her attention to the bike and unhooking the trailer, thinking she could go much faster without it. In her clumsy haste, the coupling wouldn't budge.

Cursing at the trailer, Melanie set off anyway. Breaking the cardinal country rule to always leave a gate the way you find it, she flung open the paddock gate and roared off down the laneway leading to the workers cottage she shared with Vince. As Melanie approached the house she started screaming his name. Inside the house, Vince heard what sounded like a cockatoo being strangled. He raced outside to find his wife on the other side of the garden fence, her face white as a ghost. 'What the . . .' he started to ask.

'Don't ask,' she cut him off. 'Look after the kids.'

Almost throwing them over the fence, she flung herself back onto the bike and tore off towards the cattle yards near the house, where Les was working. Melanie quickly told him what had happened. Thinking she had said Catherine's hand had been caught in the augur, he rushed inside the house to grab a wet towel in which to wrap it. Abandoning the bike, they jumped into the old farm ute and raced to the accident scene.

Meanwhile, Margaret had heard the raucous scream of the motorbike and wondered what was going on. Having lived for years on an isolated cattle station and raised five children, she was used to dealing with emergencies. When she saw Les and Melanie tear off in the ute, she decided to follow in her Toyota RAV4 to see if there was anything she could do.

Waiting back in the paddock, Catherine was feeling surprisingly good, although it had occurred to her she might bleed to death if they didn't hurry, given the amount of blood that was pouring out of her head. 'I was really calm. I was actually very composed,' she says. 'I tried to sit upright because I was worried I might fall in the dirt and the doctor would have to get it all out of the wound. So I was sitting on the ground, squatting with my elbows on my knees, and I planted myself really square so if I did pass out, I wasn't going to fall over. I would just sort of slump.'

When the ute pulled up alongside her, Catherine even tried to stand up. Les stopped her and helped Melanie wrap his wife's head in the towel before Margaret arrived and could see the ghastly spectacle. Realising it would be faster and more comfortable than the ute, they helped Catherine into Margaret's car. Les took the wheel.

Using everything he had learnt as a police officer about emergency driving, Les pushed the small four-wheel drive to its limits as he sped towards Keith. A distance of 27 kilometres over both gravel and bitumen roads, he made the trip in about ten minutes instead of the usual seventeen or so. Catherine sat in the front seat, rocking backwards and forwards, humming a tune to keep herself focused. 'I sat there the whole time hanging on to my face and thinking about all the positive things I could to keep myself alive. I have no idea what the tune was but I was thinking of the children the whole time.'

Bringing the vehicle to a screaming halt outside the hospital's emergency entrance, Les carefully picked up his wife and carried her into the waiting doctors and nurses. Catherine says she was such an appalling sight even the medical staff had to receive counselling afterwards to help deal with the memory.

The augur had removed her scalp, starting behind the left ear, and then tearing across the nape of her neck, up over the back of the right ear and across her lower forehead, removing her right eyelid before ripping across the top of her nose and along the left eyebrow. With the screwing motion of the machinery pulling her head around in an arc, it then tore away part of her left cheek under the cheekbone, and returned to the base of the left ear. When the augur stopped, her scalp was hanging from the side of her head by a small piece of skin.

'It was like a B-grade horror movie,' Catherine says with gentle humour, completely unfazed by describing her gruesome injuries. 'There was blood and muscle and ooze all over my face, and my scalp was hanging off and pressure had built up around my eyes, which were jammed shut. So it looked pretty ordinary,' she says with massive understatement.

Realising she would require major surgery and specialist care, the hospital called the state's medical emergency helicopter retrieval service based in Adelaide. Catherine was lucky. Keith lies at the eastern-most edge of the zone covered by the helicopter, making it an important emergency centre for the many accidents which happen along the Dukes Highway, connecting Adelaide to Melbourne, and the Riddoch Highway, running south to Mount Gambier. It is one of the points being emphasised repeatedly by the local community as it fights to secure enough funding to keep the hospital and its emergency ward open.

While one look at her injuries sent the hospital staff into emergency mode, at the sight of the doctors their patient relaxed. 'And as soon as I let go I went into shock,' she says. 'I started punching and kicking, and they had to strap me down. Apparently I was like that for the whole hour it took for the helicopter to arrive.'

Coincidentally, the helicopter was piloted by a guy who had served in the Northern Territory police force with Les. When she realised they knew the pilot, Catherine was embarrassed he should see her in such a state. She remembers having two other extremely odd thoughts. The first was dismay that she wasn't wearing matching knickers and bra when they cut her clothes away. 'How anal is that,' she says now, laughing at the stories of mothers who warn their children to always make sure they are wearing clean underwear in case they get hit by a bus. The other was far less amusing—maybe her husband would finally leave now she had lost her hair and good looks.

The helicopter brought two doctors from the Royal Adelaide Hospital, who anaesthetised Catherine and continued administering blood. She does not remember anything from this point until when she woke up in Adelaide a few days later. Doctors told her that by the time she reached the hospital, they had transfused about twelve units of blood, the equivalent of her body's entire supply.

Catherine's luck continued to hold as she was rushed into the hospital. Waiting for her was a team from Adelaide's famous Australian Craniofacial Unit, led by internationally renowned surgeon Dr David David. She was wheeled straight into surgery, which lasted a staggering fourteen hours. A large team in fact operated around the clock, bringing her out of the anaesthetic briefly after ten hours to give her body a rest, and to assess the success of the surgical techniques being used to reattach her face and scalp. The network of veins they had painstakingly reconstructed was not functioning properly. Surgery resumed for another four hours to try again.

On at least two occasions during the surgery, Catherine flatlined and they had to restart her heart. There wasn't a repeat of the near-death experience she'd had in the paddock, but she does recall feeling incredibly suffocated, like she was being sucked into a deep, black, swirling sinkhole. 'I didn't like those experiences at all,' she says. 'Someone suggested that it might have been when they were trying to bring me out of the anaesthetic. They were quite different to what I felt in the paddock, I think because they were clinical.'

Waking up in the intensive care unit was quite a shock, and not just because of her injuries. One of the first things she saw as she slipped in and out of consciousness was a nurse attaching leeches to her face. She couldn't talk because of the incubation tube down her throat but she was disgusted by the squirming creatures, and still shudders at the memory. The leeches were being applied to help drain deoxygenated blood from her swollen face and scalp and prevent clotting, which could lead to the wounded tissue dying. Over the next two weeks, they would be applied for twenty minutes every three hours as part of Catherine's recovery treatment.

She also became aware that Les was sitting beside the bed. After spending the first night with the children, he had driven up to Adelaide. Walking through the ward, he failed to recognise his wife because her entire body was so swollen from the trauma. 'He said I was the size of the bed,' Catherine says. 'And I had tubes up my nose, in my mouth, and in my heart.'

On coming to, one of her first concerns was Melanie. 'Straight away, for whatever reason, I just needed to speak with her and tell her it wasn't her fault,' she says. And she started worrying about Brett, who was about to attend his first day at school. 'I was really pissed that I was going to miss it.'

As she became more aware of her body and what was going on around her, Catherine discovered she was lying on a special bed with ripples designed to prevent bedsores. After a few days she was moved from intensive care to the high dependency unit, and the bed was so comfortable she wanted to take it with her.

By the ninth day, Catherine was missing her children so much she became distressed. The difficulty was that although she wanted to see them, she did not want Brett and Renee to see their mother in such a state. One of the nurses looking after her had a creative solution. He would wrap her head up in so many bandages they would only be able to see her eyes; he figured the children would be expecting bandages anyway, and that it would be better than seeing the bruising and scars, and her bald head.

While the children travelled up from the farm, the tube in Catherine's heart was removed. 'I will never forget when they took it out. It was a plastic pipe as thick as a finger. They said, "Now, just relax and take some really deep breaths. This is going to feel really strange, but we have to try and do it between heartbeats." They just dragged it out. I felt it slide out, which was a bit freaky.' Then she was able to have her first shower. With various other drips and tubes still attached she was wheeled to the bathroom, where she sat under a handheld nozzle for an hour or so, savouring the therapeutic feel of warm water cascading over her skin.

Gradually she regained enough strength to manage short walks down the hospital corridor. One day she met a doctor who paused when he saw her and said, 'So you're the one who stopped the hospital for fourteen hours!' Only then did she realise that she had become something of a medical celebrity. In fact the surgery and her recovery had gone so well, she was the subject of a case study put together by Dr Margaret O'Donnell, a plastic and reconstructive surgeon visiting from Dublin, Ireland, who worked closely with Dr David. 'She was lovely,' says Catherine, reflecting that she did not fit at all the reputation surgeons sometimes have for poor bedside manners.

She also had the chance to meet Dr David about ten days after her surgery and question him about her recovery. 'Will you give me a straight answer? Is this going to work or not?' she asked him outright. He was equally direct. It was probable that with additional surgery they would be able to successfully reconstruct about 90 per cent of her scalp and face. Catherine had no idea the odds were so good. She was immensely relieved. 'Thank God for that,' she thought. 'At least it's pretty well all there and functioning. It's just a few scars.'

After about two weeks in the hospital, she left the high dependency unit for a surgical ward, but she had to face another two skin graft operations before going home. 'That was actually the most horrific part,' she says. Catherine was appalled to discover a considerable amount of the scalp on the back of her head had died since the first operation and had to be replaced. 'I was so devastated. I was a hairdresser and I knew hair doesn't grow on a scar. And I used to be a hairdressing model. I had amazing thick hair you could do anything with. I had a boring face so you could make me up to look like anything you wanted. It was a blank canvas so people liked using me as a model for hairdressing competitions and stuff like that. So I had gone from that to this thing that didn't even resemble a human being.'

Catherine was in the Royal Adelaide Hospital for a little more than six weeks. At one stage during her recovery she succumbed to several different types of staph infection, including golden staph and methicillin-resistant *Staphylococcus aureus* (MRSA), which is resistant to the antibiotics commonly used to treat ordinary staph infections. Before they diagnosed the problem, Catherine was so frightened she was going to die that she made a nurse sit with her through the night. 'I knew if I could hang on to her hand I wouldn't die, but I was sweating all night. I lost kilos . . . When the doctor finally came and told me what was wrong, I thought, "Oh, is that all," and I went to sleep straight away.'

The doctors were more concerned. Their main fear was the infection might enter her heart where the tube had been inserted, and they wanted to administer the strongest possible antibiotics intravenously. Catherine does not like antibiotics and demanded to know if there were any alternatives. Trying to be helpful, one of the nurses explained that sometimes there was no option but to have treatment that might do some damage along the way in order to survive. She gave the example of chemotherapy. It was the wrong comparison for someone whose father had died after receiving exactly that treatment for cancer. Turning to another nurse in the room, Catherine insisted: 'Surely there must be something else?' Avoiding looking at her colleague, the nurse suggested sitting in the sun. Catherine tried it and the infection cleared up.

With tests showing her red blood cell count was not as high as the doctors would like, Catherine also talked to a hospital dietitian about changing her diet. A keen student of human nutrition, she wanted to incorporate more into her diet than the high-protein meals being provided. Top of the list was more fresh food and mineral supplements. Catherine sent her mother to a health food shop with a list, and asked her to start preparing home-cooked meals.

Six and a half weeks after that gruesome afternoon on the farm, Catherine was finally allowed to leave hospital. Walking out the front door onto North Terrace in the centre of Adelaide was a major psychological hurdle which took all her courage. She felt like everyone was staring, although a cap, scarf and large-framed sunglasses covered the worst of her injuries. Perhaps it was because she looked incredibly thin. Naturally of light build, she had lost about 14 kilos since the accident and her clothes hung off her emaciated frame in loose folds.

The doctors ordered their patient to remain in Adelaide for another fortnight so they could monitor her progress. Staying with her mother at a motel with in-room kitchen facilities, she started to rapidly gain weight. 'All I did was eat and I couldn't go for five seconds without a drink of water. I was thirsty constantly, drinking 4 or 5 litres a day, and I wasn't going to the toilet every five minutes either.'

On one occasion, when Les and the children came up from Keith for a few days, a friend with the best of intentions arranged to take them to the Big Rocking Horse at Gumeracha in the Adelaide Hills for a bit of an outing. Afterwards they went back to the hotel where their friend was staying and sat around the pool, while the children played in the water. It was all too much for Catherine. Not only was she feeling very weak, but she was incredibly self-conscious about her appearance.

She was completely bald. A black scar ran across her face from one side to the other, just above her eyes and curving down to her ears. The skin above this line had turned black because of the trauma and the amount of deoxygenated blood trapped there, and there was swelling around her eyes. 'I had to wear a hat and a scarf and tonnes of makeup to hide the black skin. I had these big sunnies on and I wouldn't take them off. I looked like shit, and I hated being out. I tried to do it but I had to leave early. I just couldn't deal with it. There were all these nicely dressed people with wicked hairstyles, and I kept thinking, "I used to look like that once".'

Finally, she was given the all-clear to return to Keith. She was missing her children enormously and couldn't wait to be with them again. Back at home, she learnt how much the district had rallied around. Many people had called, wanting to know how she was progressing and offering assistance if it was needed. Neighbours had helped care for the children, and they kept an eye on the farm when Les, Margaret and Melanie were in Adelaide. Nurses from the local hospital now came daily to check her wounds, change the dressings and monitor vital signs.

The care and concern of local people made it both easier and more difficult during Catherine's first public outing in her own community. It was the annual primary school athletic sports day in Keith. Renee and Brett were taking part and she did not want to miss it. Just getting out of bed and dressing took most of her energy. At the sports field she was surrounded by people extremely pleased to see her and wanting to wish her well. 'I was just swamped by everyone, to the point where I had to sit down frequently. Everyone's energy was sapping, but it was also refreshing. They meant only the best, and they would come and give me a cuddle.' Most were unfazed by the evidence of her scars peeking out from behind the ubiquitous cap, scarf and sunnies. What shocked them was the amount of weight she had lost. Friends were frightened by the sight of shoulder bones sticking up through her shirt and to feel her ribs as they gently embraced her.

Once the bandages were removed and the nursing stopped, Catherine visited specialists from the craniofacial unit about once a month so they could monitor her progress and plan the next phase of recovery. She would need a series of corrective operations to repair her face and minimise the scarring, but Dr David wanted to wait a while so her body had a chance to recover. Catherine also wanted to delay any more surgery until her weight had returned to normal. Keen to be as fit as possible, she swallowed extra vitamins and minerals and ate plenty of fresh food. And she took to going for walks around the farm, not only to improve her physical strength but because she had heard horrifying stories from other farm accident victims about the dangers of blood clots after reconstructive surgery. 'I was going for walks every day, and I started to feel really good.'

Gradually the skin on her forehead returned to a normal colour, although it took almost a year and the scars remained strikingly obvious. Once the swelling settled down Catherine was surprised with how smooth her scar-line was, and how well the surgeons had managed to realign things, but she had no left eyebrow and as it healed the skin tightened and twisted her features to one side. Chewing hurt for a long time because of the damage to her left ear and the cartilage linked to her jaw. Her hearing seemed to be okay but part of her face around the left cheek was numb and didn't move because of extensive muscle and nerve damage. While most of her hair grew back, there were large permanent bald patches across the back of her head because of the scar tissue.

As her body started to heal, one of the most disconcerting aspects was the sensation of nerve endings reattaching. 'It was like there were ants crawling through my scalp,' she says. 'Nerves are one-27th of a hair strand in thickness—that's how fine they are—and they had to find their way back to where they were before the accident. A lot haven't, but a lot have, and it's amazing. When they were attaching I would get this massive shock. Even though I was actually numb when I was in hospital that lightning trigger was happening daily, and that little crawly feeling.' It continued to happen to a lesser degree for up to eight years after the accident.

As the time for reconstructive surgery approached, Dr David's office supplied a preferred list of plastic surgeons, and she arranged interviews with four or five of them before making a decision. In the end, she selected Dr James Katsaros. 'He was amazing,' Catherine says. It took two and a half years and another ten operations before he was done, with his patient returning to Adelaide every few months until after the final operation in May 2000.

People meeting Catherine now would find it almost impossible to tell what she has been through. There is a faint scar around one eye near the nose, and one eyelid is just a tiny bit shorter than the other. It doesn't close properly, so at night she wears an ointment to stop her eyeball from drying out. Part of the right-hand side of her forehead is still numb, which makes it feel heavy at times and occasionally affects her peripheral vision. She still has the bald patches but she wears her hair long and pulled back to hide them. She carries a large scar on the back of her leg too, where skin was removed for the initial skin grafts, and there is a long, thin, white line on her inside forearm revealing where the surgeons harvested some veins. 'I actually ended up with more scars from the operations than I did from the bloody accident,' she jokes.

About two months after her last surgery, Catherine had the chance to celebrate more than three years of hard-fought recovery in a special way. She was selected to participate in the Sydney Olympic Games Torch Relay when it passed through Keith on 17 July 2000. Thousands of Australians took part in the longest torch relay in Olympic history, carrying the flame more than 27 000 kilometres before it was used to light the cauldron at the opening ceremony. Unbeknown to her, Catherine had been nominated by Renee, who was extremely proud of her mother's achievements.

It should have been an exciting day for Catherine, but in what marked the beginning of the end for her marriage, Les managed to ruin it. He told her she was embarrassing everyone by putting herself on public display, and that he was the real hero in the family for saving her life in the first place with the emergency dash to the Keith hospital. 'The day of the relay was horrendous,' Catherine reveals. 'He was pissed to the max that I was getting all this attention.' Les was particularly infuriated that a journalist from *Woman's Day* magazine was in attendance to research her story. 'He threw a public fit and his mum saw it happen. Even she was gobsmacked,' Catherine recalls with a grimace. His resentment worsened once the article appeared and other media started to take notice.

It was the final straw. Catherine had attempted to end the marriage several times over the past eight or nine years, but she had always caved in because of the children. This time there was no turning back. Les had never been physically violent towards her, but he had developed a flash-point temper which seemed to be getting worse and he had become emotionally abusive and more controlling over the years. After returning from Adelaide, where she had sought the advice of a solicitor, Catherine fronted him and said: 'I've got something to say, and you are not going to butt in until I have finished. What I have got to say is my final decision. You are leaving.' Even then, she gave him until the end of the month to pack up and go.

With Les gone, Catherine quickly settled into managing the farm in her own right. They had purchased the property the year before as part of family negotiations following Fred's death, and finding the money to pay Les out put Catherine under considerable financial pressure, but she wanted to stay. Looking back at the support shown by the local community, she realised this was home. With newfound confidence, she was more than a little nonplussed by the real estate agent who showed up not long after the marriage breakup, convinced the property would be going on the market now there was no man around.

During the coming months, Catherine had the time of her life. 'It was bloody good. I could do whatever I wanted, whenever

I wanted to do it,' she says. While people coping with relationship breakups often take to reading self-help books, Catherine became a farm course 'junkie'. Belying her lack of interest in school, where she particularly disliked science, she signed up for all sorts of seminars and short courses on everything from soil chemistry and biology, to plant nutrition, financial and pasture management and stock handling. Melanie had by then bought her own farm a few kilometres down the road, but she was willing to help keep an eye on things and look after the children so Catherine could disappear for a few days at a time to attend more intensive programs. 'At one point I was away nearly every other month,' says Catherine. 'I was trying to work out what I was doing and it was really good for me. I feel like I have a lot of knowledge now, and it's pretty diverse.'

She was encouraged down this path after participating in a grazing management school less than a year after the accident. For some time, she hadn't been all that happy with the conventional approach being used to manage the property's pastures, which not only seemed inappropriate to the Australian landscape, but was costing a fortune in chemicals and fertilisers in an attempt to grow more grass. 'I drove around here and it was looking more like a mown English park. To me it just didn't sit right,' she says. She wanted nature to be given more of a chance to make a contribution, even if it did look a little untidy by comparison.

One day she was having a drink at the Willalooka Tavern, almost the only building in the 'township' of Willalooka and a popular watering hole for local farmers. She started talking to a neighbour who was a bit of a lateral thinker and had just completed a course about an alternative and more profitable approach to grazing. Catherine decided it was worth exploring and signed up herself and Les for the next program, which was being run across the Victorian border in Ballarat by a private agricultural consultancy.

The eight-day intensive management school aimed to provide graziers with holistic insights into the many factors affecting their farms. The idea was that graduates would be better able to manage their livestock enterprises, not only reducing overheads but improving stock health, making more efficient use of water and the pasture they grew, and increasing the number of livestock it was possible to run. Participants also developed skills in planning, how they worked with their family or employees, and how to better manage their time. Much to Catherine's delight, there was also a strong emphasis on sustainability and creating healthy ecosystems, rather than relying on pesticides, heavy applications of fertiliser and constantly resowing pastures. She says, 'I sat in that room and everything seemed so obvious. It made perfect sense. I understood what they were talking about straight away. It didn't seem foreign to me at all.'

Shortly after returning from Ballarat, she and Les sat down over a giant aerial photograph of the property to redesign the way it was set up as an important first step in taking a completely different approach. Indiana actually comprised two neighbouring sheep farms bought separately in 1984 and 1985. Tricia and Lance had installed a central laneway and built some cattle yards; and there was a combined total of 42 main paddocks, including two significant areas of remnant native scrub.

The grazing school advocated cell grazing, a concept which involves running as many livestock as possible in small paddocks, and moving them frequently so the pasture is rested and allowed to regrow between grazings. How often the cattle are moved depends on how quickly the pasture recovers. The idea is to encourage the cattle to eat all the plants evenly, and to encourage the plants to develop larger and stronger root systems so they can make better use of the nutrients and water available in the soil. In spring when plants grow quickly, the rest time between grazings is relatively short. In winter and late summer the rest times are much longer. 'It makes it really easy to understand what you should be doing, and when and how,' says Catherine.

To make the concept work, Indiana had to be divided into paddocks no bigger than 10 hectares. Overlaying the aerial image with tracing paper to sketch out a new plan, they realised there was no need to start from scratch with the fencing. Most of the existing paddocks could be split into ideal sizes, ranging from about 7.5 to 9 hectares, simply by dividing them into wedges, radiating out from a central watering point. The initial work to set up the paddocks was finished by the time Les left, but Catherine had considerably more work to do redesigning the watering system so a single trough could deliver enough water fast enough for the mobs in each paddock.

The extra courses Catherine was completing were now pushing her even further towards the idea of farming organically. She had stopped using conventional fertilisers and pesticides some time ago, so converting the farm to an organic operation proved reasonably straightforward. The property received an official tick of approval from one of several organic schemes operating in Australia in 2003, but Catherine later decided not to worry about formal certification because of the significant expense involved. However, she did go to the effort of creating a brand, Indiana Organics, and devoted hours to researching potential markets, testing her product, and then going out to meet butchers and convince them to take it on.

Today Indiana runs about 450 breeding cows, mainly crosses of British and European breeds. The colour doesn't matter too much as long as they have the right build to carry enough muscle, without being either too fat or too lean. About 250 of the best male offspring are sold each year to the organic market, with about ten slaughtered every fortnight, and the carcases or boxes of premium cuts go to select butchers in Adelaide, Melbourne and Sydney. Because the market for organic meat is still relatively small, the property also buys in young cattle every year which are fattened and then sold to feedlots and local saleyards to generate more income. 'Feedlots are totally against my idea of animal husbandry but you have to survive,' Catherine says.

'We try to turn over between 800 and 1000 stock a year,' she explains while driving around the property on a wet Sunday afternoon, checking the various mobs and frowning over the damage some recently purchased shorthorn heifers have been doing to the fences. They were all pregnancy tested before the purchase and the plan is to wait for the calves to drop, re-mate the cows and then sell them again. Although it can be a useful way to make money, buying what are known as trade cattle from unknown backgrounds has its drawbacks, such as discovering they are not used to being handled. 'You have no idea whose trouble you are going to get,' she says. 'They wreck the fences and you can't muster them. They run a million miles from a motorbike, and they won't go through gates.'

By comparison, the cattle raised on Indiana walk towards the fence, stand quietly and stare at the vehicle as it pulls up at a gate leading into one of Catherine's favourite parts of the property. This area of remnant native vegetation thick with a rare species of callistemon is now fenced off as part of a native vegetation agreement she negotiated with the state government. At its heart is a small clearing where the family often gathers with friends for picnics and bonfires. When they were younger it was popular with Renee and Brett, who would often camp there overnight. Not far from the clearing, perched high in a red gum, is the massive, intricately woven form of a wedge-tailed eagles' nest. The birds return every year, adding even more twigs.

Catherine is pleased to see quite a few gum tree seedlings are starting to germinate. They are coming up in the paddocks too. She is convinced cell grazing is contributing to the natural revegetation process, because the cattle are moved before they start eating them. She also believes the native plants on Indiana have been doing better since she stopped spreading superphosphate fertiliser some fifteen years ago. As part of the organic philosophy, Catherine prefers biological solutions that encourage natural microbes to build up in the soil. The pastures also benefit from manure left behind by the cattle, which she says carries more nutrients these days because of the way the cattle are being fed. Portable bins containing nutritional supplements are set up in the paddocks so they can help themselves when they feel like it. The 'lolly trolleys' provide different mixes and stock licks such as seaweed meal, humates, vitamins and the all-important trace elements.

Recognising the link between soil, plant and human health, it is an extension of the care Catherine takes with her own diet. She has long been concerned about the effects of eating processed foods and food additives, becoming an inveterate label-reader years before it became a topical issue. She was spurred on to learn about nutrition when Renee developed eczema as a baby; through a process of elimination she worked out it was caused by a drink containing preservatives and reconstituted fruit juice. She became even more intensely interested when her father was diagnosed with cancer a few years later. Looking for ways to build his body's ability to fight the disease, she consulted alternative therapists and read extensively. Fred took her dietary suggestions on board and survived for another four years; the doctors had predicted he might live for only a few months.

During her 'course-junkie' phase, she attended as many human nutrition and personal development courses as she did farm seminars, and for some time now she has been studying part-time for a bachelor of health science focusing on nutritional health. At one stage she travelled to the United States for treatment to reduce the scarring from her accident, and took time to visit Dr Arden Anderson. An agronomist who ran one of the soil biology courses she had attended in Australia, he also happens to be a practising physician extremely interested in nutrition and its contribution to human health. 'It all seems pretty left wing,' Catherine says, admitting some people in the district still look at her sideways because of the far from conventional path she has taken.

It is a sunny afternoon in the middle of July, and in a ritual that has drawn together rural communities for decades, people are gathering at the Padthaway oval to watch a game of Australian rules football. Saturday arvos at the footy remain a tradition in many country towns, where it is a rite of passage for boys to play in the junior competition and then work their way up to the senior A-grade team, providing they are good enough. If they shine and someone notices, they could even find themselves joining the big names in the Australian Football League (AFL) and play at the Melbourne Cricket Ground, known affectionately as the 'G'. If they are really fortunate they may get to experience the thrill of running onto the hallowed ground on the last Saturday in September when two teams of blokes in tight shorts traditionally fight it out in the grand final. It is not a completely unrealistic ambition for a young country boy given so many of the league's best players come from the bush, and it is has driven Catherine's son Brett since he was big enough to tie on his first pair of footy boots.

Brett is out there today, wearing number 18 for the Padthaway Lions. He drove down this morning from Adelaide, where he now lives and works. He and several other Adelaide-based players make the trip to the South East every weekend during the football season, recruited by the Lions to help bolster numbers so there are enough players to field a team. Every one of the eleven teams in the Kowree Naracoorte Tatiara Football League resorts to bringing in players these days. It is a sad reflection of the shrinking population of young people in most rural districts.

Standing proudly on the sidelines watching her son's every move is Catherine. With half-time approaching she is still wearing the blue and gold one-piece dress that makes up the uniform for Padthaway's netball teams. She has just finished her C-grade game, where she usually plays the position of goal defence. Football and netball competitions go hand in hand in country leagues, and at 45 she reckons it's a good way to keep fit and 'a bit of a giggle'. Besides, these days it's something of a family commitment to be involved in local winter sporting competitions, with her partner Simon coaching the A-grade football team.

Although she doesn't remember it, Catherine first met Simon about ten years ago when she was a guest speaker at the Elmore Field Days in Victoria. At the time, she was often invited to talk to groups about her accident and its impact on her life as part of programs highlighting the importance of working safely. Then a workplace safety inspector with the Victorian government, Simon was in the audience. He was there the following year too, when she was invited to address a dinner at Maffra in Gippsland. That year Simon reminded her of their first encounter and the two enjoyed a few drinks.

A few months later, his own marriage over, Simon gave her a call. He wanted to come over for a visit and get to know her better. Cautious after previous experiences and determined to put her children first, Catherine told him he needed to spend some time 'getting his shit together' first. A few months later he tried again, and eventually ended up moving to the farm at Willalooka, although initially Catherine had to convince Renee and Brett it was a good idea. 'I had said to my children when Les left that there would never be a man in the house again . . . but they warmed to Simon pretty quickly. He was really good with the kids, and he is so laid back. He got on really well with them, and we did things together, like going away on holidays, that we had never done before as a family.'

Simon and Catherine now have two young children of their own—Summer, who is five, and three-year-old Scarlett. Catherine absolutely adores being a mother, and has spent less time out on the farm since they were born.

Raised near Benalla in Victoria, where he spent time on an uncle's dairy farm, Simon has taken to farm life and stepped up to look after most of the daily tasks, although Catherine continues to take primary responsibility for animal health, all the paperwork and marketing. Before Summer was born she was out on the farm every day, and she is still very much hands-on when it comes to drafting, marking and weaning the cattle. A talented welder, she maintains the steel cattle yards and manufactured a set of forks for the tractor. She loves doing maintenance work, gaining quiet satisfaction from repairing things properly so they will last. 'I love being able to put everything back together again, looking spick and span,' she says, acknowledging she becomes very impatient if something takes longer than expected or the results are not quite what she wanted. 'If I can't do something about it, I have to go away and do something else,' she confesses.

In the past few months, Catherine has started harnessing her long-standing interest in human health and nutrition to build a new venture offering people advice. She has spoken to quite a few groups, sharing her personal story and explaining the basics of healthy eating and why it is so important. The business is growing rapidly and taking her quite frequently to Adelaide, where she stays in a house bought when Brett started playing football in the city, hoping it would save money in the long run and make life a bit easier.

When Brett was only five, Les had forbidden him to play football even though he showed obvious talent and was desperate to join the local Auskick competition for young children. Simon changed all that, giving him 'a life in football'. After moving to the South East, Simon quickly became involved as a player and then coach with the Keith football team, which he led to a premiership. Catherine saw no reason why Brett shouldn't get involved too. By the time he was fifteen Brett had played in his first premiership with the Keith senior colts and had started playing A-grade football. He was spotted by South Australian National Football League scouts and played for North Adelaide's under 16 and under 18 teams. Last year, at the age of nineteen, he was in the reserves for the senior team and on the AFL draft list when he broke his leg. The games at Padthaway are helping to rebuild his match fitness, and he is hopeful of finding his way back to major competition.

Catherine loves watching him play, but becomes anxious in the final quarter when she sees her son knocked to the ground and not get up immediately. By then she is over by the coach's box, where Simon is sitting in a deck chair paying close attention to the game and swearing in frustration when a passage of play doesn't go quite as it should. The visiting team from Border Districts started to close the gap in the third quarter, but Padthaway are beginning to regain control now and will end up winning by 25 points. A group of supporters gathered in front of the outdoor bar cheers raucously as the final siren sounds. Spectators sitting in cars and utes parked around the oval join in with honking car horns—no country footy match would be complete without the sound.

Game over, Catherine walks across the field to round up her two youngest children. They have been in the care of a local lad who earns pocket money every Saturday by babysitting so she can help with gate duty at the oval and play netball without having to watch them. A lot of young families are involved in the club, so there are plenty of other children to play with as everyone gathers in the clubrooms for the post-game presentations to top players and an early meal cooked by rostered volunteers. Tonight it's a choice of the traditional country favourite, corned beef with white sauce and vegetables, or chicken at the bargain price of only $10. At the bar, adults settle for a beer or an excellent wine from the local Jip Jip Rocks winery at prices so low it would have city drinkers crying into their sauvignon blanc.

Although they both appear relaxed and are sitting comfortably together at a table while the children pick at their food, Simon and Catherine are going through a difficult time in their relationship, and everyone around them knows it. Simon recently had a brief affair with another woman involved with the netball club. Describing it as the worst mistake of his life, he admits it was wrong and is fiercely committed to repairing the damage. Catherine is highly appreciative of the effort he is making yet she is equally committed to making it clear not just to Simon, but the wider world, that while having an affair is not considered anything out of the ordinary these days, in her eyes it is totally unacceptable behaviour which society should condemn and not condone. With a strength and determination that is no surprise to anyone who watched her fight to recover from the accident, Catherine is now applying herself to dealing with the situation and renegotiating their future.

'The way I view my life now and beforehand, Simon and I got along so well that our life was like travelling on a five-lane freeway above everyone else. We were cruising along and everything was very easy and comfy, with no need to take any of the exits and get off,' she explains. 'Because we got on very well and were really good friends, there was nothing that made us stop and take time to explore the relationship in depth to see if there were any problems. We enjoyed doing lots of things together and we knew what each other liked, but we didn't check in with each other very often about how we were doing or what we were feeling.

'Then this big hole in the road appeared, and suddenly we have been diverted off the freeway to the streets below. Now we are coming across all these obstacles—roadworks, speed humps and the usual traffic jams. The affair has made us more exposed to all the things we haven't encountered before or had to think about. But now we are travelling at 15 miles an hour instead of 100, which means we have time to talk and to listen, and to actually hear what we are saying to each other. I think now that we are working at it, our relationship is coming back stronger than ever,' she continues.

'For Simon, he came into a family that was already set up and doing well. Renee, Brett and I were strong, independent and secure, and looking after each other after all we had been through together. When he arrived it took a while for the children to accept him, but he is very likable and he soon won them over. He is a nice bloke, a good father and well liked, which is why I think all of this has been such a shock to everyone. I was confident about what I was doing, and had a clear direction that I was going in already, and he didn't have to worry too much about anything. For a long time I was focused on him and the farm, and then we had two little ones and I changed my focus to look after them.'

Catherine acknowledges that although her miraculous survival and recovery from the accident may seem like a storyline straight from Hollywood, life rarely delivers the perfect happy ending. In fact, her story is still unfolding. While she is convinced it is her destiny to help others by sharing her experiences, warts and all, she still has plenty of lessons to learn too. 'The way I see it, the day you stop learning is the day you die,' she says.

8

KEEPER OF COUNTRY

Keelen Mailman, Augathella, Queensland

White fellas call it Lost City. In the language of the Bidjara people of central western Queensland it is *Dhigarri*, meaning 'white cockatoo'. For Keelen Mailman it is both a place of work and a place of enormous cultural significance which she feels connected to on a very deep, spiritual level. Maybe it's the name that conveys the sense of archaeological ruins belonging to a lost civilisation. Or it might be the layers of towering rocks and hidden caves standing silent like empty tenements. Whatever the reason, there is something about this beautiful, rambling sanctuary set amid virgin bushland that takes hold of the soul.

Keelen was brought here for the first time about fourteen years ago by a Bidjara elder who was trying to recruit her to work on Mt Tabor station. The Indigenous Land Corporation had purchased the isolated property of more than 70 600 rugged, uncleared hectares north-east of Augathella because it encompassed country of cultural importance to the Bidjara people. The local community was looking for someone to manage it, and Lost City was one of many sites they wanted help protecting as part of the job.

At the age of only 31, Keelen was a remarkable choice which caused more than a little controversy within her own community, let alone among neighbouring station owners. Not only was she young and female, she was a single mother with two children and she had no real experience. Despite the seemingly obvious drawbacks, the elder, 'Sugar' Ray Robinson, saw something in the young Bidjara woman and wanted to give her a go. When they shook hands on the deal they made history. At that moment it is believed Keelen became the first Indigenous woman in Australia to manage a cattle station.

It is late morning on Mt Tabor and Keelen is hefting 30-kilogram bags of stock lick into the back of a ute, ready to make another run over the sandy tracks they call roads in this part of Australia. It is a grand term for the rough trails forged through dense bush by station owners needing access to vital watering points and boundary fences. Even after a bit of homegrown maintenance to smooth over the worst patches, they challenge the suspension of four-wheel-drive utes carrying only moderate loads. Months after some of the worst flooding in living memory, many are still impassable, the ground so soft it swallows vehicles to the axles.

At one stage Keelen spent eight days straight with a shovel trying to dig out her Nissan four-wheel-drive station wagon. It sank so far she couldn't open the doors. She was 20 kilometres from the homestead on what serves as the main road from

Augathella—'The worst bloody road in Queensland,' jokes Keelen, knowing full well there are far worse. She was doing about 60 kilometres an hour and applying her considerable driving experience when the vehicle stopped as if it had hit a brick wall. 'It just sunk like I was in quicksand,' she says. 'The mud was right up to the black strips on the door.'

Her grown-up children, Allan and Kristy, and Kristy's husband Mark were travelling with her at the time. They all had to climb out the windows—no problem for Keelen, who is of relatively small build, but a contortional challenge for Allan, who is 184 centimetres tall and weighs more than 100 kilograms. 'It was so hilarious,' she says, using one of her favourite phrases.

She wasn't laughing quite so much the next day after driving back in the station ute to start the salvage operation. Ten metres from the Nissan, the ute became bogged too. Highly embarrassed, she picked up the satellite phone once again to call the same neighbouring stockman who had come to collect them the day before. 'It was an absolute nightmare,' she says. 'I don't want to see a shovel again in the whole of my life.'

Her rescuer was Dave Hagger, who lives in a small house across the homestead paddock and works as a stockman for one of Australia's largest cattle operations, Australian Country Choice (ACC). Owned by the Lee family, ACC supplies 50 per cent of the beef sold by the massive Coles supermarket chain. Apart from feedlots and meat processing plants, they own fifteen cattle stations covering 365 000 hectares of Queensland, including neighbouring Babbiloora where Dave spends most of his time working; and they lease additional properties so they can run an average of about 80 000 head at any given time. Among them is Mt Tabor, which carries up to 2500 head depending on the season. In what Keelen considers a mark of faith, ACC approached the Indigenous Land Corporation in 2002 to lease the property, wanting to keep her on as manager. She was happy to agree as long as maintaining fences, roads and bores, checking watering points and putting out stock lick didn't interfere with her primary responsibilities caring for the property's cultural sites.

Now in his 70s, Dave has worked on stations across this part of Queensland since he was a teenager. For the past two months he has been helping with the annual muster, which usually only takes about four weeks on Mt Tabor using horses and large teams of working dogs to push the cattle out of bush so thick in places that good dogs are indispensible. It's been a long, drawn-out affair this year because of the floods. Torrents of water bursting through the gullies tore down fences, scattering the cattle, and have made the ground so boggy even the horses sink in some places.

When Keelen looked out her kitchen window first thing this morning she noticed the mustering team had left. They stayed in the workers' quarters with Dave while they worked this end of the station. Now he is heading off to join them at a campsite on Babbiloora, where they are due to start the next muster. After refuelling the ute from a large drum of diesel, Keelen heads over to see him before he goes. She is going to be keeping an eye on the nearest section of the neighbouring property while he is away and wants to check any last-minute instructions. She is also keen to find out what he knows about road conditions at the top end of Mt Tabor, which he passes through regularly. A group of Bidjara representatives want to go there and further on to the boundaries of neighbouring Carnarvon station and Dooloogarah, which is managed by Dave's son Pat. They are trying to visit cultural sites in preparation for a land rights claim that has been dragging on for years.

The news isn't good. Dave gets down on his knees in the dirt to draw an old-fashioned mud map explaining a complicated detour she might have to take to avoid getting bogged in deep sand or soft ground where seasonal springs are still running in steady trickles. An exceptional bushman and a father figure who Keelen greatly admires as a steadfast friend and 'true old gentlemen', he knows the country like the back of his hand, but it's an area Keelen doesn't visit too often and getting lost or stuck so far out would not be a good idea. Even riding a quad bike, Pat had trouble for months leaving Dooloogarah because the roads were so bad, and Dave was lucky to get back from one bore site just a few days ago. The trip will have to wait a bit longer to give the ground even more time to harden up.

Dave knows Keelen can be relied upon to look after things in his absence. He has worked for more than a few owners and station managers in his day, and ranks her pretty highly in his understated way. 'She's a good woman, one of the best, eh?' he says, using the final exclamation that regularly ends conversational sentences in this part of the world, more a gentle full stop than a question despite the inflection. 'She has had it hard too, eh? She has battled. When I first came over here, she was out shooting kangaroos nearly every night. You would see her out there with the light, midnight or later, skinning roos to get enough money to bloody survive. You wouldn't see many women doing it, eh?'

Keelen heads off to the workers' quarters to have a word with Colleen, one of two women who take it in turns cooking and mustering with the team. She has stayed behind to stock up the supplies of cakes and biscuits. Keelen's youngest daughter, twelve-year-old Charlee, doesn't want to go on today's lick run. She would prefer to spend time with Colleen instead, taking advantage of the rare visit. Colleen has no objection and sends Keelen off with a container of Anzac biscuits, still warm from the oven. 'Better make a mile,' Keelen says, smiling goodbye as she climbs into the ute and heads back to the homestead to deliver the good news to Charlee and collect her foster child Maggie, who is still keen to ride along.

Now fourteen, Maggie is the youngest of five children Keelen took under her care about ten years ago 'to get them out of a bad situation'. Originally from the northern Queensland coast, Maggie loves station life and goes out with Keelen on a regular basis. Her elder brother and sisters have all left home now, and next year she and Charlee will be going to boarding school in Toowoomba, leaving Keelen with no-one but herself to look after for the first time since she was a small child.

Keelen Mailman was born at Clermont in central Queensland on 29 November 1966. She was taken back to the *yumba*, an Indigenous word for a town camp, at Augathella, when she was only a few months old. She had very little to do with her father, a Kooma man from the small town of Cunnamulla. It was her mother, Betty Saylor, and the extended Mailman clan who raised her and were the most powerful influence in Keelen's early years, teaching her to respect others and passing on the Bidjara culture.

Betty was raised on country, a term referring to the traditional land linked with each Indigenous language group or community. In the case of the Bidjara, it covers a huge expanse of central western Queensland, stretching from Mitchell in the east, up to Emerald and Clermont in the north, across to Aramac and south as far as Wyandra, the other side of Charleville, although the accepted extent of the boundaries is still a point of legal debate as part of a land rights claim that is far from resolved. For Betty, the heart of her world lay on Mt Tabor and the neighbouring station of Binnalong, where she spent much of her childhood camping with her people.

When she was only sixteen, Betty left her community and entered a world now virtually forgotten in today's era of mass-produced entertainment. She became a performer in a travelling vaudeville tent show that moved around Australia, setting up at agricultural shows in the days when attractions incorporated an eclectic mix of boxers, wrestlers and theatrical acts, as well as games and rides. Betty was working as a housemaid at a Charleville pub when the 'showies' arrived in town for the local annual event. Among those who came in for a beer was a bloke who ran a tent show featuring exotic dancers and other acts in the tradition of American burlesque. Betty was a stunning young woman with long, curly black hair and a flashing smile, and she caught his eye. He asked her to join his troupe as a dancer and she accepted, tempted by the considerable amount of money being offered, which would make all the difference to her family.

Young and inexperienced though she was, Betty quickly became a star. She performed under the soubriquet Jedda, taken from the name of a famous movie released in 1955, about a young Indigenous girl from the central Australian desert. Over the next few years, Betty not only stripped and danced with snakes but 'wrassled' too, taking on men from the audience in what proved to be a popular feature of the program as the troupe toured from Tasmania to Sydney and Darwin. Supple and surprisingly strong, Betty usually won.

In later life she talked a great deal about her adventures, telling her daughter, 'I had a ball'. Keelen says her mother was a strong woman who 'wouldn't take crap from anyone'. She had great memories of her days as Jedda, which inspired Queensland playwrights Margery and Michael Foorde when they created *Way Out West*. Commissioned to mark the centenary of Australian federation in 2001, the piece of musical theatre told the stories of people from western Queensland. Betty was sitting in the front row when a performance by the La Boite Theatre Company opened in Charleville not long before she died. 'They were in tears when they realised Jedda was still alive,' says Keelen. 'I was sittin' there with her and I cried too because she had her memory flashing right before her. It was so touching.'

By the late 1960s, Betty had given up touring and was living with three children among her own people at the *yumba*, tucked away in the bush on the outskirts of Augathella. It was a marginal existence, with only one tap providing water to seventeen families living in rough, tin shanties. There was no electricity or proper sanitation either, but to Keelen Mailman it was home, in between extended periods camping out on nearby stations. These are the places where she started to learn about her culture and how to live off the land, collecting seeds and berries from native plants, hunting echidna and fishing for yabbies, or *booglying*, in the Warrego River. Years later when she was a teenager living in town, she would often walk out to the *yumba* for sentiment's sake. By then most of it had been demolished but one hut remained, providing shelter to an old stockman from the Northern Territory who spent his days sitting in the dust, making things out of green hide.

For the first years of her formal education, Keelen had to walk 1.5 kilometres into Augathella every day to attend the local state primary school. About the time she started year 3, someone found her family a house in town, making it considerably easier. Betty's partner was away a great deal, working as a mechanic and stationhand on sheep and cattle properties in the area, and the family had grown to seven children. Keelen had an older brother and sister, Charlie and Brenda, who helped raise her, and four younger brothers and sisters; Jenice, known as Dom, Kenny, Cissy and Carl.

It is an understatement to say that as a child Keelen would rather be anywhere than school. The local police officer regularly had to escort her to the classroom to make sure she turned up. 'I had no interest in school. All I wanted to do was get out and go bird hunting or fishin' or something else,' she admits. 'When I was growing up I was the biggest tomboy in the country. Don't talk about a doll. I had nothing to do with dolls whatsoever. I was into slug guns, making shanghais, marbles. I always had marbles and slugs in me short pockets. Dresses—don't even go there. I think maybe me sex got mixed up somewhere,' she says, laughing. 'Cars, fighting with the boys, footy—that was me growing up as a kid. I was full on.'

Another favourite pastime was heading out with her siblings and friends to a swimming hole about 10 kilometres out of Augathella. It usually meant walking because no-one had access to a car, but occasionally they would all combine the few dollars they had between them and take the local taxi. More often than not, the driver would forget to come back and collect them so they had to walk back home along the hot, dusty highway.

Sport was the only exception when it came to Keelen's general aversion to anything related to school. Talking about it brings back both some of her happiest memories and some of the most bitter. 'The biggest love I had for school was sports. I never missed sports time, sports training, sports practice. Sitting in the classroom, every time I could jump the fence I'd do it, but sports I loved.' A natural athlete, Keelen proved to be an extremely fast runner over short distances—so fast she is said to have clocked times quicker than Australian Olympic medal winner Raelene Boyle, who made headlines for her achievements in 100- and 200-metre events while Keelen was growing up. But no-one got to hear of the young girl from Augathella, thanks to a gut-wrenching example of discrimination.

When she was about twelve, Keelen was selected to represent western Queensland in a major sporting competition at the Queen Elizabeth II stadium in Brisbane. It was a rare opportunity for an Indigenous child from the bush. Recognising her extraordinary talent, the school principal was very excited about the potential it offered for a better future, especially given Brisbane was due to host the Commonwealth Games in just a few years time. Betty had recently suffered a stroke, but he arranged for another parent to deliver Keelen to the stadium because he was anxious she didn't miss out.

Keelen was extremely excited. On the morning she was due to leave, she was up early and waiting outside the house ready to go. The principal had already been past in his bright orange Valiant Charger, after going to see the woman who was giving her a lift. He wanted to make sure everything was organised. He was going to Brisbane too, but the woman assured him there was a place for Keelen in her car. Moments later, the woman pulled up alongside Keelen and told her she couldn't go. 'She left me,' Keelen says, the devastation and bewilderment of a heartbroken child still strong in her voice. 'I watched the orange Charger and the dust behind it go over the hill, and she told me she couldn't take me.'

Keelen begged the woman to change her mind. She refused. She had a young baby and it might catch something because Betty was sick. 'My mum had a stroke,' Keelen points out in disgust. 'What was the little fella going to catch?' In desperation, Keelen implored her to race after the principal and send him back, but the woman again refused. 'It was bad, bad—such a sad, sad memory that I will never ever forget and forgive. Who knows, I could have ended up running for our country. But no-one knows because the chance was stripped from me in a minute. I cried and cried and cried,' says Keelen. 'And all it could have come down to that day was that I was black and she didn't want me in the car.'

Struggling to get over the disappointment, Keelen continued running in local competitions and dragged herself to school whenever she couldn't get away with not going.

With their mother now an invalid because of her stroke, Charlie and Brenda acted as surrogate parents to keep the family together. But when Keelen was old enough to start high school, her older siblings moved away. At the age of thirteen, Keelen stepped in and took their place, nursing her mother and looking after her four younger brothers and sisters. It was an enormous responsibility for someone so young, with so much to learn. 'I didn't know much about anything,' Keelen says, recounting an instance when her stepfather had returned home after six months or so working on a station to find there was no food in the house. He always ordered in a large supply of non-perishables before leaving and the family usually topped it up with fresh food purchased on account at the local store.

'How come youse are pretty much starving?' he asked.

Keelen explained their home supplies had run out and the amount owed at the general store was so high the shopkeepers were refusing to provide any more until it was settled. She had no money to pay the bill.

'But where's your mother's money?' he asked.

'I don't know, but I've got all these things in here,' she told him, opening a drawer full of envelopes with her mother's name on them.

'You silly, silly, little girl.' He laughed hard at her foolishness then explained the envelopes contained her mother's pension cheques. All she had to do was take them to the shop, which would exchange them for cash after deducting the amount owed.

'We had heaps of money. Every fortnight those pension cheques had been comin' in and I just put them in my drawer,' Keelen says. 'I didn't know. I was going without my food to give it to the younger ones.'

It wasn't the only struggle. Once she had finished primary school, with no high school in Augathella, she had to get up early enough every morning to catch a bus at about seven o'clock to Charleville, the major service hub for the region. By the time she got back to Augathella it was usually 4.30. Then there were clothes to wash, meals to prepare and homework to do. 'I was missing a bit of school, but I tried to do the right thing,' Keelen says. She persevered for about six months, at which point it all became too much. 'I had to choose. I wasn't getting enough sleep. By the time I finished washing and cooking tea I was too tired to do any study. So I thought, "Fuck it, I love me mum and me little brothers and sisters more than I love school," so I just ditched it.'

There was one not-so-small difficulty associated with this plan. Legally, she was required to attend school until the age of fifteen, and the local police sergeant already had his eye on her as a persistent truant. He warned that if she and her siblings didn't go to school, the authorities would take them into care. In a sign of the dogged determination and quick thinking that has seen Keelen through much of her life, she came up with a solution on the spot one day when Sergeant Wheeler spied her in town yet again during school hours. 'No, it's okay, Mr Wheeler. I'm goin' on the bus to Brisbane tonight to my big sister Brenda, and I'm goin' to school down there,' she told him convincingly.

'Thank the Lord he never checked the bus stop, cos I never got on no bus,' she says. Instead, for the next twelve months, Keelen hid in the house while continuing to care for her family. No-one found out about the subterfuge until she emerged on her fifteenth birthday.

It is hard to imagine the tenacity and strength of mind it took for a young girl to pull off such a feat, especially in a small country town of just a few hundred people where everybody notices everything that happens pretty much all of the time. She had to give up her sport and her friends, who missed her but couldn't be told in case they inadvertently let the secret slip. She couldn't go swimming at the waterhole or walking in the bush, or visit her people at the *yumba*. Her days were made up of caring for her mother, keeping the house clean, washing clothes, raising her siblings and dreaming of the freedom she would have once the magical birthday came around.

'It was quite amazing, really, when I look back on it . . . I was only a kid. Now I can see how big it was, but to me then it was nothing as long as I was home and we were all together, and the days seemed to pass quite quickly, strangely enough.

But looking back now, I don't know how I done it either, eh? It was obviously meant to be. No-one come to the house to visit us . . . It was like we were an Aboriginal family that was forgotten about.'

The deception not only placed pressure on Keelen, but her brothers and sisters too. The youngest, Karl, was only about five and Cissy was only eight. Remembering not to tell anyone or say anything that might reveal the secret was a big thing to ask of them, but Keelen reinforced every morning just how important it was not to give her away. The older children—Kenny, who was about ten at the time, and Dom, who was twelve—were able to help a little more with things like shopping and paying bills, although Kenny was tempted at times to hold the secret over her, threatening to tell people when his big sister had cause to discipline him for something.

Finally the day came when Keelen could step through the front door and out into the street, 'proud as punch'. It was 25 November 1980.

Sergeant Wheeler spotted her soon after. 'Miss Mailman, where did you come from? Why aren't you at school?' he asked.

'No, Mr Wheeler,' she replied. 'It's my birthday today. I am fifteen and I am allowed to leave school so I'm back home.'

It wasn't until a few years later when she tracked down a copy of her birth certificate while applying for a learner driver's permit that Keelen discovered not only had she been celebrating her birthday four days earlier than her actual date of birth, but she was a whole year younger than she thought. 'He could have busted me,' she says, laughing. 'You have no idea of the look on my face when I saw the date.'

It wasn't the only revelation. The certificate also showed she had been going by the wrong name. In fact, there were so many discrepancies, she actually wondered if the authorities had produced the right document. Trying to sort out the puzzle, she asked Betty. Keelen learnt she had been named after an

Irish nurse who had been kind to her mother while she was in hospital and filled in the paperwork registering her birth. She spelt her name 'Keelen' but with her accent it sounded like Kaylene. Keelen decided it was not too late to remedy the situation, and immediately started going by her correct name. Some people who have known her since she was a child still use the old version, or its abbreviation, Kay.

After coming out of hibernation, Keelen continued to care for her family until, at the age of only sixteen, she herself became a mother. Allan was born in August 1982, followed by Kristy in June 1985. Despite her age, she loved being a mother and it seemed to come naturally after so many years caring for her younger siblings. But she was not happy raising her children in Augathella, where she had experienced so much discrimination as a child.

'Growing up in a little town, there was massive racism. It gave me a childhood with a lot of very hurtful memories, which is heartbreaking too, really, because it was home,' she says. 'You know, people see you when you are a grown, adult woman and they think it's all fine and dandy, it's water under the bridge. But they forget that people were scarred way back when they were children, and that's left something embedded in your memories.'

Keelen says many locals tried to ignore the existence of the *yumba* and the Bidjara culture. Widespread assumptions were also made about alcohol and drug problems. 'Those people knew me. I never drank in my life. I have never done drugs in my life, and to be continually judged and criticised for that sort of stuff, I just don't like it. We never stole, we never broke into anyone's homes, and we weren't allowed to be disrespectful to other people or we copped it.'

Determined to bring up her children in a different environment with more opportunities, Keelen moved to Brisbane. As a single parent, for the next twelve years or so she worked hard to earn as much money as she could so they didn't miss out. That often meant holding down several jobs at the same time and working night shifts. She tackled everything from operating machinery on production lines in a large factory, to harvesting vegetables. 'Relationships just didn't work out and I just thought, "Oh well, I'll do it on me own".'

Then, towards the end of 1997, Keelen had what she describes as a 'spiritual calling' to return to Augathella. 'I just wanted to come home,' she says. 'And it was probably the best calling that I'd ever had because I got to have six more years with my mum that I wouldn't have had.' Betty was living in a nursing home at Charleville and continued to suffer more strokes. Keelen was devastated when the doctors eventually warned her to enjoy 'every minute of every hour of every day' because her mother could die at any time.

Betty passed away in 2001. Keelen still thinks of her often. A photograph of her mother takes pride of place in the lounge room at Mt Tabor, which is filled with family photos and precious mementos she has squirrelled away over the years. Recalling her mother, Keelen says: 'She was one of those that never carried grudges, ya know . . . She'd always say, "What's the good of it. You only live once. Live a happy life, a good life. Treat everyone good. Just be happy and always grateful for what you've got and achieved. Don't hold grudges. They can be here today and gone tomorrow and you don't get a chance to say sorry." And it's true.'

Keelen had been back in Augathella little more than six months when she was offered the job at Mt Tabor. She bumped into

Ray Robinson at a funeral and he told her to come and see him. When word got out about what he intended, the Bidjara elder attracted an enormous amount of criticism from his own people. 'I copped a lot of shit but so did he,' Keelen recalls. 'They said to him all the crap under the sun—single woman doing a man's job, out in the bush, blah, blah, blah. But he said, "She'll be right." It was him that took that step of believing in me as a single mum, believing that I was capable as a woman to come and do the job . . . It was that man that shone a light on me, so to speak, and I sort of hope that I have made him proud since then.'

To this day she is not altogether certain what Ray saw in her that made him take such a chance. It may have been her reputation for working hard to keep her family together, or the fact that she doesn't drink alcohol and has never taken drugs. Keelen likes to think it had something to do with all these things and with her being a hard worker and a straight talker, someone who can be relied on to take her responsibilities seriously without supervision. 'I do a day's work. I don't need anyone here to see me clock in and clock out,' she says, pulling up the ute at the first of a series of troughs she will visit today to distribute stock lick.

A tailored mix of nutritional supplements, the lick is designed to provide essential minerals and proteins to the cattle which they cannot absorb in sufficient amounts from native grasses. They don't need much, but they need it regularly to stay healthy and gain weight. Bound in bright yellow plastic, the lick has to be lifted into the ute one bag at a time, from pallet loads delivered to the station. This vehicle can only carry up to twelve bags when the roads are soft, so Keelen has to make runs almost every day to cover the station often enough, depending on how many cattle there are and where they are gathered. Most lick troughs are placed near watering points so the cattle don't have to walk any further than necessary in the rugged terrain. Each trough is an individual work of art; a rough, organic sculpture carved out of an old tree trunk, preferably box or ironbark because it lasts longer. Dave made most of them but Keelen created a few too, using a small chainsaw to hollow them out where they dropped. When they start to disintegrate, another tree is selected and cut down to replace them.

As the ute appears, the cattle start to walk out of the bush and gather in anticipation. Used to seeing Keelen on a regular basis, they are extremely quiet and walk right up to the trough while she is still cutting the first bag open. One particularly impatient cow even puts her head into the back of the vehicle before being shooed away by Maggie. ACC uses Mt Tabor to run mainly breeding stock. The cows and their calves come in all shapes and sizes, the colourful mix of British, European and *Bos indicus* breeds ranging in hues from black to ghostlike silvers and soft peachy reds.

Climbing back into the ute, Keelen heads further east into more open, flinty country where swathes of wattle drench the senses with broad splashes of brilliant yellow and sweet-smelling pollen. Six different varieties of the popular Australian native plant can be found across Mt Tabor, transforming the landscape in the winter and early spring, when most wildflowers start to appear. Dropping down into a gully and heading cross-country to avoid a badly eroded creek crossing, Keelen emerges from the scrub to spot a mob of brumbies cantering off into the distance. A large pinto stallion, obviously in charge of the group, turns and faces the vehicle in strong protective mode. Head up, nostrils flaring, he snorts and stamps the ground with fierce authority, giving the other wild horses a chance to head off into the bush before he turns to follow. There are about 600 brumbies on the station, with a government monitoring program keeping an eye on the numbers.

Pausing to roll one of many cigarettes she smokes during the run, Keelen recalls her first days at Mt Tabor. She was brought out to the station by another Bidjara elder under instructions from Ray. 'Take that girl out there and let her see if she likes it,' he suggested.

Something about the place, its raw natural beauty and the peacefulness touched her soul straight away. 'The wattle was out like now and the wildflowers were starting to come out, and it just got my heart, the bush, and wanting to be out here,' she explains. 'And that was it.'

Within a short time Keelen, Allan and Kristy had moved into the homestead, a small transportable house with no garden set in an open paddock where the grass had grown metres high. The property had been stripped of every possible fitting, even the bore pump, so she had to go back to Augathella and cart out enough water for the first week while it was sorted out.

Once the initial problems were resolved, Keelen didn't mind the isolation at all, although the children were initially nonplussed to find there was no ready-made entertainment in the way of broadcast television or even radio. The very idea would appal Charlee and Maggie, who love watching the latest cable shows and video music clips via satellite on a large flat screen, and rely on internet connections for distance education lessons as part of School of the Air. Keelen thought the complete absence of such things an excellent opportunity to spend quality time with her children, and for all of them to really get to know each other. 'And the kids loved it,' she says. 'Half the time we didn't know what day it was, and it was quite hilarious. We were already close, so it was just more good memories. We would sit around and yarn and yak, and they survived.' As a treat, Keelen would organise for the mail truck to bring a few videos from the newsagent in Augathella. The truck came twice a week, delivering groceries and other orders as well as the post.

When it came to work, Keelen didn't even have a map to show her the layout of the station, let alone much of a briefing about what she was expected to do. Initially, the main requirement was to maintain the house and keep a general eye on things. The corporation was yet to stock the property with its own cattle, so there were no lick runs, or trips to pump bores, which was just as well because she wasn't too sure where they were. 'It sort of started off quite strange in a sense. I had no idea what was where and how to get there,' she admits. 'It was a long time before I got a map so I just had to find my own way around.'

With the main fire danger season approaching, the first chore she decided to tackle was burning the house paddock to clear away the long grass and create a fire break. This is a common practice in the semi-arid station country of south-western Queensland towards the end of winter when things are still dry but cooler temperatures ensure slow burns and overnight frosts help extinguish the embers. The burn-offs not only help to reduce the danger of intensive bushfires in the hotter months, but remove old, rank grass that cattle won't eat and encourage fresh, green growth when the season breaks in about October.

'Apparently the place hadn't been burnt for six years. In the house paddock, the grass was probably my height double—that's how much grass there was,' Keelen explains. Knowing the then manager of Babbiloora, she rang him for advice about what was involved in applying for a permit to carry out the burn and how to go about it. He was very pleased to learn her intentions and encouraged her to burn off as much of the property as possible. 'So we lit the bloomin' thing up and let it go ... It burnt for weeks. We would be sitting on the verandah at home having a cuppa in the afternoon, and you could hear timber dropping from kilometres away ... It was unbelievable,' she says.

Over the next few years, Keelen gradually explored the property as she worked seven days a week to restore some sort of order to the fencing, roads and watering points, and to identify and start fencing off important cultural sites. She was determined to make her people proud, and not a subject of ridicule for how the station was being run. A fast learner, she took advantage of Bidjara elders who were experienced bushmen and stationhands, and of her neighbours, who were mostly welcoming and helpful.

Initially, one of her greatest allies was Bob Mailman, her mother's only brother. He offered to come and stay for a few months and teach her what he could. When he wasn't there in person things were explained over the phone, with Keelen urging him to go slowly while she attempted the task as he described exactly what to do. While several family members helped along the way, Keelen turned mainly to Uncle Bob, who showed the most patience 'because I was his pet', she confesses sheepishly. 'I could ring him a million times a day . . . although sometimes I felt like he really wanted to say, "For goodness sake, Keelen, go and get a grip on yourself". It was very hard for a little bit.'

Much to her pleasure, later on he told her: 'Mate, you have done well. I am that proud of what you've done and how you've done it. You're a quick learner.'

In the early stages, not everyone was so convinced. When she was first given the job, a small group of Bidjara men started placing bets about how long she would last. Some only gave her six months, but one old fella challenged them all. 'She'll prove youse all wrong,' he told them. 'I know that girl. She was the biggest tomboy growin' up. You have bet on the wrong woman. I'll bet she'll be there for a lot of years.' Keelen only found out about the wager years later. By then the old bloke had claimed his money.

It is close to midday and Keelen has encountered the first of several unexpected water-related problems she will have to deal with before the day is done. Out here the job description for a station manager covers an extraordinary diversity of skills but knowing how to maintain and fix bore pumps would rank among the most essential. Livestock cannot be left without water for long in this country, and cattle need a significant amount to survive. A cow feeding a calf in hot weather may drink 100 litres or more a day, and even a young steer might need at least 20 litres in the cooler months.

Making regular runs to check water levels in the dams and holding tanks is essential. When levels at the tanks are low, they must be refilled from an adjacent bore. Mt Tabor has 26 dams that cattle and horses can drink from when there is enough rain. Even after floods during the first half of the year, not every dam is full but at least they are all holding reasonable amounts of water at the moment, and the natural waterholes and springs are flowing. Besides the dams there are two main bores—one near the homestead and another at Foal's Gully on the eastern side of the station. Keelen is planning to work with contractors to put down another bore in the northern reaches, so cattle in that part of the property don't have to walk so far for water and Mt Tabor can run more livestock. An attempt was made last year, but a different set of drilling contractors made a mess of the work, annoying Keelen greatly because it can be so hard to find viable underground sources.

Today it's the bore at Foal's Gully that is causing grief. It is fitted with a diesel pump which Keelen has topped up with fuel and started easily enough, but it's not pulling any water. Keelen calls out to Maggie for the spanner set she always carries in case of such emergencies. Maggie digs it out of the big tool chest on the back of the ute and climbs over a timber fence to deliver the bright yellow bundle. Meanwhile, Keelen is applying all her strength to undo the couplings that fix a thick black length of hose running from the bore up into the air a few metres away where it is attached to a metal pipe suspended on timber posts.

The pipe runs straight into a large, open galvanised-iron tank, partially set into a raised mound of earth. It is about half-full with dark green water reflecting the image of a cluster of small peach trees, covered in beautiful pink blossom; it brings an unexpected touch of European softness to the landscape. A keen gardener constantly looking for new treasures, Keelen some time ago dug up one of the seedlings and transplanted it to a corner of her garden where, much to her surprise, it thrives. After a brief struggle, the coupling has finally given in. Keelen decides to try and prime the pump by pouring some water down it. After a few attempts, it does the trick and water starts bubbling up out of the ground. She carefully reattaches everything and leaves the engine running after topping it up with just enough fuel to refill the water tanks. It will save her having to wait or come all the way back to turn the pump off.

Back at the house later that night more water problems emerge. There seems to be air in the pipes and no water is coming through here either. Cursing, Keelen heads back out into the dark to check the holding tank and the pump for the house, so she can have a hot shower after a hard day's work. She is back inside and finally relaxing in front of the television when Maggie tells her there is nothing coming out of the tap that brings precious rainwater into the kitchen. The small electric pressure pump that pulls water from the tank adjacent to the house doesn't seem to be working. That problem will have to wait until morning, a Sunday. Never mind. With another lick and bore run on the agenda anyway, it wasn't exactly going to be a day off. In fact, there are few days when some kind of work doesn't have to be done on the station.

Keelen's life sounds demanding, and it is, but nowhere near as challenging as the years when she was raising six children at the same time. She had been on Mt Tabor for a few years when she finally took a well-earnt holiday to travel up north to Ingham and visit relatives. During the trip she discovered the four girls and a boy from one family were living in a 'bad situation'. Without being explicit, Keelen explains she decided to apply for custody so she could bring them back to the station and care for them as her own.

Winning custody was not going to be easy, although it's fair to say Keelen had no idea just how difficult it would prove. Her job came with housing, but she was only earning $175 a week at the time, which is all the Bidjara community could afford to pay with support from a government CDP program. It took a long time to save even a small amount of money and she had to make multiple trips to Townsville to lodge papers and appear before the children's court. It was a struggle to find enough to cover the travel costs, let alone engage a lawyer, so she decided to represent herself.

The enormous amount of paperwork involved was intimidating for someone who only made it part way through the first year of high school. She also had to find the courage to stand up in court before a judge and the lawyers representing the child protection agency. The Indigenous legal service in Charleville offered a few pointers, although it was outside their field of expertise, and Keelen's sister, Dom, who was a teacher's aide, helped with the paperwork. 'It was all new to me and I often thought, "What the hell am I doing?" It was quite scary,' says Keelen.

The worst moment came when she arrived at the Townsville courthouse ten minutes later than the appointed deadline to file the main application. She had been given very short notice to make the drive of more than 1000 kilometres and she had to borrow money from family and friends to cover the fuel costs. 'I've fuckin' failed them,' she thought to herself as she rushed into the courtroom after driving all night. 'God, it was horrible,' she recalls. 'It was the start of a big circus for me. In we go, into the courtroom, and I was like, "Oh, my God," looking around the building. I had never been in a court before. And straight away they had their barrister and they were talking all these words and I had no idea what they were saying.'

Heart in mouth, Keelen rose to her feet and asked the judge: 'Excuse me, your honour. I don't mean to be rude, but can they please break it down for me so I can understand, because I have no idea what they are talking about, and I don't want to be agreeing and disagreeing to something I don't bloody know.' The opposing barrister stood to argue the point. He mocked her abilities and 'trashed' her for arriving late. But the judge intervened. Instructing the barrister to get on with it, he gave Keelen credit for only being a few minutes late instead of a whole day given the circumstances. 'I don't know what he thought of me, but I think I blew the old judge away as well,' she says, grinning.

What happened next astounded Keelen. Word started to spread within the legal fraternity that an Indigenous woman was trying on her own to win custody of five children. Keelen was back on Mt Tabor when the phone rang. It was a solicitor named Ann from the North Queensland Womens Legal Service in Townsville. 'What I actually do is pro bono and I have heard along the line that you are struggling a bit,' she said.

'Mate,' Keelen stopped her, 'can you please tell me what pro bono is first?'

Ann explained it involved members of the legal profession working for free. 'Oh mate, that's lotto to my ears,' a delighted Keelen replied with relief.

So Ann stepped in to help finish the application process, and she brought on board a whole team of people working pro bono as the case progressed through a ten-day trial. 'I ended up having half a dozen barristers and solicitors that were all with me. It was wonderful . . . They were lovely people and I will always be indebted in my heart and mind to those guys,' Keelen says. 'There are so many beautiful people out there, eh?'

Sole custody was eventually granted to Keelen and reality set in. She had to set up the homestead to cater for five more children, starting virtually from scratch when it came to organising enough things like bedding and even clothing. She went heavily into debt to do it, but Dom and her partner Rob pulled together some money to help and arranged to deliver the children as far as Torrens Creek, south-west of Charters Towers. 'So that's where my big extended family happened—out on the Torrens Creek road,' Keelen says simply. Joining her and Charlee, who was two and a half at the time, were Elizabeth, aged eleven; the only boy, CJ, who was ten; Fay, aged nine; six-year-old Donna; and Maggie, the youngest, who was four.

With Keelen doing all she could to make them feel loved and protected, the children quickly adapted to their new life, despite the isolation. 'They just felt so free, and they had all the love I could give,' she says. When Charlee was little, Keelen had taken her out on the property while she worked, but with so many children that was no longer an option, and the older ones had to settle down to lessons at home via School of the Air. A series of carers from the extended family helped to keep an eye on them during the day, including Betty's youngest sister, Aunty Clare, Allan's wife Sonia, and Dom's son Codey.

While there was love to spare, money continued to be an issue. Things improved about a year later when ACC came on the scene and started paying Keelen to look after their cattle, but she was constantly looking for ways to save and make more. An excellent shot, she decided to take on roo shooting. As long as she had a gun licence and followed regulations controlling the culling of kangaroos in Queensland, she could make reasonable money selling the skins to accredited buyers in Charleville.

Keelen soon discovered it was a tough and bloody business. To make as much money as possible, for a period of about five years or so she went out almost every night in a ute mounted with spotlights. Then she had to skin every animal, salt the hides to preserve them and tag them ready for delivery. She even made her own bullets by saving spent shells and refilling them with fresh primers, projectors and gunpowder, more than halving the cost of buying new ones. 'I tell you what, mate, that was hard yakka,' she reflects. 'Sometimes I ended up with a thousand dollars in my hand after tax, and sometimes five hundred. The only time I would miss going out was when it was rainy . . . I never had a lot of sleep. It seemed like I burnt all me candles at both ends.'

Another option was shooting dingoes. The local shire council at the time paid a $10 bounty for every scalp received, later increasing it to $30. The idea was to encourage landholders to help reduce the large numbers of wild dogs roaming the area. The only trouble was Keelen, for some reason, just couldn't bring herself to scalp one. The issue came up when much to her astonishment she was named a finalist in the 2007 Queensland Australian of the Year Award. Without her knowledge, she was nominated by Kristy, who was extremely proud of her mother's achievements.

'Is there anything you won't do?' the interview panel asked, obviously convinced by the application there wasn't too much she was frightened to tackle.

'Yes. I can't be comin' at scalping a dingo,' she replied without hesitation. They burst out laughing. 'Well, it's like I'm scalping my own dog,' she added, in her own defence.

Keelen got around her squeamishness by putting a proposition to the older children. If they agreed to do the scalping and salting, she would shoot the dingoes and organise delivery of the scalps to the council via the mail truck. In return, they could keep the money and share it between all six of them. Fay and CJ agreed and it turned out to be a lucrative deal. One year each child received $260, an extraordinary sum in the scheme of things.

❖ ❖ ❖

Sunday morning and after a bit of a sleep-in, Keelen is sitting on the front verandah in one of her favourite spots, sipping a cup of tea. Apart from the occasional mournful caw of a large black crow standing on a nearby timber railing, it is so quiet in the garden she can hear the somnolent buzz of bees hovering around the peach tree blossom. The garden is Keelen's pride and joy, the place she most often comes to relax and enjoy her own company. With occasional help from the family, she has created it from nothing. There were a few large box eucalypt trees not far from the back door when she first moved in, but that was it. Now there are shrubs and small fruit trees, and a series of flowerbeds that burst into life in the spring, framed by small rocks Keelen has gathered up on the property.

She is constantly on the lookout for new treasures to improve the landscaping. Her elder sister Brenda calls her a bowerbird, and looking at the eclectic assortment of bits and pieces which decorate the garden it is not hard to see why. There is a stump of petrified wood, pieces of metal and old machinery fashioned into sculptures, stone-coloured figurines and brightly painted garden gnomes, a miniature windmill, and some fascinating boulders. Keelen found the small, red stones on Babbiloora and, with permission from the manager, lugged them home. They are perfectly symmetrical, shaped in a slightly flattened sphere, and some are carved out in the centre, like a hard-boiled egg with a single scoop spooned from the top.

Alongside the back fence is a small shelter protecting an outdoor table and chairs. It is a simple timber structure with rich cultural meaning. The roof is fashioned out of thick, fibrous sheets of budgeroo bark. While pastoralists prized the budgeroo tree to make fence posts and strainers because its wood is both termite and fire resistant, the Bidjara people used the bark to make coffins. It was wrapped around bodies and tied with long strands taken from Kurrajong trees, and the coffins placed in hidden caves. The bark is also waterproof, making it a favourite choice for shelters. The open-sided version in Keelen's backyard was built with help from Allan and her nephew Ben, who decided to finish it as a birthday surprise while she was away.

From her seat on the front verandah, Keelen can admire another construction effort—a large, shallow pond she dug out with a front-end loader. At one end it has a small waterfall fashioned out of stone and concrete. Especially in the summer, she loves sitting here at night after a hard day's work, listening to the soothing murmur of water as it trickles into the pond.

This morning her gaze is fixed further afield, on the home paddock and the tall stands of grass that sprang up after all the rain. It is dry now, of no interest to the stockhorses roaming the paddock, and a potential fire danger once the weather warms up. Keelen is itching to clear it away. The forecast is for cool, calm conditions and maybe even a little rain, perfect for burning off. She heads inside and picks up the phone to call her good friends Kelvin and Louise, who live on a neighbouring station. Kelvin is a registered fire officer with the Queensland Rural Fire Service and can issue the required permit.

He isn't in so she leaves a message and then sets to work checking out the recalcitrant pressure pump. It is tucked under the raised floor of the kitchen, alongside a 5000-litre plastic tank that collects water from the homestead's simple, gable roof. Crouching down, she uses a shifting spanner to wrestle with the connection between the pump and the waterpipe which has seized up. If she breaks it, the repair job will be even more time-consuming so she takes it steady. With a screech, the coupling finally gives way so Keelen can pull the pump out from under the house and take a closer look. She takes it apart, methodically checks all the moving parts and the electric motor, and decides it's a job for the dealer in Charleville. In the meantime, she can borrow a similar pump from Dave's house and install it while she gets this one fixed.

Another cup of tea and a cigarette, and it's time to do a lick run over into Babbiloora. Dave wants her to check out Black Springs, not far over the boundary, to pump the bore, and put out a bit more lick along the way. There is a large mob of cattle camped alongside a massive dam and they are going through it pretty quickly. This is one of Keelen's favourite runs because it gives her an excuse to visit an old campsite that was used by Billy Geebung, a skilled tracker, a respected horseman and her great-grandfather on her mother's side of the family. She didn't know about this place until Dave showed her. As a young stockman, he visited the campsite and met Billy. Keelen was astonished to learn parts of the camp were still standing.

It is tucked away off a side track overgrown with stinking Roger, a type of daisy with a strong, unpleasant smell which she is reluctant to walk through. Pushing the weed aside, she follows the track on foot, pointing out paw prints left behind in the soft sand by some dingoes. They are barely discernible but with a glance she has worked out that there are several pups in the group. A few steps further on, she leaves the track and heads up into long grass, which parts to reveal some old timber posts set either side of what was obviously a stone fireplace. 'This has been here for close around a hundred years. It always makes me so proud to come here . . . It's so old but it's still here, and it's just so special. This was their camp. This is where they cooked, this is where they hung their billies . . . I love it—it's a very special spot deep in my heart.'

Billy's daughter, Sissy, married Keelen's grandfather, Dan. Dan's father, Charlie, was the original Mailman, who had the local mail run 'back in the horse and wagon days'. He acquired the surname after a misunderstanding one day when his wife Lucy was trying to explain who her husband was to some white people. She spoke only a few words of English and they had difficulty understanding her. 'You know. Charlie. Does the mail,' she tried to tell them.

'Oh, right. Charlie Mailman,' they said, and it stuck.

The surname has since become well known to many Australians through the actor Deborah Mailman. Her father Wally was a celebrated rodeo champion who is honoured in the Stockman's Hall of Fame at Longreach and also on a wall built quite recently in Augathella as part of a new community park. Keelen's grandfather and Deborah's grandfather were brothers.

As an older woman, Lucy was forcibly removed from Bogarella station and taken to Cherbourg, an mission set up in the early 1900s about 170 kilometres north-west of Brisbane, as part of a government policy to segregate Indigenous people from the rest of the Queensland population.[39] Children and adults from dozens of cultural groups were taken there over several decades, separated into dormitories, forbidden to speak their languages and forced to work. 'Old Granny Mailman mourned and mourned for home. She wanted to come back to her country and her family,' says Keelen, explaining that her sons worked for years to save money and send it to the authorities so they would let her out. 'Such a lot of sadness,' she adds.

The visit to the campsite reinforces yet again Keelen's sense of connectedness with this part of the world. She was raised from an early age to respect her culture, learn the Bidjara language and how to live off the land, and to know the Dreamtime stories explaining how it was created, which have been handed down from generation to generation since the beginning of time.

Driving back from the campsite she shares one of her favourite stories about the giant *goori goori* bird which lived high in the ranges and preyed on Bidjara children: 'He told them to climb on his back and he said he would take 'em for a ride . . . but the parents would never seem 'em again. He actually took them back to his nest and ate them. One little fella, Wangurd, was pretty clever one time . . . He jumped off and escaped, and he ran back and told the elders and his family what had happened. So the warriors all went out with fire sticks and hunted. They seen a big nest in the highest tree in the country, on the side of a hill. So they waited for him to land, and then they lit it on fire. And when he landed his feathers caught on fire, and as he flew he sent out the sparks that created the stars and the smoke that created the Milky Way.'

Another important Dreamtime figure is the Rainbow Serpent, or *Moondungera*. 'He come down out of the stars, out of the sky, and created all the rivers, all the waterways,' Keelen says. 'If there are water places that don't go dry, that's where the *Moondungera* lives. You can have the biggest drought in the country but that water won't go dry because it's the home of the *Moondungera*.'

Part of Bidjara beliefs is that the rainbow colours of the Rainbow Serpent are so dazzlingly beautiful that if you let him catch your eye, even for a moment, he will mesmerise you and fill your body with poisons so that you die. Keelen recounts a story about her grandfather, who was riding back to camp one night when he saw a bright light. It was the *Moondungera* collecting leaves and making a nest. Her grandfather became very sick, but Billy Geebung and an old uncle, who was a 'clever man', the term for doctor, sang powerful healing songs over him all night to remove the poisons and he was cured.

'All the Dreamtime stories, they are a big part of us,' Keelen says. 'People think it's hogwash . . . but if they can believe a lot of laws and powers in other people's cultures, why can't they understand we have a culture too that is very strong and powerful and we are trying to tell it?'

Keelen is extremely committed to passing on these stories and other elements of her culture to younger generations and even the broader community. She has made a point of teaching her children and grandchildren, relishing the two years or so Allan spent back on Mt Tabor with his own family when they decided to escape the Brisbane 'rat race'. At one stage troubled youth from Charleville were also coming out regularly to stay on the property for some tough love to help them break away from a cycle of alcohol and drug abuse. As part of building their sense of self-respect, Keelen showed them how to live on the land and told them about Bidjara traditions.

On another occasion a large group of Bidjara elders and schoolchildren travelled out from Charleville as part of a generational learning project organised by local Indigenous and community health agencies. They were taken to different sites of cultural significance where the students interviewed the elders about the sites, and then created digital stories. 'A lot of kids don't get that sort of opportunity to learn about their culture and I think there should be more of it,' Keelen says. 'Because I am so proud and passionate about my culture, I love to teach it.'

Putting words into action, not far from the old campsite Keelen brings the ute to a sudden stop and hops out. She has spotted one of her favourite bush foods and is keen to share the taste. The native blackberry, or *burrumu*, starts to appear in the early spring and these are the first fruits of the season. Shaped like a small black olive, they grow on a bright green bush with thorns. They are crunchy and sweet, like an apple, with tiny seeds. *Burrumu* are Charlee's favourite bush tucker.

Keelen's favourite is echidna, what she calls porcupine, or in Bidjara, *barrbirda*. When it's roasted underground or in an oven, the meat is rich and the skin turns into crackling, like pork, but the taste is apparently quite different. 'To me it's got its own complete taste,' she says. 'But there are a couple of glands and if you don't get them out, don't even bother eating it. It's like you're sitting there eating ants.' She was shown how to track echidna by her Uncle Bob. He would take her out after it had rained or there had been a heavy frost, when the tracks were easy to spot in the damp sand. 'They are not hard to catch, once you know how,' she adds. 'You might have to walk 2 kilometres, or more, before you find them but you will find them.'

Betty taught her how to find witchetty grubs, or *dhambun*. Traditionally, a stem of grass with a natural hook-shape at one end was used to reach up under the bark and drag them out. It was a delicate operation which had to be done slowly so the grass didn't break. These days most people use wire instead. One day Keelen was out on the property with Charlee and some of her friends when she overheard her daughter sharing the same knowledge. Calling her friends over, Charlee told them: 'See this stuff around the tree? That's *dhambun* shit. This is where you will find a *dhambun*.'

'What's that?' they asked her.

'A witchetty grub that you eat,' she replied.

'Eeww,' they exclaimed in apparent disgust before begging her to show them.

With Keelen's help, they retrieved one of the largest *dhambun* she has ever seen, cooked it and gave some to the visitors. 'I was that proud of her,' Keelen says, 'and they were just blown away, those little fellas.'

Because they are her totems, Keelen is not allowed to eat red kangaroo, emus or brown snake, although she has tasted another species of snake. She tried it as part of a 'welcome to country' ceremony in Western Australia's Kimberley region, during a personal and professional development course run by the Australian Rural Leadership Foundation. Keelen was one of 32 people selected to participate in the prestigious program, which takes about 60 days to complete over a period of seventeen months. The trip west in May 2009 was the first time Keelen had ventured outside Queensland. Later on she not only got to travel to other states and meet leading business people and politicians connected with agriculture, she made her first journey overseas, to India. While she has great memories of the adventure, for her the trip to the Kimberley was one of the best parts of the whole experience. 'I had always wanted to go—it was a dream come true for me—and I had always said if I was going to eat snake, I wanted it to be on country, in the Kimberley, with the traditional owners.'

Keelen's mother also made sure her children learnt the Bidjara language. Betty was a hard taskmaster. 'Pronounce it properly or don't say it all,' she would tell them. Aside from ensuring the language wasn't lost for at least another generation, Betty's strict teaching had other unexpected benefits when a Federal Court of Australia judge visited Mt Tabor in 2000 to gather evidence as part of a land rights claim. He had come on country early in the process to hear from elders whose health was fragile. One of the barristers heard Betty and another elder, Uncle Rusty, 'rattling the lingo' while they sat on the verandah. 'Wouldn't it be good if one of you young ones could speak the lingo and they knew what you were saying, and you could translate it for the judge,' he remarked.

'I can do that,' Keelen volunteered.

'So I rattled the lingo off at Uncle Rusty. He just jumped up, pulled his strides up, tilted his cowboy hat back and said in English, "No bloody fear. People have got to pay a lot of money for our language." It was an absolute classic and so funny the way he done it; he was quite a character. Our barrister said it was excellent because it showed the judge on country that someone my age spoke the lingo and that an elder who was 30 years older understood me perfectly.'

Proving ongoing continuity of culture across the generations and links before European settlement are essential parts of making a land claim under the Australian Native Title Act. Native title is the recognition by Australian law that some Indigenous people have rights and interests to land that come from their traditional laws and customs. In this case, the process is attempting to legally define the boundary of Bidjara country so they have rights such as protecting cultural heritage sites within the area.

Acting under power of attorney for her Uncle Bob, Keelen is part of a group representing the Bidjara people in a frustrating process that began more than a decade ago. In that time many witnesses and all the original applicants except Uncle Bob have died, including Betty and Uncle Rusty; six elders passed away in just one 45-day period in the same year Keelen lost her mother. Now the next generation of Bidjara is stepping in to take their place. 'It really saddens me because it seems like it's neverending,' Keelen says. 'You get something ready, then they want something else. Then you get that ready and they want something else.'

One of the unfortunate side-effects is that members of the Bidjara community not involved directly in the process do not always understand just how much work is required and why it's taking so long. Keelen has spent many days and hours along with the other applicants attending meetings with lawyers and mediation sessions in Brisbane and Charleville, helping to prepare evidence, checking and signing paperwork. But she is determined to hang in there. 'To me it's all about my people, my family, my grandkids, and plenty of generations to come. What we leave behind now will hopefully be a great benefit to them in the future. But we want to make sure everything is right, as spot-on as possible,' she says. 'A big wish for me is hoping we get it all sorted before I go, before I pass, so that the next generation don't have to go through such a struggle.'

Although ongoing access to Mt Tabor is not in question because the property was purchased by the Indigenous Land Corporation, one of Keelen's major contributions is mapping heritage sites on the station. Once they are identified, the next step is to put up fences to protect the sites from horses and cattle.

The plan is to install simple, four-strand barbed wire fences around every area, and then later on reinforce the perimeters with mesh, cemented into the ground to exclude feral pigs and other smaller pests. With help from Ray's son Floyd Robinson, she has located more than 50 important sites, and is in the process of plotting their precise location using GPS.

While the technology is great for pinpointing exact coordinates, identifying culturally significant sites in the first place relies heavily on Keelen's knowledge as a Bidjara woman. 'There are places I will go to and I will know it's not a women's place, and I shouldn't be there. It's a spiritual thing. I just get that feeling. And I will ring Floyd and say, "Listen, mate, I have found something here but I'm having a bit of an uneasy feeling, and I think it might be a men's place." And he will find time to come out. Then there are a lot of women's places that he can't go to, and he will call me. I was told by me mum what to say in the lingo to let the spirits know I am meaning no harm and what I am doing, and I think a big part of my journey out here has been through the spiritual looking-after of my ancestors because they can see what I am doing and know that I am doing the best I can and not letting anyone do any harm.'

Sitting on a favourite slab of rock in the heart of Lost City, Keelen pushes her Akubra to the back of her head and digs the heels of scruffy elastic-sided boots into a crevice for extra purchase. While contemplating the view, she reaches into the front pocket of her green-checked flannelette shirt and fishes out the makings for another cigarette. Stretching out to her left is a clearing smattered with raggedy boulders and low-growing shrubs, which drops away to a heavily timbered valley. In front stands a ridge-line of ochre-coloured sandstone topped with a distinctive slab of dark grey rock. The sandstone has weathered away and the harder layer protrudes like the cap on a mushroom. Astonishingly, a large gum tree appears to be growing out of the solid surface, its very existence both a puzzle and a reflection of the unfathomable tenacity of nature.

The oddly shaped outcrops which make up Lost City provided shelter for thousands of years to the Bidjara people. Stories relating to this site are still handed down from one generation to the next, and it remains an important place of pilgrimage. Archaeologists and experts from Bush Heritage Australia have come here to add their knowledge about its plants and animals, and the paintings and engravings scattered across dozens of caves and sheltered walls. The hand prints stencilled in white at the entrance to one cave are so bright they could have been painted yesterday, but Keelen has been told they are thousands of years old. Further along, smaller prints in a less sheltered space are softly faded. Markings at the entrance tell her this was a women's place, most likely used to give birth. Around another corner, in an alcove which stays cool even in the summer, are engravings shaped like emu tracks. Sadly, some have been obliterated by graffiti carved over the top during the past 100 years or so, before public access ended.

'Coming here, you can understand why my culture is so deep and so strong. Every spring I fall in love with this place all over again,' Keelen says, contemplating her first visit all those years ago. 'The elders more or less made me a keeper of all this cultural stuff, and that is a great honour to have handed to me . . . Passing on the culture is not a big thing, it's *the* big thing. You have to keep your culture alive. It is very important to let my kids and grandkids know their identity and their culture, their country, where they come from, where they belong. It is a big part of our being.'

Watching the sun as it drops lower, casting a golden light across a small clearing where the first tiny purple wildflowers of the season are starting to emerge, she reflects: 'There is some country here, mate, beautiful country, eh? Rough and rugged. It's really unique, different in every section you go, and I love that it's untouched because it holds its own beauty . . . They always said this is a healing place. A lot of people have come here that have been a bit mucked up or emotionally down, a bit lost within themselves, and they have left here with a good feeling.'

She pauses, thinking of her beloved sister Dom, who begged Keelen to go to Ingham for her 40th birthday party. Much to Keelen's regret she couldn't afford the trip. A few months later Dom was dead. Distraught at the loss and working too hard in an effort to cope with the grief, Keelen thought about leaving Mt Tabor but Dom had loved the station too, so she stayed. 'She would come home for a visit and drive around, just feeling free. She loved it.'

A few years on, Keelen is not too sure how much longer she will remain. Like her sister, she feels free here, but she has almost completed the property management goals she set herself some time ago. 'When I first got offered the job, I didn't know how long I was going to be here, where it was going to take me. I had no idea. I just went day by day . . . Looking back over the memories, God, I battled it. I really battled it. That is why I am proud of me achievements . . . but I know one day this has to come to a closure.'

Although she has no wish to move into a town again after the peace and quiet of Mt Tabor, she can see herself living on a few acres somewhere quiet but more convenient, and spending a little more time with her 'bunch of little lovelies'—the four grandchildren she adores, Owen, Malita, Leon and Jamahl. She feels privileged to be young and fit enough to kick a footy with them and chase them along the beach. 'That's a great gift, eh? Bless their hearts.'

In the short-term, she is looking forward to a year without children and some 'me' time so she can focus on her own needs a little more, and properly process the grief relating to Dom's death. With the newfound confidence and skills the leadership course provided, lately she has also been thinking that perhaps the time is approaching when she needs to go back out into the wider world and share what she calls her 'true heart story' to generate greater understanding and reconciliation between Indigenous and non-Indigenous Australians. 'There are a lot of beautiful and good people in the world but there is still so much discrimination too,' she says, with great sadness. 'We are not all drunken, bludgin', no hopin' blacks, and I guess I am an example. So I'm thinking that maybe there is a bigger purpose for me out there somewhere to tell my story and give people more of an insight.'

No matter where her future takes her, there is one thing about which Keelen is certain. She will always return to Mt Tabor, because this land is in her blood. She says, 'That's something born within me. It will never change.'

EPILOGUE

As the minibus pulls to a stop next to the paddock gate a burble of voices becomes clearly audible, punctuated by a sudden burst of laughter. The sliding door of the bus is flung back and the passengers reluctantly break off their conversation to climb out. As each one emerges they give me a kiss on the cheek and a heartfelt hug, delighted to be together at last and in my home territory.

The women of the land—Mary, Lynette, Jan, Nan, Susie, Cecily, Catherine and Keelen—have just met each other for the first time. They have travelled from across Australia to attend the national launch of the book that captures their personal stories and remarkable everyday lives. Over the past hour the bus has dropped in to various hotels and holiday apartments to collect them one or two at a time, and carry them to a farm in the beautiful Adelaide Hills. In a part of the world where the climate is highly variable, even the weather seems to be celebrating the occasion. It is an absolutely perfect autumn morning. The air is still, the sun is shining in a clear blue sky, and the temperature is already warm after a mild night.

In the adjacent paddock, Bob Evans sits on his tractor, front-end loader resting easy on the ground. His wife, Jean, makes her way towards us, glancing over to where a quiet mob of cattle are contentedly munching on grass hay. A beautiful, wooded valley and the receding hills of the Mount Lofty Ranges provide a picturesque backdrop.

Jean and Bob have kindly lent their paddock and their cattle so we can all have our photos taken in a setting appropriate to the women and their stories. A photographer from the local daily newspaper has been colluding with Bob to arrange the 'set'. Old hands at working with animals, Bob and Jean arrived at the shoot with a large round bale of hay ready to feed out and make sure the cattle stand in the right place and stay put.

It is proving not so easy to manage the women. Excited about the day and eager to find out more about each other, they are far more intent on talking than standing in the right place to have their photo taken. Joking reference is made to fetching a border collie to help round them up and usher them to a large, strategically placed log. The surface worn smooth and bleached silvery grey by the elements, it makes an ideal prop. In between various combinations of shots, the women continue to talk, learning each other's stories, asking questions about each other's farming enterprises, and chatting away to Jean and Bob while the cattle quietly ignore the interruption of a peaceful day's grazing.

Despite coming from diverse backgrounds, it's as if the women have known each other for years. The conversation is easy and natural, the things they find in common so numerous they could be mothers, daughters, sisters. At one level, it is the camaraderie of people who make their living from the land and deal with the same immutable challenges—weather, market forces, rising costs and fluctuating prices for the food and fibre they produce.

Six months later, the pattern of life at home hasn't changed that much for Mary Naisbitt since my visit to Lake Grace in May 2011 except for one important factor. To everyone's relief the cropping season brought rain. Across the region, tractors took to the paddocks in the last weeks of autumn, sowing thousands of hectares of cereal crops which quickly emerged from barren soils, creating rolling carpets of brilliant green and reviving a sense of cautious optimism in households down to their last loan extensions from the banks. The rain kept coming as the season progressed, producing the best crops Kevin had seen since he came home to the farm in 2003 to work alongside his mother.

With follow-up rains continuing into the spring, there was a lightness of spirit about the celebrations held in September to mark the centenary of Lake Grace. The resilient community had survived another bad spell, and there was plenty to celebrate. Former residents and descendants of the local settlers 'came out of the woodwork' for the program of events, helping to make it a roaring success, according to Mary. 'It was unreal,' she says.

But every farmer knows from bitter experience the dangers of counting proverbial chickens. In a paradox that is all too common in the history of Australian farming, the rain following the drought became a curse, continuing to fall and wiping out its beneficent promise. After three years of one of the worst dry spells on record in Western Australia's southern wheat belt, it was so wet during the summer harvest that machinery bogged in the paddock. Kevin and his neighbours often had to make several attempts to reap their grain, desperate to salvage what they could before it was downgraded in value because of the damage.

In a lighter moment, at least for Kevin, Mary was finally forced to climb up behind the wheel of the massive John Deere tractor that he had been trying to get her to drive for some time. She continues to prefer the trusty International that was delivered on Kevin's third birthday, dubbed Nanna's Tractor by his eldest son Griffin. But in much the same way as circumstances forced her daughter Diane to conquer her anxiety and drive the little red tractor to her mother's rescue when she became bogged alongside a dam, Mary had to overcome her own concerns about tackling the giant green tractor when she was called on one day to help tow the harvester out of the mire. 'I only had to move it ten chain or so to get him out of a wet spot,' she says. 'It's easy enough to drive really, but the size of it . . .'

While the crops may not have realised their earning potential, Jenakora's sheep, on the other hand, prospered with the extended wet conditions. There was so much feed in the way of pasture and unharvested grain that Kevin bought another mob of ewes to eat it all. Because the sheep were in excellent condition, lambing rates were higher than usual, and there was grass to spare to make hay.

It was yet another reminder of the constant swings and roundabouts that come with earning your living from the land, and Mary has seen plenty of them over the years. It will never stop her loving the farm. Despite a promise to herself to take things a bit easier in her 'retirement', she still helps out regularly and continues to be heavily involved in community organisations and activities. 'I keep saying I am getting too old and I'm going to slow down . . . but I like to keep busy,' she confesses.

Keeping busy is no trouble at all for Lynette Rideout. She is now juggling motherhood with the demands of running an orchard and an expanding fruit and vegetable retail operation. Baby Robert was born in October 2011, seventeen days after the death of Lynette's mother, Audrey. With the circle of life bringing both birth and death to the family within weeks it is an understatement to say it was a challenging time for Lynette and her husband, Chris. 'It was bittersweet, but what can you do?' reflects Lynette.

Extremely well cared for in a nursing home not far from Oakdale, Audrey was suffering from dementia and she did not always recognise her daughter in the final days. Lynette says there was a moment of clarity about a week before she died when Audrey reached out and touched her distended belly and said, 'I wish this baby would hurry up.' But the due date was still more than two weeks away and Robert was in no hurry. 'She just didn't get to see him, although we had an ultrasound done and I blew it up so she could see his face,' Lynette recalls quietly. 'Then the day before she died she was really struggling . . . You could see she was fighting it so I told her we had the baby and it was all fine . . . and she just let go.'

Audrey died on 1 October 2011. She was buried next to her husband, Leo, in the grounds of an historic church at The Oaks, a town not far from Oakdale. A simple rustic timber slab building, the church was built some time around the late 1830s and restored in the 1980s by the local historical society of which Leo and Audrey were active members.

Lynette and Chris crossed their fingers that Robert wouldn't come early and upset the funeral arrangements. He was due three days later. When Lynette still showed no signs of going into labour eight days later, her doctor decided it was time to induce the birth. It proved to be a long and difficult confinement, with a few complications that gave the expectant father some frightening moments, but the baby finally arrived at eight o'clock on a Tuesday evening. 'Chris was absolutely fantastic,' says Lynette proudly.

It surprises no-one that within a matter of weeks Robert was following in his mother's footsteps and spending considerable time out in the orchard at Top Forty. Not that there was much choice. The hectic Christmas tree season was upon them so he slept nearby in a stroller while Lynette served the regular influx of customers. Robert's first solid food was stewed apple, and well before turning one he had his first set of blue overalls, just like those Lynette wore as a child. And just like Lynette, the increasingly active child has an apple bin as his first play pen. Lined with blankets and carpet, it can be hitched up behind her tractor and carried out to wherever she is working. 'I park the bin, put him in it and away I go. When I am picking or pruning, he goes with me,' she says.

While he is a few years off being able to help his mother in the orchard, Robert is already proving an asset at the farmers markets where Lynette sells her produce. He not only helps keep the customers amused when things get a bit busy, but he has perfected the art of staring at people until he gets their attention, and then giving them a big smile, as if encouraging them to come over and buy something. 'He has gotten quite used to the market crowd, and the other stallholders are like a family. It's not unusual for another stallholder to come and collect him and take him for a walk, and he loves people,' Lynette says. 'He is a wonderful little boy. Being a mum is one of the most fantastic things in a world. I couldn't be happier, but my goodness isn't it challenging.'

Challenging or not, Lynette and Chris are talking about the idea of having another child, and the arrival of the next generation is already reshaping the orchard. In winter 2012, Lynette took delivery of 63 rare and heritage apple varieties to plant out a new section. 'I have named the block Robert's Applery because by the time they are bearing in commercial quantities Robert will be old enough to help pick them. I am planting them for his future,' she says.

As the new trees testify, Lynette is still forging ahead in her constant quest to diversify and boost the small orchard's ability to generate money. The number of apple varieties alone on Top Forty now adds up to 95, most of them never seen in supermarkets or shops. Lynette sells them at farmers' markets in the Sydney area. During the past 12 months she has become a foundation member of the Exeter market, and started selling produce at Lane Cove and Bowral, as well as Thirlmere, Camden and Picton. Meanwhile, Chris has bought a truck and set up his own delivery business.

Lynette admits she is constantly on the go, helping Chris at times with deliveries as well as working in the orchard. Someone comes in two days a week to look after Robert, and Chris's mum and friends step in occasionally too so that Lynette has 'tractor time'. 'I've got a certain number of things I want to achieve and I have every reason to try because I have a new "boss"—the baby. It's his future,' she says. 'And just because you've got a baby and you are a new mum it doesn't mean you can't do stuff. I've had people say to me that I'll have to give up the farm work a bit with the baby but I can't just switch the farm off.'

Switching the farm off is far from Jan Raleigh's mind too, although at the age of 66 the Timboon dairy farmer is taking steps to plan for her retirement. In June 2011, she took on a farm manager. Philip is in his mid twenties, married with two young children. Jan and her farm adviser found him after advertising in *The Weekly Times*, a weekly rural newspaper based in Melbourne which has been delivering news to farmers for more than 140 years.

Although he didn't grow up milking cows, Philip left school at the age of 15 and found work on a large dairy farm near Mount Gambier, about 230 kilometres west of Timboon. Now studying for a diploma in agriculture, he responded to the ad because the idea of managing a farm, rather than just working as one of the milk hands, really appealed to him. 'He's really passionate about the dairy industry and working in it, and that's what's encouraging to me,' Jan says. 'We are going to set up a sort of succession plan so he can buy into the cattle and the farm.'

Philip had already made a start building up his own herd when he arrived at Timboon. He brought with him 15 young Friesian–Jersey heifers. Much to his delight, the first calf he bred from them was born on Father's Day in September 2012. The newborn was a heifer so it will potentially join the milking herd one day. Philip is also gradually acquiring shares in Jan's Aussie Red calves, with the idea that one day he will end up owning 50 per cent of the farm's dairy cattle. That is no small thing given Jan's beautiful herd of pedigree Aussie Reds were ranked number one for the breed in Australia in 2011/12, according to the system used to objectively measure the national herd.

Meanwhile, Philip is responsible for organising where the milking herd grazes each day and what pastures are grown. He brings the cows in and milks them too, with Jan helping to clean up afterwards. She doesn't get off quite so lightly during the calving season, when the herd is split into 'fresh' cows that have just come in for milking after giving birth, and those that have been milking for a while. Then there are the first-time milkers to handle as they get used to the shed and the milking machines. And there are the calves to raise—50 or more depending on how many heifers are born. The bull calves are sold but the heifers are kept for the milking herd. Feeding them and monitoring their health is a big job. 'It takes a lot of time, and then you get the odd one that gets sick. If one dies I get so upset it's not funny,' confesses Jan. 'You have to watch them hard because you need to pick up early if they are not doing well.'

Jan is enjoying having Philip around to help with the calves, and all the other daily farm chores. 'Feeding the hay and other things are just so much easier with two of you. We have usually finished milking by eight o'clock and fed the calves by 8.30.

Philip has breakfast with me, and we talk about what we are going to do for the day, and it all works out well.'

With Philip on deck, they are milking the cows the more conventional twice a day, instead of only once, so they are back in the dairy in the evening. As a result, the cows produced 37 per cent more milk last year than the year before, attracting a significant financial bonus from Fonterra, the company which buys Jan's milk. It cost more to produce because a dryer than usual summer and autumn meant a crop of turnips sown to provide autumn fodder to the cows failed to come up. Instead, she had to spend a lot of money buying in feed. 'But it kept the cows milking really well. It was hard work . . . but we certainly got our money back.'

At least she had help this time. Jan is delighted with how quickly Philip has settled into the farm, and how compatible they are proving to be as a working team. 'It's sort of uncanny in a way. We almost think alike. It's really weird. He'll be thinking something, and I'll mention the same thing, and he'll say, "How did you know I was thinking that?" And he really loves the red cattle. He's got right into them and he's got a good memory for all the animals.'

Jan is hoping one day that Philip will be interested in buying the farm. Single and without any children of her own, she says none of her extended family are interested. 'So I may as well sell it to someone who is keen on the dairy industry and wants to be involved because there is not enough of it.'

The other major change in Jan's life came with hip surgery in 2011. She hadn't realized quite how debilitating the constant joint pain was until after it went away. 'It made a huge difference. I sort of feel a different person all together.' She was only in hospital for five days, resisting a doctor's insistence that she should move into a rehabilitation centre to recover from the surgery rather than going straight home. By then she was already tackling stairs with the aid of a walking stick and itching to get back to the farm where a New Zealand couple had settled in to milk the cows and generally look after things. 'They parked their van on the track in front of the house, and they used to come in at night and talk to me, and watch television. I had my bed brought into the lounge room because you are meant to lay fairly flat for first six weeks, and I would lie on the bed in front of telly,' she says.

In the past fourteen weeks, Jan has also been following a 'Healthy Weight for Life' diet, organised by her insurance company. She has already lost 10 kilograms. Combined with the benefits of the hip replacement, she is feeling like a new woman.

Across Bass Strait, Nan Bray is venturing into an exciting new phase in her wool enterprise too. The Oatlands farmer has decided to produce tops and yarns from her own wool and market it under her own label—White Gum Wool. The name was inspired by the beautiful white gum trees still growing on the highest point of Lemon Hill. The accompanying logo is an image of her stockman Davey Carnes and some sheep near one of these trees.

To say bringing the concept to reality has involved negotiating a few hurdles is an understatement. Finding businesses able to clean, card, comb, spin and dye her wool has been a fraught reminder of the crumbling state of the manufacturing sector in Australia, and the almost complete demise of local wool processing. Then there has been the extremely time-consuming and frustrating process of navigating bureaucracy, not just in one country, but, out of necessity, two.

Nan has persevered because she believes consumers care just as much about the wool they use and wear being produced ethically and sustainably as she does. She wants to produce tops and yarns whose origins are traceable and held to account. She can prove to the people who buy them that the sheep have been run in a way that respects the environment, and without using the controversial practice of mulesing.

After tracking down a company still in business and prepared to handle small quantities of wool, Nan sent her first bale for scouring in June 2011 but it took almost six months before it was ready for the next step. In the meantime, she found a small company able to comb the wool but she was still having trouble locating someone who would spin it to the standard she required. Nan finally hooked up with an Australian company prepared to try spinning her fibre but by the time her wool was ready, they had decided to get out of spinning altogether. Another well-respected company wasn't able to take on her fibre because it was too fine for their plant to handle. Another cottage spinner was too small to handle the quantities needed to make it worthwhile.

In the end, Nan felt she had exhausted the Australian options and turned to a company in New Zealand. They would comb, spin and dye her wool, and then wind it up into standard sized balls and label them as long as she was prepared to produce no less than 300 kilograms of finished yarn at a time. They were also happy to use the unique dye colours Nan had designed by Tasmanian textile artist Wendy Koolhof, using the rugged landscape of the Tasmanian midlands as her inspiration. With the processing and freight costs it wouldn't be cheap, but the end product would be equivalent to the high quality yarn used by Italian fashion designers and should sell for a premium. 'I just wanted to put my toe in, but at this point I had to make a serious commitment,' Nan says.

People got to see some hand-dyed tops and the new logo for the first time in June 2012 at the Campbell Town show, one of the most important agricultural shows in Australia for sheep and wool producers. A highlight is always the fashion parade showcasing garments made from wool. As an initial marketing exercise, this time it featured a stunning wedding dress and two bridesmaid dresses made out of Nan's wool by Brisbane textile artist Svenja. Nan also set up a trade display which won a trophy after being judged the show's best trade exhibit.

It was a very promising start, but three months later Nan was still waiting for the first delivery of yarn from the processors. This time the issue was the quarantine requirements between Australia and New Zealand. Apparently Australian veterinarians from the quarantine authority were not prepared to sign a form introduced by the New Zealand authorities relating to biosecurity. The Australians wanted to use another form but it was not acceptable to the New Zealanders.

Nan and the shipping agent worked to resolve the problem, and Nan thought things were finally in hand, and then her agent became ill with the flu and was out of action for two weeks. When the wool finally did reach New Zealand, the required paperwork was missing. 'The best way to make me determined to do something is to put boulders in my path,' says Nan. 'There was a point where the whole thing unravelled in a weekend so I really had to sit myself down and work out how much I wanted to do this. But once I found the guy in New Zealand I was pretty confident it would work.'

Back on the farm, Davey and Nan have seen through another two lambing seasons. The oldest ewes on the farm now were the first lambs raised in family groups five years ago, and Nan has been consolidating her approach to running sheep around the principle of nutritional wisdom. The 2012 clip shorn from the pregnant ewes in August was the best yet—clean, bright fleeces and no tender wool. Nan even tried her hand at classing the clip, working alongside her regular woolclasser who is retiring soon.

At the moment, she is looking forward to the fun she and Davey are about to have training four new pups. The first she has bred in some years, they are the progeny of her sweet little long-haired border collie, Janie, and a New Zealand-type slick coated dog called Ted, owned by Nan's occasional stockperson Karen Fish.

Janie had seven pups. Two have gone to homes where they will work as sheepdogs and a third provides companionship for a young boy from Hobart whose parents are friends of Nan. The pup stays with the boy's grandparents who have a farm where the boy spends most weekends and time after school. 'He called him Buddy, and they are inseparable,' Nan says.

Nan kept another two for herself and gave the others to Davey who selected them from the litter not long after they were born. The first he chose was Blaze, the smallest and darkest of the litter. Then there is Joker, the only slick coated pup left behind, whose face is half white and half black. A 'thinker' who watches the other dogs carefully, he may be Davey's but he won't let Nan out of his sight when they are out on runs. 'He is a bit special,' she admits. Then there is Flynn, who takes after his father because 'he has long legs and runs like the wind'. And finally there is Pearl, named after her great grandmother who died in her sleep in June 2011 at the age of 15 while Nan was overseas.

Nan and Davey will train all four pups together. Nan has never worked alongside Davey training dogs from scratch before and she is looking to seeing what she can learn from the very experienced stockman.

Susie Chisholm is also looking forward to learning something new when it comes to breeding beef cattle on her property near Adelong. In September 2012, she attended a workshop and farm tour organised by the Te Mania Angus stud for producers who are part of Team Te Mania. There are about 40 of them now, and Susie came back energised from spending time with them, reconnecting with old friends, and hearing about the latest research and technology to help her be a better cattle producer. They sent her away with a laptop computer loaded with the latest software that will make it easier for her to record information about each animal when she brings them into the yards.

She is particularly excited about the idea of using emerging DNA technology to identify the sires of her calves. She is planning to make a start next year. She wants to be able to run more bulls and cows in each paddock, but it is important that she knows which bulls mate successfully with which cows so that she can record the precise family history of all the offspring. Taking DNA samples will enable her to do this. It's a practice not that widely used by Australian beef producers because the tests are so expensive, but the cost is dropping as more farmers take it on and more commercial players come into the market offering the service.

Susie's passion to be the best commercial beef cattle producer she can possibly be is infectious. She is extremely enthusiastic about anything that will help her to breed cattle that produce even better quality meat. The feedback she puts most value on comes from the processor, who sends her 'kill sheets' recording the details of each carcass. She is delighted that she is often matching the quality of elite wagyu animals known for producing meat finely marbled with fat, which makes it tender and tasty.

But she is also grappling with the more mundane daily challenges of running the farm. In recent years floods have swept through various parts of her property on four occasions. The most recent in April 2012 destroyed most of the fences surrounding her lucerne stands on Wyuntha. It's been a cold start to spring since then too, and feed is short for the cows trying to raise this season's calves, so she is spending a bit of time feeding out hay, hoping that the sun will soon emerge and encourage the grass to grow. Recognising it's an area where there is room for improvement, she is bringing in some professional advice to improve her pasture management skills.

And she continues to refine her approach to handling cattle, talking enthusiastically about the benefits of patience and relying on natural instincts rather than trying to push them too hard. 'I don't muster up the cows and calves any more. I move them in small lots, focusing on the ones closest to the gate, and I just sit patiently to encourage the lead cow so the mob follows her, and then tickle up the stragglers. It's about sitting and waiting and letting the cattle move away from you,' she says.

With summer approaching, she is starting to think about gathering her family around at Christmas, and lazy mornings swimming in the Murrumbidgee with her granddaughters who are all growing rapidly and continue to delight their grandmother. Further reading over the past 12 months has increased her fascination with the idea that legendary Australian overlander Joseph Hawdon and his companion Charles Bonney crossed the river somewhere near Wyuntha in the early stages of their famous trek to Adelaide. She has managed to get hold of a recently published version of Hawdon's diary and finds him a fascinating figure. 'It's such a good yarn. I have read it about four times and every time I read it I get more out of it,' she says. 'There are little bits in it that are real gems.'

By comparison life on Barnoolut has been 'fairly uneventful' during the past 18 months, although there still seems to be plenty going on. Now in her early 80s, Cecily has had some frustrating moments of ill health, forcing her to slow down a little and spend more time than she prefers with her feet up. But she has some new part-time help on the property, the dams are full after a wet winter, and she is starting to feel like her efforts to improve the property are coming to fruition.

Work has even started on renovating the old homestead, with considerable input from her daughter Edwina, who became foundation provost of Monash University in September 2012. The appointment makes her the chief academic officer of the university responsible for managing faculty operations and academic portfolios, and Cecily could not be prouder.

Unfortunately the past year has also marked the passing of her black Labrador, Pepper, and one of her treasured mares, a descendant of the remarkable Arabian stallion Riffayal that Cecily brought back from England just after the Second World War. 'That was a great sadness,' she says. 'She was nearly 30, and she couldn't get up one day. I had to have her put down. I was away and I had to make the arrangements on the phone which was very upsetting. I knew the time was coming and what I had to do, but I didn't want to do it.'

On a happier note, the last foal that she bred, Barnoolut Rimini, is back home after competing in shows with considerable success under the guidance of an experienced show rider. One of the people helping Cecily part-time has been using him to do some stock work, and he is showing natural ability. Cecily is very pleased about this given it was always a priority at the Barnoolut stud established by her parents Edwin and Nancy Crozier to breed useful horses.

She also has a new house companion—a dachshund called Teea. The five-year-old dog ended up with Dachshund Rescue Australia in Sydney after being left to fend for herself and being hit by a car. Edwina found the rescue service on the internet after her mother confessed to missing Pepper. Cecily was interviewed and 'put through the seventh degree' before the service decided she was the right person to adopt Teea, who was understandably nervous after her experiences. Even though she has a penchant for hunting Cecily's chooks, she is much loved and has quickly settled into her new home.

Out on the farm, Cecily is still focussed on slowly building up the numbers of sheep and cattle. Admitting that she has never come to terms with computers, she nonetheless continues to win the admiration of her family and farm advisers for taking an active interest in the latest innovations in livestock breeding and pasture management. 'The place has to pay for itself and it has,' she says. 'We are part of it and it would break everybody's heart if it went out of the family. That is happening a lot in farming these days but hopefully Barnoolut is secure for another generation.'

Catherine Bird is spending more time thinking about future generations too these days, and the legacy of today's farmers and community leaders. Her accident and the response to her story have made her determined to make a worthwhile and lasting contribution of some sort to society, although she is still working out what form that might take. While she gains tremendous satisfaction from guiding people on health and nutrition, she is also becoming increasingly concerned about the health of the farming sector and rural communities.

'There comes a time in your life where you realise the only reward is giving. When you are young it's all about doing things for yourself—buying a house, building a career . . . But then you come to a part of your life when you realise, hang on a minute, it's not about assets or being financially rich. For me it's about trying to improve the situation for everybody,' she says.

What particularly concerns her is finding a way to make farming more sustainable as well as more profitable, which she strongly believes will in turn generate more sustainable and vibrant rural towns and businesses. She has spent considerable time thinking about this since she experienced 'a light bulb moment' during the Keith community's ongoing battle to retain the hospital that helped save her life.

'I understand the drive to save the hospital but there is a bigger picture that has to be addressed, and if we do that the hospital will be saved,' she explains. 'If you help farmers improve their livelihoods they will spend more in their rural towns and they will start growing again. That means there will be more people in the town and that will make the hospital more viable.'

Catherine also wants to see a reversal in the trend that has seen four farmhouses near Indiana become empty because people were forced to cut back on employing the workers that would once have lived there, or the farm had been sold to the next door neighbour in a 'get bigger or get out' process that is seeing the number of Australian farmers dropping constantly. 'We have to find a way to fill those houses,' she says.

Like many rural Australians, Catherine is also becoming increasingly concerned about foreign ownership of Australian agriculture. There have been more than a few sales to overseas investors in her area, and she has been following with interest the political debate that emerged in 2011, when the issue started to grab the national headlines. It was driven in part by independent South Australian Senator Nick Xenophon, who she admires greatly. He has been a strong supporter of the Keith Hospital too, helping to lobby the state government, advise the community and agreeing to have his portrait painted for the prestigious Archibald Prize so it could be auctioned afterwards to raise money.

Catherine says selling off farms to foreign investment makes no sense, either to rural communities or the environment. She strongly believes it would be better to leave the land in the hands of families who know it and love it and can farm it sustainably, than have it owned by large corporations.

The issue that lies behind most of these problems is that the economics of family farming has been out of balance for years when it comes to income versus expenses, and farmers are just not paid enough for their produce. She has some ideas about how to address the situation, although she admits she has no idea if they will work. She plans to spend more time researching the issues and talking to people before deciding what she can do in a practical sense.

Catherine clearly understands there are no simple solutions, just as there have been no quick fixes to the challenges she has been dealing with in her personal life. She and her partner Simon are still together. People have been surprised at how frank Catherine has been about the affair that rocked her marriage. 'As many people talk to me about that, as they do about the accident,' she says. 'The amount of people that have been through the same thing is appalling. It just blows me away that it has become so acceptable in our society. It's a bit like the farming industry—if something isn't done about it, it's going to become just par for the course.' That is what motivated her to talk about it so openly.

Catherine likes to think that she and Simon have become stronger through the experience, and that their relationship is richer, with them offering each other more compassion and support. 'There is a lot more substance to it now,' she admits. She continues to be amazed by the strength and maturity of her oldest children, Brett and Renee. 'There is no way I would have dealt with the whole situation as well without them,' she says. And she is particularly proud of Simon and the way he has worked so hard to redeem himself and demonstrate that he is prepared to stand up for what is important to him. He has had to do that in his sporting life too.

At the end of the 2011 football season, Padthaway dismissed Simon as coach of their senior team. Rather than walk away from football, he offered his services to the club at Bordertown. Just twelve months later he led them to their first premiership since the local football league was formed in 1994. Very much the underdogs, they defeated a team that had lost only one match in the whole season. In a bittersweet moment, Bordertown had to beat Simon's old club to make it into the preliminary finals.

❖ ❖ ❖

And Keelen? Well, despite the last two children heading off to boarding school in 2012, opening the door to a more reflective year of her own company, life has been 'flat tack' at Mt Tabor station. For the third year in a row, floods swept across the property, damaging fencing and roads, and causing massive erosion wherever the water rushed through. Over just two days in February, the station received 12.5 inches of rain. 'It was just shocking,' says Keelen, reflecting that stockman Dave Hagger had never seen anything like it even though he is in his 70s and has spent most of his life working on Queensland stations. 'When other places were not getting much we were getting inches. Springs were coming up everywhere.'

The water created a gully near the horse yards and swept sand down through the sheds in the homestead paddock. It was six months before the country was dry enough for her and Dave to make their way cautiously to some places to check out the damage, with long grass hiding deep holes and enormous washouts. Six months later parts of the station are still inaccessible by vehicle, including the magical Lost City. Some of the tracks through the station are in such a bad state that Keelen has decided to make new ones rather than attempt to repair them.

The ground was still so wet in August that even the cattle and horses were bogging when mustering started up. This year, much to Keelen's excitement, the contract mustering team is made up of five young Indigenous men from the remote Northern Territory community of Borroloola in the south-west region of the Gulf of Carpentaria. Aged between about 16 and 21, they are staying with Dave in the workmen's quarters. 'They are kids doing a man's job but they are out there, and they are lovely little horsemen to watch,' says Keelen, whose extended family includes champion rough riders and generations of respected stockmen. Some of these young men also ride in rodeos in their spare time, and one of them did some mustering for Baz Luhrmann's Outback film, *Australia*.

Away from the property, Keelen has made a few trips in her role as a member of the Australian Landcare Council. The council advises the Australian Government on landcare issues, with Keelen offering them an Indigenous perspective. At the end of February 2012 she went to the first national landcare conference held in New Zealand, freezing in unseasonal cold weather, and in September she attended the National Landcare Awards gala dinner in Sydney. She came back to Mt Tabor very excited that it had given her the chance to meet former Prime Minister Bob Hawke. 'I didn't mind old Bob, bless his heart and soul,' she says.

Keelen and her best friend Nicky have also started running cultural awareness training as part of the induction process for mining company employees. Keelen was asked to do it before but there was never enough time. With Charlee and Maggie at boarding school in Toowoomba she decided to give it a go. 'I do the traditional welcome, and then translate that into English, and then we get into a slide show with a massive amount of cultural stuff. We have had really great feedback,' she says.

After more than fourteen years of good intentions, she has finally, officially, received her certificate to operate a chainsaw. More than a dab hand at using one already, it took the instructor just half a day to pass her instead of the usual three days of training. With everything she had on her plate at the time, Keelen was more than a little relieved to save the time. She has also been working on a book of her own, telling her life story in more detail. There has been an extraordinary response to her story, and there is plenty more to say.

But all these achievements and challenges pale into insignificance compared to an extraordinary weekend in April when Bidjara people travelled from far and wide to attend a special event in Augathella. After extensive negotiation and planning, the Queensland Museum finally returned to country some ancestral remains and sacred objects taken from the area many years ago. Keelen played a key role in organising the repatriation ceremony for this momentous occasion. 'It was the most powerful spiritual feeling that I have ever had,' Keelen says.

Truth be told, having their stories captured in a book has not really changed the lives of Mary, Lynette, Jan, Nan, Susie, Cecily, Catherine and Keelen in any significant way. Quiet achievers who have spent most of their lives heads down and working hard, they remain extremely surprised and a little embarrassed that others find their lives remarkable in any way. After reading each others' stories, they feel honoured to be included in such company.

What has in fact given them the most pleasure from the experience is having the opportunity to get to know each other. Normally reticent about meeting strangers, Mary relished her time in Adelaide with the other women, which she shared with her daughters Trish and Diane. 'I just felt like I knew them always,' she says. The youngest of the group, Lynette also felt a strong sense of connection despite the age differences. 'We are all different, but we are all the same ... We didn't have to explain ourselves to each other.'

For Lynette attending the launch was extra special because it was the first holiday she and Chris had shared in eight years, and their first holiday with baby Robert. Susie also loved being able to share the launch with her daughter Melissa. 'It gave Melissa and I the most wonderful opportunity to have time together, and I thought it was so great that everyone made the effort to get there. I felt like I connected with each and every one of them,' Susie says.

Juggling the demands of organising the repatriation ceremony, Keelen was very pleased that she managed the long trip. 'It was an honour and a privilege to be part of it, and to meet those beautiful ladies,' she says. Echoing the sentiments of the others, she adds: 'It was like we were all part of one. We have all had our heartaches and sadness, but we have had our good times too, and we all have good memories to share.'

A week after the launch something amazing starts to unfold. Having met face to face, the women start exchanging emails. A dab hand at communicating via skype and email thanks to having a daughter living overseas, Mary starts what turns into a series of ongoing conversations in which they share experiences back on the farm, offer each other support and encouragement, and seek advice.

The emails are still coming six months later, although more sporadically, with people diving in and out of the conversation depending on the season and how busy they are. Susie reports excitedly on a three-week holiday in Sri Lanka, followed by a quick return to reality when she came home to start preparing the cattle for spring calving. Keelen writes about the never-ending rain and flood damage. Mary, Catherine and Jan, anxious about getting enough rain for pastures and the crops, marvel at the idea of too much water. Jan writes that she having trouble finding good quality hay to keep the dairy herd going, and Nan shares some of the lessons she learnt from trying to get animals through three years of dry conditions in the late 2000s.

Writing on a day when she is stuck inside because of torrential rain, Lynette shares a lovely story about slow combustion stoves, inspired by reading about Cecily and her Aga. When Lynette's parents were first married her mother had enormous difficulty mastering the secondhand wood stove installed in the house they built together, so when they could finally afford it Leo bought a new one. 'He said in jest to his mum, who was a fantastic cook, that if Audrey couldn't master the new Rayburn then he would have to trade her in for another wife because he is not going to get another stove. Nan Gertrude thought that Dad was serious so she threw herself wholeheartedly into teaching Mum how to use the stove. She liked Mum and didn't want to have a different daughter in law!!!'

As the months unfold Nan tries to keep her sense of humour as the whole saga of producing her yarn continues to unravel. In an exciting side-development, she and Lynette make arrangements for Lynette's young farmhand Elizabeth to visit Lemon Hill on work experience. Inspired by her days at Top Forty, she has made up her mind to be a farmer and, potentially, breed rare sheep. She has just been accepted into a leading agricultural college to study agriculture. In a country where farmers are constantly worrying about how to inspire the next generation to stay on the land, there could be no better outcome.

Liz Harfull
September 2012

NOTES

1 *The West Australian*, 18 May 1911, page 8
2 *Western Mail*, 11 November 1911, page 3
3 John Bird, *Across the Lake*, Guildford WA, 1992, page 37
4 ibid., page 38
5 Jamie Kirkpatrick and Kerry Bridle (eds), *People, Sheep and Nature Conservation—The Tasmanian Experience*, CSIRO Publishing, Collingwood, 2007, page 3
6 Mary S. Ramsay, *Eliza Forlong and the Saxon merino industry*, Tasmanian Historical Research Association Papers and proceedings, vol. 51, no. 3, September 2004, pages 121–35
7 Used to measure the diameter of wool, a micron is just one-thousandth of a millimetre. While the definition of 'superfine' is sometimes open to variation and takes in more than fibre diameter, it usually applies to fleeces with fibres which average between 15 and 18 microns.
8 Heritage Highway Tourism Region Association website, viewed 11 July 2011, http://www.heritagehighway.com.au/home
9 Barry Humphries, *More Please*, Viking, 1992, page 151
10 'Scott, Andrew George (1842–1880)', *Australian Dictionary of Biography*, Online Edition, Australian National University, viewed 8 August 2011, http://adb.anu.edu.au/biography/scott-andrew-george-4546/text7451
11 *The Australian Women's Weekly*, 25 July 1936, page 2
12 *The Sydney Morning Herald*, 5 October 1923, page 5
13 *The Argus*, 14 October 1893, page 11
14 Mary Hannay-Foott, 'Where the Pelican Builds Her Nest'
15 *The Sydney Morning Herald*, 28 July 1849, page 8

16 Alan Gross, 'Hawdon, Joseph (1813–1871)', *Australian Dictionary of Biography*, Online Edition, Australian National University, viewed 12 August 2011, http://adb.anu.edu.au/biography/hawdon-joseph-2168/text2781

17 State Library of South Australia website, viewed 8 August 2011, www.slsa.sa.gov.au/fh/passengerlists/1838LadyMaryPelham%20 Hawdon,Joseph.htm

18 Rodney Cockburn, *Pastoral Pioneers of South Australia*, vol. 1, Publishers Limited, Adelaide, 1925

19 *The Adelaide Advertiser*, 28 December 1910, page 12

20 References are contradictory about whether the mail contract was run by Joseph or John, with an extensive account of John's life published in several parts by *The Sydney Morning Herald* in 1929 claiming they operated it together.

21 Adam Lindsay Gordon, 'Ye Weary Wayfarer', originally published in *Sea Spray and Smoke Drift*, 1867

22 Moving Here website, managed by the National Archives (UK), viewed 18 June 2011

23 *The Adelaide Advertiser*, 30 December 1937, page 6

24 *The Adelaide Advertiser*, 26 March 1949, page 7

25 Moving Here website, viewed 18 June 2011

26 Jacqueline Peck, *Porlock Vale Riding School, History and Memories* website, viewed 21 June 2011, www.angelfire.com/ab5/ jacquelinepeck/

27 History of Casterton and Surrounding Districts, *Significance Assessment 2010*, Ballarat and District Genealogical Society website, viewed 24 June 2011

28 The Working Kelpie Council of Australia website, viewed 21 June 2011, www.wkc.org.au/Origin.php

29 John Cornish and Keena Le Lievne, *Deeds Speak Louder than Words*, Mt Waverley, c 2009, page 37

30 *Portland Guardian* (Vic.: 1876–1953), Thursday 23 July 1925, page 3

31 Alan Barnard, 'Guthrie, James Francis (1872–1958)', *Australian Dictionary of Biography*, Online Edition, Australian National University, viewed 18 June 2011, http://adb.anu.edu.au/biography/ guthrie-james-francis-450/text11171

32 *The Argus*, 25 September 1929, page 20

33 Cornish and Le Lievne, *Deeds Speak Louder Than Words*, page 1

34 The University of Adelaide website, viewed 21 June 2011, http:// ebooks.adelaide.edu.au/m/mitchell/thomas/index.html

35 *The Advertiser* (Adelaide), 15 March 1935, page 23

36 Pearl Powell and Eileen McRae, *By Packhorse and Buggy*, Australian Outback Printing and Media Museum, Alice Springs, 1996

37 *Northern Standard* (Darwin), 24 January 1928, page 4
38 Powell and McRae, op. cit.
39 Cherbourg Aboriginal Shire website, viewed 24 August 2011, http://
    queenslandplaces.com.au/cherbourg-aboriginal-shire-council

ACKNOWLEDGEMENTS

This book would not have happened without the serendipitous moment created by ABC Landline reporter Pip Courtney. My heartfelt thanks to Pip for her ongoing encouragement, and her skilful television piece about my research for a different book on a subject dear to both our hearts—the traditions of country show cooking. It generated such a staggering response from viewers that it opened up amazing opportunities to me as a writer and changed my life forever. I am not sure how I can ever repay you.

My sincere gratitude goes to Allen & Unwin associate publisher Claire Kingston for her faith in me as an emerging author, and for her willingness to allow me to tell the stories of rural Australian women in my own way. To my managing editor Aziza Kuypers, for shepherding the book so ably through the production process and to editor Susin Chow, who polished the manuscript and nurtured my creative ego with pencil notes of positive feedback. And to the rest of the team involved in creating this book—I have enjoyed enormously the experience of working with Allen & Unwin.

Many thanks too, to my agent Fiona Inglis, for her willingness to take me on and her enthusiasm for the project. And a

347

very special thank you to my fellow Moggies—you know who you are—and the South Australian Writers Centre, for their professional support and friendships, and sharing the excitement. We often work in such isolation, but your generous support and our regular gatherings, accompanied by the odd glass of red wine, kept me going under the weight of what seemed like impossible deadlines.

To my friends and colleagues in the rural world who embraced the concept for this book and helped track down many of the extraordinary women it features—what talented talent scouts you proved to be. And thanks to the farmers and farm advisers among you, who helped me to understand some of the more technical aspects of farming beyond my own experience and to find ways to explain them without putting everyone to sleep—I hope I have done you proud!

To my much neglected friends, thank you for putting up with me disappearing from your lives for eight months while I worked on this book, volunteering your services as house sitters, providing accommodation when needed as well as the occasional meal, and for calling every now and then to check I was still alive. A special mention in particular to Cheryl Kennedy, who set aside the demands of her own life to read the early chapters and provide invaluable feedback.

As always, love and gratitude goes to my family for their love and support, for helping me to keep my feet on solid ground, and for giving me my own life on the land. No matter how long I live away from it, the farm at Mil Lel will always be my spiritual home.

And last but not least to Mary, Lynette, Jan, Nan, Cecily, Susie, Catherine and Keelen. Thank you for allowing me to tell your stories, and for your open-hearted approach to sharing your lives and your place on the planet. It is an honour and a privilege which I do not take for granted.